The Virtual World of Work

How to Gain Competitive Advantage through the Virtual Workplace

The Virtual World of Work

How to Gain Competitive Advantage through the Virtual Workplace

by

K. J. (Ken) McLennan

Scottsdale, AZ
www.virtualworldofwork.com

INFORMATION AGE PUBLISHING, INC.
Charlotte, NC • www.infoagepub.com

Library of Congress Cataloging-in-Publication Data

McLennan, K. J. (Ken J.)
  How to gain competitive advantage through the virtual workplace / by K. J.
McLennan.
     p. cm.
  Includes bibliographical references.
  ISBN-13: 978-1-59311-872-3 (pbk.)
  ISBN-13: 978-1-59311-873-0 (hardcover)
  1. Telecommuting. 2. Work environment. 3. Employees–Effect of
automation on. 4. Virtual reality in management. I. Title.
  HD2336.3.M35 2007
  658.3'123–dc22

                                                            2007047348

This book is dedicated to my wife Margaret—
Without her love, support, encouragement, and persistence
I would not have been able to accomplish this goal.

To my sons and their families—
They helped me keep focused through the many months,
and gave me an audience.

And to Ray Kissinger—
A friend, colleague, and client, whose memory helped provide
the passion to follow through on this project.

Acknowledgments

I would like to thank all those who have contributed:

Bronwyn A, Ken M, Marina M, Dave C, Mary-Rita C,
Mike G, Tracy B, Edna S, Rodger T, Sherwin D,
Alaina B, Bill J, Linda L, John H, Kathy H, Greg F,
Doris P, Tom K, Ricardo B, Ray M, Mike M, Gene H,
Chris R, Kathie L, John T, Dean S, Gene G,
Hans G, Agnes L, Jim C, Mark M, John N, Eli K.

CONTENTS

Section Three

Will the Virtual World of Work Continue?

Section Four

How Will the Virtual World Work?

Section Five

How to Architect the Virtual World of Work?

INTRODUCTION

HOW WE DO OUR JOBS

Is It Changing?

How we do our jobs is changing so dramatically the impact is altering our long established concept of work. Flexibility is replacing predictable schedules and management is transitioning its focus from people and time to effort and output. For the information workers that adapt, new opportunities will emerge and for those that do not, the loss of their job is probable. This book explains why this is happening and what information workers and organizations need to understand to continue to survive and prosper.

There are four irreversible forces coalescing that are changing forever how we think about work and how we will perform our jobs in the future. These forces are fundamental to the formation of the *virtual world of work*.

- **TECHNOLOGY**—The rapid introduction and acceptance of incredible technologies (computers, hand-held and wearable devices, communication networks, security, and software) are enhancing human capabilities and enabling mobile connectivity for the people of the world.
- **ATTITUDES**—New attitudes, habits and mental models are altering how we think about ourselves, family roles, communications, technology, security, collaboration, and knowledge—changing who, how, when and where we work.
- **DEMOGRAPHICS**—The retirement of the baby boomers, reduced birth rates in the developed countries, and the transition to the new

The Virtual World of Work, pages xi–xix
Copyright © 2008 by Information Age Publishing
All rights of reproduction in any form reserved.

generations (X, Y, & N) of information workers is forcing transformation of the workplace.

- **GLOBALIZATION**—The reduction of physical, geopolitical and mental boundaries are enabling the integration of national economies into a truly global economy—providing new markets, know-how, innovation, resources, opportunities and problems.

Let's define what is meant when we use the term *information worker.* The information worker *creates, analyzes, communicates,* and/or *uses* digital information every day in performing their jobs. It is for the information workers, at all organizational levels that I have written this book. They will be the ones intimately involved with the emerging changes in *who, how, where,* and *when* information workers get to perform their jobs. Their workplace has changed and it will continue to change even faster in the future. This is the transformation of those once called the "white collar worker, office workers, and suits."

Microsoft has legitimized the term by using it to describe both their customers and their business group responsible for developing and delivering technologies for these customers. The objective of the new work enabling technologies is to impact information workers to be more productive, with more control over their time and more opportunity to realize their potential. Once we have set the context for the key messages we will explore the four transformational stages and how these stages represent the evolution of the information worker's capabilities. We will chronicle their progress from the 1960s through to the 2030s. The book is an aggregation of personal research, observations and conclusions. These have been accumulated from my experiences, interviews and surveys, as well as the accounts of the most notable experts and the experiences of those organizations leading the transformation to a virtual world. The outcome is a new vision called the *virtual world of work.*

The transition to a more flexible work environment is not a passing movement. The forces (technology, attitudes, demographics and globalization) have been emerging quietly for some time, they are picking up support, and will continue to strengthen and accelerate whether you are ready or not. There will be many people-related problems and technology issues surfaced during this transition because attitudes, habits, and mental models, along with organization and government policies are difficult to change. The speed at which the young employees can adapt and new technical breakthroughs can be introduced will exceed management's ability to control the pace of change enabled by the new virtual world of work.

Much of our current social and work related thinking was born with the Industrial Age and has been reinforced over the last two hundred years. The concepts of commuting to work to do work, attendance, centralized assets, organization dynamics, management practices, pay for time, even being an employee are all strongly rooted mental models of how most people think. Until these remnants of the Industrial Age are forgotten, we will not have fully completed our evolution to the Information Age, or as it is called, the *Digital Age*. Experience shows that some will never embrace the change, most will take time, but still others will make the adjustment with ease.

The future of who, how, when and where work is accomplished in your organization is rapidly changing. Will you embrace these changes, will they change you, or will you try to preserve the status quo? We will see over the next decade, who is successful and who will be the casualties of the new virtual world of work.

Information technology (IT) has evolved tremendously over the last several decades. So much so that on a visit to the Microsoft museum in Redmond, WA, I discovered that I have personal experience that predates their earliest exhibits.

This book is based on my journey as an information worker and the changes experienced over the past 40 years. This will set the context for how we got to where we are today. To appreciate the extent of how dramatic the technological change is, let's take a quick look back at the early electronic data processing (EDP) technology of the '60s and '70s. This technology was responsible for replacing the earlier manual processes and tabulating equipment.

The first computer facility I worked in was on the ground level, with floor-to-ceiling glass, so people passing by on the busy street could see and marvel at the new IBM/360 model 20 and 40 computers we worked with. The people were fascinated by the flashing console lights, spinning tape drives and the printers spewing paper. You will never see that today. After a few similarly located data centers were attacked in the late '60s, the computers were quickly relocated into more secure locations. Computers were so environmentally sensitive and valuable they became housed in separate, non-accessible facilities, and were the sole domain of the new specialized computer people.

Business managers had no direct access to this new powerful technology. To gain indirect access to the amazing new capabilities the departments had to manually complete paper input forms and deliver those to the key punch department. There amongst the unit record equipment the data was keyed and verified into machine readable card stock and prepared for entry into the computer. The operations manager would process the input, usually over night, according to preset turnaround schedules. Printed reports were the only availability business users had to the data. The correction of errors followed the same process and the turnaround could take days.

The next major breakthrough was the *dumb terminal.* These were introduced for use in work areas that were located close enough to the computer to be directly connected by heavy cables. Raised floors were introduced to accommodate the endless miles of cable. The terminals were also known as *green screens* and supported most of the early information workers. Although they were limited in their capabilities, they survived for many years as the dominant computer tool of business.

A little later *micros* began to emerge, today called PCs (personal computers). At first they were treated like toys by the "real" IT professionals and not considered appropriate for corporate business. As the micro computers evolved, supporting new software applications, people started to use them for business functions outside the control of the computer department (a major shift). I observed many DP (data processing) managers, called CIO's (chief information officers) today, fighting with business managers to stop the introduction and use of these micros. I find it very ironic that in such a short period of time those leading-edge technologies and work processes, which I was so proud to be part of, now look so antiquated and cumbersome.

Jumping forward, it is incredible to see the extent of the technology explosion and the amazing acceptance of these new tools into all aspects of our life. We now use mobile technologies not just for work, but for learning, playing, entertainment, news, navigation, and communications. The vast community of knowledge gained over the last few decades about the use of these technologies is a key enabler to why we can now achieve tremendous advances so rapidly. And as they say, you ain't seen anything yet!

Today, there are a seemingly endless number of devices used interchangeably for business and personal purposes, all connectable to everything and everyone. Telephony and computing have become inseparable. Communication is global, high speed, secure, and wireless. Cell phones, PDAs, Blackberries, laptops, and the latest hand held devices all work over the ubiquitous Internet. To accommodate the required access into organization intranets, there are fire walls and sophisticated security software. For those with the right VPN (virtual private network) tokens, codes or biometrics, access is no longer a limiting factor to virtual work. People can, and are, working from anywhere at any time. The work week and work day have literally been enabled to 24 by 7.

The existing technology primarily provides tools for the individual worker, but the next generation of software technology will enable breakthroughs in group, team and collaborative work from nearly anywhere on the planet. The collaboration techniques will deliver stunning advances in the efficiency and effectiveness of the workforce and will forever change the information worker's world of work. These advances make work flexibility possible in ways that we could not imagine, at least I couldn't, just a few years ago.

The opportunities for who, how, when and where we work are truly infinite. The line between when we are working and when we are not is becoming obscure. The concept of an eight-hour work day and a forty-hour work week is irrelevant for most information workers. Workers that travel extensively are equipped with technology that allows them to become more and more comfortable with working while remote from the office. This has already enabled some 25 million U.S. employees to work from home at least part of each month, according to the U.S. Census Bureau.

When calling an office looking for somebody, you may get this type of response, "the person you are trying to reach is working from home today—please feel free to contact them, it's OK, they are really working." It is interesting; many still feel the need for some sort of explanation or excuse for being at home during what was the traditional workday. Most people accept working while on the road but there is much evidence that many are not comfortable with work being performed primarily from home. The more technology makes it possible to connect remotely and work extra hours, the more internal competition is fueled by that, and it becomes an imperative if you are a career driven employee.

Young workers are less inclined to depend on others to manage their careers. The changing attitudes will increasingly enable the new generations to make their own independent decisions about where they will live, who they will work for, and what is important to them. The ability to have greater work flexibility, enabled through technology, is creating a realization that they can better balance their lives in ways not previously available. I use the word *balance*, because a change to ones work environment will demand change to their whole life, including where they choose to live.

Here are a few of the additional factors which I believe have profound social impacts on attitudes and why the new generations think and act different than previous generations:

- A second generation of dual working parents has changed traditional family dynamics and the relationships that exist in many homes.
- The younger generations are blending their work and family responsibilities with greater opportunities to put more balance in their lives.
- More complex lives caused by an overload of information, unlimited options and choreographed schedules are common for the young programmed generation.
- Faster paced lives mean things change quickly with little predictability, familiarity or dependability.

- More money, debt and choices allows instant gratification of their desires.
- Greater self-focus is contributed to by smaller families—the "me-generation."
- Risk adverse environments in which children are much more protected, thus they have little practice evaluating or taking responsibility for risks prior to adulthood.
- Individuals are most familiar with making decisions based on the benefit to them and expectations are very high.
- Young business people today can and do "vote with their feet, "—changing jobs when it makes sense for them.
- Net-gens have lived their whole lives in a digital society and are not intimidated by technology and cannot imagine doing work without the latest tools.

Personally, I have a lot of old attitudes, habits and mental models that made, "going virtual," working permanently from home, difficult. It was different than working from home on the odd day, evenings and weekends, while I still had my own office "at work." Work has become so synonymous with a physical location that, as I just did, we use the verb as a noun. We will know we have made the transformation to a new virtual world of work when the word is no longer used to describe a physical place.

One critical realization for me was my work environment influenced how I viewed myself and in turn my self-image impacted how I felt about what I was doing. This was a critical realization for me in adjusting to the virtual world of work. Another important lesson learned was that my wife had a tough time adjusting to me working from home. I discovered it may be our home in the evenings and weekends, but during the week, it was her home. This was a major change in our lives and I needed to be sensitive, and not be perceived as an intruder.

These are all extremely important lessons that must be taken into account when planning a virtual work environment. Decisions about working from home, dictate the whole family should be involved, and everyone's needs and feelings taken into consideration. Do not underestimate the effect your family and friend's reactions will have on you when you start working from home.

But, not all workers will be able, or want, to take advantage of the virtual world of work. Most non-information workers truly need to be on-site to do their jobs. This will cause strong feelings and bring out differences in attitudes among workers. At first, expect the virtual workers to be considered different, isolated and/or even inferior. Over time these feelings may actually be reversed and lead to envy and great dissatisfaction.

These workforce pressures will need to be closely monitored and managed. This in itself may be difficult because those with the most inflexible attitudes are most likely the managers. HR (human resources) needs to be deeply involved from the very beginning of a change to the more flexible work arrangements that will result from virtual capabilities. Management will be required to design new policies, procedures and measurements related to employee contributions, classification, benefit eligibility, time reporting, compensation, expense reimbursement, personnel reviews, and career management. The anticipation and resolution of conflicts in this kind of change management program will be difficult for most traditional large organizations.

If we combine these incredible enabling technologies, with the social and personal attitude changes taking place, we have the necessary conditions to ignite a quantum leap in how we think about work. This change is just starting to emerge, evolve and pick up momentum. The pace of this evolution is controlled, not by capabilities or availability of technology, but by attitudes, habits and mental models. These inhibitors will quickly weaken or be eliminated, and those with the most inflexible attitudes will either retire or be forced to change. Organizations will then create new definitions for what constitutes an employee, and rethink new possibilities for how work and careers will evolve.

Workforce demographics are leading to a dramatically reduced resource pool in the industrialized nations over the next decade. One of the causes is the "graying" of the workforce which refers to the tremendous number of Baby Boomers that will leave the traditional workforce in the next decade. This boomer bulge in the workforce, caused by the higher than normal birth rates after WW11, has started to retire. Further compounding this fact is the birth rates in most developed countries have come down to well below the rate at which they will be able to supply the necessary future workforces. Also, the choices available to students today are resulting in a reduced number of future information workers graduating in the disciplines valued by business. Immigration and productivity increases will not meet the demand of a growing economy. This is necessitating a movement to a more international workforce.

Globalization is causing an enormous change in the world of work. This is having a huge impact on where and who will perform work. It is opening new markets for the exchange of products, services, assets, capital, resources, and knowledge. In just the last few years the world's largest countries (China, Russia and India) are emerging and integrating their national economies into the global economy which was dominated by the U.S., Europe and Japan. The move to global recruiting will become very competitive and absolutely mandatory. As globalization opens our thinking and expands our horizons the successful organizations will reach out to the rest of the world and offer new business arrangements for the performance of work without the requirement to immigrate.

The new generation of information workers is viewing their jobs through very different mental models than those of the current middle and upper management. This is referred to by an ex-colleague and author, Don Tapscott, as the "net-gens meet the baby boomers." In my interviews it seems the net-gen's distrust in corporations, unions and governments are very tainted by the constant business events reported on the news. Some have already been impacted by negative work related experience. Others are aware, through their parents or friends of layoffs, cutbacks, rollbacks, outsourcing, and downsizing that has caused many to be disillusioned with the public and private work sectors. There exists an imbalance in negativity verses trust by both the employees and the organizations.

My hope is that people will identify with the messages and conclusions contained in this book, allowing them to relate to the forces and the possibilities for human-centric change. Use this information to embrace the change, be more effective and become a more valuable resource. I encourage everyone to think about their use of time and technology, and imagine new ways of structuring their work lives or freeing themselves from unnecessary structure. Hopefully, you will have the opportunity, or responsibility, to influence your organization in creating new work related policies and procedures to support mobile and virtual work environments. The purpose of this transformation is so organizations can redefine how, where and when employees can increase personal productivity, find ways to deliver superior value, and provide more work flexibility for the employees to achieve better work/life balance for the good of both employers and employees.

To me it is clear, if organizations do not embrace these changes and offer new flexibility and technologies to their employees, they will become unattractive employers. This will show its ugly head through failures in hiring and retaining the best resources. The outcome of such failures will cause organizations to struggle in meeting their goals and they will fall short of the expectations of their workforce and their investors—putting them out of business!

Summary

- Our long established concept of work is rapidly changing, it will lead to greater opportunities for a better future for those ready for the challenge.
- Technology is enabling new human capabilities that will change everything.
- Flexibility is replacing predictable work schedules.

- The management focus is changing from people and time to effort and output.
- The four irreversible forces enabling the future world of work are:
  - Technology
  - Attitudes
  - Demographics
  - Globalization
- Information workers create, analyze, communicate and/or use digital computers and information daily in doing their jobs.
- Who, how, where and when information workers do their jobs is changing, allowing more control over their time and opportunities to realize their potential.
- The vision is a new virtual world of work where everyone is connected to everything they need, regardless of geography, culture, language or time.
- Changes will happen so fast management will not be able to control the pace.
- We are still not complete in our transformation from the Industrial Age to the Digital Age.
- The early information worker processes now look so antiquated and cumbersome.
- The work week and day have been literally enabled to 7/24.
- There are 25 million employees working from home in the U.S. at least part-time.
- Mobile work habits are accepted but working from home makes many unease.
- The new generation is more independent about where to live and work.
- Work creep is making work/life balance critical.
- Work has become synonymous with a place—not just an action or output.
- A person's family needs to be involved in preparing for a home office.
- Not all workers will want or be able to work from home.
- The pace of the change to a virtual environment is control not by technology but by attitudes, habits and mental models.
- Demographic studies show our workforce will be substantially changed.
- Globalization of the work world will change our thinking, society and workplace.
- Think about your use of time and technology and imagine new ways of working.

Section One

WHAT IS THE VIRTUAL WORLD OF WORK?

CHAPTER 1

SECTION INTRODUCTION

Words, words, words—like so many today, once popularized, they take on many meanings. A quick Internet search in April 2006, for the following rather straightforward terms, illustrates the point by revealing these incredible results:

- Information worker   52.4 million hits
- Mobile worker   9.3 million hits
- Virtual worker   5.0 million hits
- Knowledge worker   16.5 million hits

The volume of hits makes it essential to create a narrower context of these terms and their prescribed meanings. With a short read of this section, you should have no trouble deciding how you feel about the vision present, and how this book will help you and your organization realize value. To make the journey to this new world of work easier to understand, the information worker's world of work has been segmented into four stages that correspond to the four terms used in the above search. Thus, the stages are:

- Information Worker Stage.
- Mobile Worker Stage.
- Virtual Worker Stage.
- Knowledge Worker Stage.

In each stage the capabilities of the information worker are enhanced through new techniques, attitudes and technologies.

The first stage chronicles the early business use of computing to perform commercial work. The focus is on how the information worker came

The Virtual World of Work, pages 3–11
Copyright © 2008 by Information Age Publishing
All rights of reproduction in any form reserved.

about and how their efforts have computerized the current world of work. The period covered in the first stage is from the 1960s to the early 1990s.

The second stage is organized around the enablement, advancement, and productivity increases associated with being connected and able to work while traveling or remote from the office. It is in this mobile stage that the majority of organizations are functioning today and the greatest improvement realized is through responsiveness and individual productivity. Most organizations will function primarily in this stage, taking us into the 2010s.

The third stage is built on top or cumulative to all of the developments enjoyed in the first two stages and covers the impact caused by having a significant percentage of the information workers working primarily from home. Their ability to work effectively in teams will be enabled by advances in technology, communications and new collaboration software. Some organizations are just entering this stage and will over the next 5–10 years learn to leverage collaboration and knowledge. It is in this stage that productivity will be increased dramatically. Productivity gains will be realized through a combination of increased hours, fewer interruptions, better tools, greater leverage of knowledge and the benefits enabled through working together in teams. The individual productivity of the previous stages will be extended to the group and team levels. These advances will forever changes how we think about working collaboratively and utilizing computer accessible knowledge.

The fourth and final stage covered is a theoretical exercise describing thoughts and observations of what the future, 20 to 25 years out, could be and how this will change everything. Throughout the book, we will deal with both the technology enabled trends and human attitude changes, and what their subsequent impacts are on business and individuals.

You might have strong but different feelings toward each of the four stages. To understand what is possible and then imagine your own picture of the future is a big step in making the future virtual world of work a reality.

The material presented is based on my experience working with some of the best clients, partners and consultants in the world. Many of the organizations are world-renowned and represent a wide diversity of culture, geography and lines of business. Although each organization is unique, they all have one thing in common, a compelling drive for performance improvement in what they do. In parallel, individuals are struggling with the time commitments necessary to better balance their personal and work lives, and enhance the quality of life enjoyed by themselves and their loved ones.

As a retired Senior Vice President of Management Consulting for Fujitsu Consulting, (Fujitsu is the 3rd largest IT Corporation in the world), I gained knowledge through both, working directly with clients and overseeing the engagements of our senior consultants. Although my specialty was process improvement solutions, my passion has always been to focus on productivity improvement at the individual level. Experience shows that if you enable the individual participants in a process to make an improvement in their personal productivity, you can realize a quantum improvement in organizational performance. We will examine why this will happen and what you need to do to take advantage of this in your life.

The newly enabled virtual work environment is a great example of Electronic Performance Support System (EPSS). The mission of EPSS is to enable organizations to achieve business performance through human performance. For more information on the "*how*," go to the society's website at www.epsscentral.com. There you can discover human-centered design techniques and how knowledge enables better personal performance that will directly contribute to enterprise value.

Microsoft, IBM, communication organizations and many others are defining standards and building software that will run on a wide spectrum of devices to deliver on a dream of seamless, on-demand computing. To the information worker this means their information will be personalized for them, there when they need it and they will not be burdened with information they do not care about or require. Information is summarized in a meaningful way and distributed to the individual or the group to use in an efficient and effective manner while they are performing their work.

The objective is to demonstrate the idea that mobile work environments enable increasing productivity "*one worker at a time*" and virtual collaborative work environments will increase and improve productivity "*one team at a time*." The definition of "*increase*" is to be a greater amount of output in the same period of time, or a reduction in the amount of time to produce the original level of output. The definition of "*improve*" is to indicate a higher level of quality that is measurable in the output. We can achieve enhanced human performance not just by how people work but also by creating greater flexibility in when and where workers contribute. Once collaborative teams are enabled and embrace new capabilities in work management and knowledge management, the increases in productivity and improvements in quality will approach those achieved by the industrial laborers over the last century.

In this material we will examine the enabling technology, collaborative methods, techniques and tools, and the changing attitudes toward work that can be leveraged to create personal productivity improvement. Equipping the worker with the right tools is the easy part. The hard part will be successfully cultivating the "*human change*."

To change the habits and attitudes that have led to the current work related policies, procedures and practices may seem an insurmountable challenge in the short-term. But, over time the necessary change will come. Do not expect to send out an email and make it so, it will not be that easy.

It may require removing those with the most inflexible attitudes, or other aggressive actions to have them change their position. The pace of changing, or eliminating these inflexible attitudes, will dictate the pace at which this transformation to a virtual world of work can progress and the benefits harvested.

To me, allowing work to be done where and when the greatest productivity can be achieved makes ultimate sense. If that is in the office between 8:00AM and 5:00PM great, but, if it is in the early morning, evening or night, no matter where they are located, why should that not be supported? Yes, I realize that collaboration has to fit with team schedules and deadlines, but I strongly believe most attitudes against working from home or the negativity toward the realities caused by globalization are shrouded in old thinking that we need to put behind us. I am not advocating unrealistic freedom of choice, security breaches or a lack of governance and management practices, but the use of new attitudes and innovative techniques to accomplish good management oversight. The desire to maintain the status quo or overzealous nationalism are very powerful emotions, especially during times of terrorist's threats, but we must not let these emotions be used to hinder or slow global progressive change.

The *vision* is for a new virtual world of work that is delivered primarily from home offices located in cooperating countries around the world. The vision includes a workforce that is:

- Enabled by advanced technology.
- Supported by new corporate and government policies and practices with regard to security, work visas and taxation.
- Employees are trusted and allowed great flexibility, not stifled by old habits, attitudes and rules.
- Employees can work from home and still have careers.
- Collaborative work practices are the norm.
- Work teams embrace global diversity.
- Better balanced lives can enhance the quality of life.
- Improved corporate performance can be measured and realized through worker productivity increases.

It will take more than token sponsorship and limited funding to achieve this vision; it will require *understanding, change, investment, involvement* and *commitment* by management, employees, governments and related organizations.

One of the main arguments against having virtual workers work from home is the human need for personal contact and the fact that much of what we communicate is through visual expression and body language. In meetings I have had to use this statement, "*I could not hear what you said; your body language was too loud.*" I believe that face-to-face is still the most effective and necessary human communication technique; it just does not have to happen daily between 8am and 5pm at the same fixed location. The human need for person-to-person social contact and stimulation is real and must be achieved, but it does not have to be satisfied through the traditional office.

As more and more success with mobile work is realized and benefits harvested, the movement to virtual work will pick up momentum. This movement will change what is acceptable for when and where information workers do their jobs. As a quick review, *mobile work* is defined as that done outside the office, initially by management and staff who travel extensively. This has already expanded to a wider spectrum of employees as the new technical infrastructures and tools are made available to many information workers. These employees whether they are on the road, in an alternate location or working from a conference room, need to be able to work in the same manner, with the same tools, as they would from their permanent business offices.

The definition used for *virtual work* is inclusive of mobile work; but it includes the incident of work performed regularly from home and the use of powerful collaborative/knowledge tools and techniques. In the virtual work scenario information and mobile workers can work from home, while traveling or from the office, but they do not have permanent facilities at the business sight. To accommodate the occasional need for workspace "*Hoteling*" is starting to emerge as a solution. Hoteling is the term used to describe a flexible workspace that is specifically designed to support walk-in traffic or those that need to reserve space for short periods of time. Their main work environment is located in their home and their normal work contact is completely enabled by the new digital world.

The quantum improvement in productivity will be realized with the development and use of new efficient and effective software enabling collaborative and knowledge work approaches. The current software suites have capability shortfalls in enabling this vision, but many suppliers are targeting different components that will eventually lead to the virtual world of work vision. The suppliers that lead the way in delivering the integrated world of work software suites will win the market share game by helping advance virtual work collaboration globally.

Kathie Lingle is Director of the Alliance for Work-Life Progress (AWLP), a WorldatWork global network component for work-life professionals. She observes "Work/life balance refers to the recognition by employers that everyone in the workplace is actively working two agendas at all times, one professional and one personal. Americans spend more hours at work than people in any other part of the world. The long days make striking a balance between the demands of work, home and personal goals a challenge."

I have worked from a home office for several years and now believe the business office environment, with all its interruptions, is not a productive environment for work. It does fulfill social contact needs and allows those with aging mental models and habits to function in a familiar setting. My studies show that people will work more hours from home than they did at the office and still have more time for themselves and their families. For me having the flexibility enabled by working from home is the answer to work creep and burn-out that has engulfed the American information worker. The virtual workplace is the only environment that will enable employees to balance their lives and continue to contribute to business performance through increased personal productivity.

The progression to working from home, for some mobile workers, may be largely invisible and painless. They could progress from spending enough time on the road that people stop expecting to see them in the office. This lack of expectation for personal contact can lead to the mobile worker increasingly taking advantage of working from home when in town. This would have to be achieved with no change in their contribution, participation or availability, and no complaints from associates. Once they are completely trusted working in this new mode and the days worked from home become the majority of the work days when not traveling, they should then have the organization eliminate their permanent office workplace and realize the savings. This scenario, perhaps not the invisible part mentioned earlier, is being enacted daily across America by some 25 million workers according to government statistics.

Currently the majority of those working from home do so only a few days a month, but the number of individuals and the days they work from home will increase very rapidly over the next 5 to 10 years. Imagine the savings that will be harvested by organizations simply by encouraging their employees to transition to virtual work and reducing the need for expensive office space. Think of the impact this will have on traffic, especially during the morning and afternoon commutes. This would save the information workers tens of millions of dollars for gas and car expenses; it could reduce our country's demand for gas by the same magnitude. It would slow the need for additional highway capacity and reduce pollution, just to highlight a few of the possible benefits. I am not predicting the virtual work environments will contribute to world peace or the eradication of hunger, but it really will make a significant difference to personal productivity and corporate performance—with some powerful side effects.

For the worker and their families it will create opportunities to eliminate old boundaries, create new flexibility and balance their family, and personal lives with their business life. It will be the worker that must take the lead working this issue because organizations will accept all the extra effort they can get from the employees.

To successfully journey to the new virtual world of work, we need to assess where we are today. With this knowledge, road maps and plans can be created that will focus on technology infrastructures, business practices, and most importantly the mind-set and readiness of the people involved. I will cover these topics in detail, later in the book.

At the 2005 Microsoft CEO Summit, Bill Gates spoke about the challenges facing the information worker. I have chosen this extract from one of his talks because it clearly articulates what he thinks, and as the definitive expert influencing what capabilities will be supported in the Microsoft software, it is important. He and his team are focused on achieving major breakthroughs in improvements in how work is accomplished. These advances are absolutely necessary for the total vision of the virtual work environment to be realized.

Microsoft has been there for the information worker over the past 25 years and will continue to put Information Worker empowerment at the center of its product philosophy in the years to come. We believe firmly that the promise of the digital work style and coming advances in smart, simple, pervasive and trustworthy technology points us onward to a more human-centric world of innovation and productivity.

Already, software is enabling shared workspaces where workers can collaborate far more effectively than in the past. There is no longer a need for team members to manually update each other on progress, for questions about who has the latest version of a project, for sending documents around, because everything is in a single place for everyone to see and routine notifications can be automated. In a new world of work where collaboration, business intelligence and prioritizing scarce time and attention are critical factors of success, the tools that information workers use must evolve in ways that do not impose additional burdens of complexity on workers who already feel the pressure of ubiquitous access and ever-rising expectations of productivity.

Information technology (IT) has played a critical role both in creating the conditions for change and in helping organizations adapt to it. As we move toward a world that is more fluid, less centralized and less certain about old assumptions and old models, IT is evolving in ways that will empower organizations, teams and individuals to realize their potentials in a new world of work.

The proliferating use of information has been instrumental in achieving better outcomes for businesses and higher productivity for workers. However, in celebrating the success of these advances, we should not forget that the ability to adapt and innovate is fundamentally a human talent. Empowering people to work more efficiently and effectively in the "digital work style" of the new world of work should be at the center of any organization's strategy as it addresses the coming era of rapid change and increasing global integration.

To read his entire speech, go to the Microsoft website, provided in the book references.

There is approximately a five-year time-frame from concept and design to software product delivery. Thus, we will be using his current ideas of the workplace to successfully compete in the information worker world in this decade. It is through the productivity and innovation of the information worker, and the organization's ability to adapt and change, that businesses compete with each other to survive and prosper. We have all heard the statement usually attributed to Darwin, "survival of the fittest," but the more correct statement is, "survival of the most adaptable."

In the past the corporate assets with the greatest value were physical. They were the buildings, tools, parts, products, physical documents; all associated with production, suppliers and customers. These were the dominant assets. Communication was face-to-face and in the business offices. So it was logical that people had to go to these assets to work. Things were familiar, predictable and for many, more comfortable. Change was at a pace that allowed people more time to adjust.

Many things have changed on the long journey from the Industrial Age to the Digital Age. Everything associated with work is rapidly changing, and so should our thinking. Today the physical assets are not as valuable as the digital assets. Knowledge, ideas, business processes, product designs, proprietary information, market strategies, innovation, et cetera are the current assets that contribute to the real value of an organization. The ability to innovate, imagine, and create new ideas are what produces competitive advantage. Things are changing much more rapidly, so they are not as stable, familiar or predictable. We have communications and technical infrastructures enabling all of these digital assets to now come to the workers regardless of time or location. We now have the ability to change who, how, when and where we do our jobs.

Section Introduction Summary

- To make the journey to the new world of work easier to understand, I have segmented the information worker's world of work into four stages:
  - Information Worker Stage (1960s to 1990s)
  - Mobile Worker Stage (1990s to 2000s)
  - Virtual Worker Stage (2000s to 2020s)
  - Knowledge Worker Stage (2020s to 2030s)
- Organizations can have great variance in their speed of transformation acceptance from one stage to the next.
- In each stage the capabilities of the information worker are enhanced through new techniques, attitudes, geopolitical events and technologies.

- Virtual work environments are a great example of EPSS (electronic performance support system) whose mission is to enable organizations to achieve business performance through enhanced human performance.
- Mobile work environments enable increasing productivity "*one worker at a time*" and virtual collaborative work environments will increase and improve productivity "*one team at a time.*"
- Organizations can achieve enhanced human performance not just by how people work but also by creating greater flexibility in when and from where workers contribute.
- The pace at which we are evolving the work world is extremely fast and these changes are causing changes in every aspect of our life.
- The pace of changing or eliminating inflexible attitudes will dictate the pace at which the transformation to a virtual world of work can progress and the benefits harvested.
- Face-to-face is still the most effective and necessary human communication technique; it just does not have to happen daily between 8 a.m. and 5 p.m. at the same fixed location.
- The virtual workplace is the only environment that will enable employees to balance their lives and continue to contribute to business performance through increased personal productivity.
- Government statistics show there are currently 25 million workers working from home at least a few days per month.
- In the past workers had no choice, they had to go to the organization's facilities to access the people and physical assets to do their work—this is not the case today, all digital assets can come to the individual regardless of time or location.
- We now have the ability to change who, how, when and where we do our jobs.

CHAPTER 2

DEFINITIONS

Words and how we use them has always fascinated me. We can take regular words that have a long history of use and put them in combination to create new meanings that define modern concepts. If we look at the term, *virtual worker*, we have a great example. The word virtual is based on the word virtue. The origin of this word can be traced to the Latin word *"vertus"* and the French word *"vertu."* Vertus mean *trust or worth* and vertu means *goodness or power.* In English we equate the following meanings to the word *virtue: efficacy, faithfulness, goodness, honesty, integrity, justice, trustworthiness.* Virtue is a good word for us to use as the basis for how we want to describe the workers in the virtual world of work.

Information is a noun and its origin is from the Latin word *"informatio (onis)"—a representation, an outline, sketch, to give form to, to inform, derived from senses, or from the intellectual faculties, communication of facts.* Today the word is very common in our language and is used to describe the representation of data. To be considered information the form of the data must be in a context such that it can be used to inform or to communicate so people can use the data to make decisions and conduct work.

Mobile can be used as an adjective or a noun. It comes from the Latin words, *"mobilis"—moveable and "movere"—to move.* The words used to define mobile today are similar to those used in Latin. They are: *not firm or stationary; very fluid; easily influenced; changeable or changing; versatile.* I think anyone, working as a mobile worker, would appreciate being thought of as versatile. Today we may use a word like flexible, dedicated or motivated as attributes for mobile workers. All of these words provide a good connotation for the meaning used in this book.

The Virtual World of Work, pages 13–16
Copyright © 2008 by Information Age Publishing

Virtual has a dictionary definition of: *being in essence or effect, not in fact; not actual, but equivalent, so far as effect is concerned.* I like this meaning, because it combines the notion of essence and equivalence with the base meaning of trust. This is a good definition for us to use in describing a virtual worker. I believe it fits well in this context because the word trust is a key attribute required for employees who work while on the road or from home.

The word *work,* can be either a verb or a noun. As a verb its meaning is: *to bestow labor, toil, or exertion upon; to produce, accomplish, or acquire; to be the cause of, to effect, to bring about, to work a change.* As a noun: *that which is done, performed; or action, deed, feat, achievement; that which is made, manufactured, or assembled; an article or product; that which is produced by physical or mental labor.* This too is very appropriate for our purpose.

The word *environment,* is used to describe; *the act of surrounding; the state of being environed; the parts or places that lie in its neighborhood.* Today we have a much greater technology focus related to that which surrounds, encapsulates or enables us.

Knowledge is defined as: *a clear and certain perception of that which exists, or truth and fact; learning or illumination of mind; skill; cognizance; recognition.* Today the word knowledge is used in many ways to support meanings that can vary widely. Chris Riemer is a knowledge guru who can be reached at "*knowledgestreet.com.*" Chris was a former colleague who used this definition in his presentations:

> Knowledge is a matter of layering context. Consider Data to be raw facts. Data becomes Information when facts are associated in meaningful ways. Information becomes Knowledge when it is linked in some way to other Information. Wisdom is Knowledge that is associated with other Knowledge over time, or with Knowledge from other domains. Knowledge is information that leads to action. People have knowledge when they know what to do. Knowledge is a renewable resource.

Collaboration is derived from the Latin words; "*con*"—*together,* and "*laborare*"—*to labor.* The dictionary definition is: *the act of performing work or laboring together, especially literary, scholarly or scientific pursuits; in association of another or others.*

I think all of these definitions work well considering they are from our family dictionary passed down from our great-grandfather. It is the *Webster Imperial Dictionary,* by Noah Webster, published in New York, in 1913. There is something reassuring to know that some things still maintain their usefulness and we can build on the knowledge or great works of the past. Not everything in our ever expanding universe has to change to be relevant.

There are some words whose usage just does not fit as well once things evolve. The image created by the pioneering word for working from home, "*telecommuting,*" will not be adequate. We need to update the term and use more visual words to paint the vision for the information worker of the future. I think a better image is created by the words mobile and virtual.

Based on the previous definitions, I describe a *virtual team* as one working from a variety of locations, brought together in essence or equivalence, to work together, to leverage individual expertise in producing a joint or community deliverable associated with a specific outcome. The purpose of the virtual team is to produce measurably superior results at an acceptable cost. The group will function collaboratively at a level which delivers greater quality, in less time, with reduced risk and cost. The team will utilize and maximize the group's expertise and knowledge. To do this effectively and efficiently the team needs a technical environment that manages the means for collaboration of each member, to function and contribute, even if the group is physically in separate locations.

The infrastructure must accommodate and actively support people working globally from different time zones; with varying skill levels, devices and expertise; in harmony with a single, shared objective. As the software tools advance, so will the opportunity to transition from working individually, coordinating and assembling the final work product; to working in unison, having the software coordinate the efforts of the group and the final iteration is the finished product.

This can and does happen today with very expensive, specialized software for specific business processes, like designing complex products. The CATIA software from Dassaut Systemes, the world leader in Product Lifecycle Management (PLM) software solutions, is used by Boeing to allow thousands of engineers from around the world, to work collaboratively, in real-time, on the design of a new airplane. As the airplane component designs progress, the software makes sure that everything will fit together and work properly. The PLM suite enables Boeing to design, build and test the airplane digitally prior to production. The difficult job of integrating design changes is handled by the software. It worked as intended and Boeing was able to sell the first 777 airplane built using the sophisticated software solution. Prior to PLM, building the initial plane was part of the design process allowing the manufacturing, tooling and engineering people to find problems and make the appropriate adjustments to the design, manufacturing, or assemble processes. This software has enabled greater quality and saved Boeing a tremendous amount of time and money by reducing rework. Complex engineering has come a long way in the last few decades, from the individual drafting boards with the thousands of paper drawings, to now having digital images generated from a single source and shared globally by thousands of engineers.

When these capabilities are available in inexpensive software, for all information workers to use, the improvement in productivity and quality will be equally dramatic. A further quantum leap in performance will be achievable when management realizes that they have the power to assemble the best resources for any job; regardless of where the resources reside. The resources may be down the hall, across town, in a different country or even at home.

Later in the book we will examine how this vision will work and provide insight to the technical environments that are available today and those that will be available in the near future. The future software and technologies will provide capabilities that can enable a much greater degree of collaboration, at acceptable costs. Personal and group productivity will be increased and corporate performance will provide competitive advantage for those that move quickly.

Chapter Summary
- The pioneering word for working from home, "*telecommuting,*" will not be adequate—we need to update the term and use more visual words to paint the vision for the information workers of the future.
- A *virtual team* works from a variety of locations—brought together in essence or equivalence to work together in association with each other, to leverage individual expertise in producing a joint or community deliverable associated with a specific outcome.
- The virtual infrastructure must accommodate and actively support people working globally from different time zones—with varying skill levels, devices and expertise—in harmony with a single, shared objective.
- A quantum leap in performance will be achievable when management realizes that they have the power to assemble the best resources for any job; regardless of where the resources reside.

CHAPTER 3

STAGE ONE: "INFORMATION WORKER"

In this stage, early 1960s to early 1990s, people are introduced to and accept computers into their jobs and their lives.

A unique categorization scheme based on worker capabilities has been created, so that types of mobile and virtual work activities can be grouped into four distinct stages for easy recognition. The segmentation between the stages will help organizations understand how far they have progressed using mobile and virtual work environments.

In the 1960s–'70s, the first half of Stage One, the office workers and management who had not previously used computers, transition to *information workers* with the introduction and use of commercial computers. The adoption of these early computers changed dramatically how work was accomplished and created totally new jobs. The acceptance of computers into our work lives has forever altered how we think about work.

The information worker stage began with the conversion of existing business processes like invoicing, accounts receivable, general ledger, accounts payable, payroll and inventory control. Some of the manual processes and most of the existing accounting machines were eventually eliminated by the automation made possible by the newly introduced computers.

There were many large accounting machine suppliers that dominated the market prior to the computers; the most common were NCR, Burroughs, Olivetti, Litton and Sharp. It is interesting that these companies, with sales and service personnel in literally every city and town, were not the ones that dominated the computer market. None of them leveraged

The Virtual World of Work, pages 17–23

their market position or their ability to influence their customers, and the opportunities were forever missed. This has created an ideal script for a great business case for educators and demonstrates what happens when the opportunity is missed because of an inability to change with the times.

These new computers were also replacing applications that run on unit record equipment and at data centers. The initial introduction of computers were to the larger companies. Gradually the small and medium sized businesses started acquiring technology and before long became the bulk of the first-time computer users. IBM saw the opportunity and quickly captured and dominated the computer market. Like in many new fields the market became controlled by the manufactures. Customers had to pay large deposits to get a delivery slot for a new computer and then wait, sometimes for over a year, for the product to be delivered and installed. The margins were incredibly high for the suppliers of the hardware and software, partially because of the uniqueness of the products and the risk associated with the large investments in technology research.

The costs of the hardware in the early years consumed the majority of IT budgets; today the costs of people and services have this distinction. In the early part of this stage the services were included or bundled with the high cost of hardware by IBM. Prices could be established by the manufacturers with little or no room for negotiations by the customers. It was a great time to work for IBM, Univac, DEC, Amdahl, Wang, to name a few of the largest computer manufacturers.

I started with IBM in the 1960s and spent my early career supporting clients with the new System/360 line of computers. I remember some friends asking me why I was pursuing a career in computing; they saw little future in that industry. Within a few years my focus changed to the implementation of mini computers for the first-time users of computers like the IBM System/3, MAI Basic Four, DEC-PDP 8 & 11, Wang 2200 and Micro Data. The sales challenge faced with the first-time users of minis was convincing non-computer oriented management that their data would be safe. The most common objection from the staff was they could not operate without the ever-present ledger cards. Most business offices had hard paper ledgers and files everywhere. Even to this day you can still see the walls of color coded paper files in medical offices.

In most cases the same report layouts, preprinted forms, and input formats could be reused with the new systems. Since the applications ran in a stand-alone manner, most accounting applications like invoicing, accounts payables, inventory, accounts receivables, payroll and general ledger could be implemented one application at a time. To automate these existing applications could each be completed in a matter of weeks.

One of the largest tasks was keying all of the history data into the computers and designing a new chart of accounts. The interfaces between applications were accomplished through manual entries or by reading the output from one application as input into another in the form of paper tape, key punch cards, and magnetic media such as tape reels or disk packs. The initial computing world of work was not very complex and most projects were actually completed successfully. The most valuable design knowledge was understanding the constraints or limitations of the particular hardware and software, and how to work within them. Today the projects are much more complex and the limitations on the technologies are much less critical. Designing new processes and integrating them into multiple sophisticated legacy environments is more difficult and unfortunately most projects in the last few decades are consistently over budget and schedule while delivering less than expected.

In the 1960s–'70s the public was very intrigued but still very unaware of what a computer could do, how it worked and the impact it would have on their lives. My first job, after months of IBM training, was working in an installation/testing facility. I spoke of this earlier but it still amazes me that some people would stand for hours at the street window to watch the lights flashing, the tape drives spinning, disk packs being changed, punch cards being feed into readers and those amazing high speed printers spewing paper. The computer was perceived to be very complex, expensive and something that the average person just did not touch. Things have certainly changed!

The computer age introduced many new terms into our language and those that could use them in conversation were given much too much credit for being smart. It was great! Computers required extensive training to understand, operate and design systems to take advantage of the new capabilities. Computers were seen by some as a threat that would eliminate many office jobs. If fact, I did not see the elimination of many jobs. Instead what happened was new jobs were created as we moved through this first stage. Today there exist millions of IT jobs supporting more and more information workers.

In the last half, 1980s to 1990s, of the Information Worker Stage, organizations started doing totally new things with their rapidly expanding computer capabilities. Projects got a lot more complex and organizations took advantage of the power, to not just replace existing processes but to aggressively create completely new ways of doing things. Clients were creating new business processes, services and lines of business. We were doing things that could not be done before by older technologies. Things like airline reservations, international banking, weather reporting, military surveillance, satellite communications, ATM machines, scanning; these high profile examples and many more less obvious systems simply cannot be accomplished without computers.

An example of an early technology introduction was described to me by a good friend. He was articling with an audit firm at the start of the 1960s when the firm acquired their first electronic adding machine. It was large and expensive, only partners could role the machine into their offices, more junior staff needed to line up to use the adding machine in the open office space. Honest, this is true. Compare that to the situation today, it seems we have adding machines with greater power in every drawer in our offices and homes. As with the adding machines most technology is not just the privy of the business world but is now totally integrated into our personal lives. This acceptance of technology is extremely relevant to our future adoption of even more advanced technologies.

We now find our society in an incredible position with regard to using technology. The vast community of knowledge that exists today, particularly in the younger people, will allow us to move forward with much greater speed and success into a totally enabled digital society. These advances in understanding, familiarity and knowledge, coupled with the more sophisticated hardware and software solutions, position us for a quantum step forward in how we do our jobs and live our lives.

The Information Worker Stage was a fantastic time in which I enjoyed the majority of my career. It was an incredible period of technology introduction, experimentation, and discovery. I am blessed to have been directly involved and working during all four decades of this stage. During this time frame information workers have participated in a vast variety of interesting and challenging projects:

- The initial introduction of commercial computers to first-time users.
- The implementation of standalone accounting applications.
- The building of automated interfaces between applications.
- The transition from custom software to COTS (commercial off the shelf) software.
- The movement from centralize computing to decentralized desktop computing, referred to as client server.
- The redesign of GUI (graphical user interface) front-ends for applications.
- The re-engineering of the legacy systems and the corresponding business processes, this was also referred to as BPR (business process re-engineering).
- The process, productivity and quality improvement initiatives.
- The projects to integrate and align business processes with the support systems.
- The programs to implement sophisticate security technologies.
- The change to just-in-time inventory systems and strategies.
- The introduction of networks and later the WWW (World Wide Web).

- The massive projects to rethink and redo supply chain management.
- The implementation of large complex ERP (enterprise resources planning), PLM (product life-cycle management) and CRM (customer relationship management) packages.
- The movement to outsourcing and the start of offshore service providers.
- The frantic time dealing with the Y2K initiatives, *"to keep the world safe."*
- The data warehousing solutions that were to deliver information anytime, anyplace and it seemed most often at any cost.
- The most interesting was the *"e"* everything race during the high-tech extravaganza, people prematurely predicted the demise of the brick and mortar world.
- The effort to extend organizational reach to customers, suppliers, employees, the public—building portals and private/public exchanges, B2B (business to business) or B2X—whatever.
- The legacy migration projects to utilize newer cheaper commodity technologies.
- The provisioning of laptops, initial mobile devices and software.
- Portfolio and value management approaches.
- The many downsizing, cost cutting, right sizing programs.
- And last but not least the compliance initiatives or SOX (Sarbanes Oxley), initiatives brought about by unbelievable fraud and lack of oversights at Enron, WorldCom, etc., that seriously damaged people's confidence in business.

During the 30–35 years covered by Stage One there have been an untold number of new amazing technologies introduced. Some were successful and some failed. The ones that I believe carried the most significant impacts were the IC (integrated circuit), desktop and laptop computers, storage devices, the Internet, satellites, mobile phones, scanning and the sophisticated software used to run computers and business processes. The point is the changes and the pace of these changes, has been nothing short of unbelievable. I think most people have adapted to these changes so well they seldom reflect on the amount of change they have personally endured. Take a few minutes to reflect on what has changed in your life time, I think you will become a little nostalgic.

During the same period individuals and society has gone through a tremendous amount of personal, family and social change. These developments have had just as significant an impact on us as the technology changes. The greatest of these changes influencing us are:

- Two working parents pursuing careers.
- The tremendous use of credit.
- The expectations and entitlement people think they have.

- The availability and variety of products and services for us to consume.
- The wide spectrum of global information instantly available to influence us.
- The pace at which we live our lives.
- The extent of the life choices we have.
- The amount of information people have.
- Our advances in health care.
- The amazing extension of the average life span.

Many things we take for granted today were not possible just a few years back. The wealth, influence and responsibility that have accumulated in a small number of high-tech innovators, even exceed that of the publishers, oil magnets and transportation barons of the past. IBM created the standard for computing in the world, Dell and HP dominate the desktop and laptop hardware markets, and Microsoft has created a whole new industry for software that we are now totally dependent on globally. Amazon has introduced a global digital capability to conduct business anytime, anywhere by just about anyone. A complete global community has been created by eBay, enabling collectors, hobbyist, individuals and small businesses to buy and sell from around the world. The Internet has become so vast and pervasive that companies like AOL, Yahoo and Google can emerge as huge entities by providing content and search capabilities. Without the digital capabilities these successes would not have happened. Each represented on this list has imagined and succeeded in making the whole world its market.

Even though the technology and social changes have an enormous impact on our lives and how we do our jobs in the new world of work, perhaps the greatest single significant outcome from Stage One is the incredible body of knowledge and acceptance that has been gained. This familiarity has changed how people think about technology and has prepared the population for much greater change. The information worker is now ready for the transformation to the new world of work.

Chapter Summary

- The categorization scheme is based on the evolutionary stages of worker capabilities.
- The stage descriptions allow organizations to measure their evolution.
- In the information worker stage, early 1960's to early 1990's, people are introduced to and accept computers into their jobs and their lives.

- The vast community of knowledge that exists today, particularly in the younger people, will allow us to move forward with much greater speed and success into a totally enabled digital society.
- I think most people have adapted to computer so completely they seldom reflect on the amount of change they have personally experienced.
- During the same period individuals, families and society has gone through a tremendous amount of change.
- Most successful organization imagine and succeed in making the whole world their target market.
- Stage One has provided an incredible change in how people think about technology and this has prepared us for even greater changes.

CHAPTER 4

STAGE TWO:
"MOBILE WORKER"

In this Stage the information worker is enabled and gains a new flexibility to be connected and work while remote from the office. This begins the always connected life style of the future and the mobile capabilities explode during the 1990s and 2000s. Because of this new capability, this Stage is named for the *mobile worker.* Pretty much all of the activities, including working longer and harder, exists because of the personal initiatives of the new mobility enabled information workers. Mobile workers are taking it upon themselves to extend the workday and the workweek. The normal time and location boundaries for work are obsolete for mobile workers. The idea of fixed times when you conduct only work, then cross an invisible line and do absolutely no work is absurd. Although these are irrelevant boundaries today, the question we must resolve is how we balance this blending of work/life. Having the discipline and the ability to start and stop work while mobile is a key skill that must be learned.

Most people who put in many hours outside of the traditional work day still feel awkward conducting personal activities during work at the office. These additional work hours have contributed to the dramatic increase in productivity across America. Without the mobile workers enablement initiatives, organizations would not be successful with the *"doing more with less"* strategy employed by most.

The dot com crash, which began in March of 2000, contributed greatly to the economic slide, which in turn led to the downsizing of most organizations. I think it fascinating that it is the technology contributions from this sector, creating new mobile work products and infrastructures that are

---

The Virtual World of Work, pages 25–30
Copyright © 2008 by Information Age Publishing

enabling the increased productivity. This in turn has contributed to the rebound of the American business sector.

Technology is being used to extend who, how, where and when mobile workers do their jobs. What I mean by these simple words is:

- **Who**—the information workers that are equipped with mobile capabilities and have security authorization to access the proprietary files, information, technology, work process and other employees to conduct work globally while away from the traditional office.
- **How**—this is the hardware devices, software, communications, security, et cetera, that comprise the mobile platforms, work infrastructures and work environments used to enable the mobile worker to connect via cable, phone lines, satellites or wireless networks and work effectively and efficiently from nearly any place.
- **Where**—the location can be anywhere you have the ability to connect with your mobile workplace, even fluid environments like planes, ships, cars, trains, cycling or walking.
- **When**—this defines the 24 by 7 time-frame in which the work is performed, this may not be as straightforward as face-to-face work environments because workers can be located on the other side of the Date Line, in different time zones and/or countries that honor different work schedules and holidays.

Being mobile can be as simple as working from different offices, meeting rooms, airports, hotel rooms, Starbucks or from home on evenings, holidays and weekends. Pretty much every organization I know is engaged in Stage Two activities. If you go to a Starbucks today you will see at least one interview, meeting or sales presentation. Clever people are realizing that mobile workers need convenient places to meet. Even office meetings have changed dramatically. Most attendees have laptops or other devices open and in use during the meetings. People are attending meetings through new conferencing and video techniques. Where people sit in meetings has also evolved. The boss seldom sits in the power position at the head of the table; instead they sit in the new "*power*" seat closest to the outlet or network connection.

Information workers are putting in extra time just to keep up or to meet the commitments and schedules dictated to them. From early morning to late night, millions and millions of workers are remotely producing, reviewing or reworking: spread sheets, reports, proposals, presentations, documents, deliverables, personnel reviews, resumes, budgets, financial statements.

Many still work remotely using paper documents but without the enabling technology they are limited in what, where, when and how much they can actually accomplish. Those that use their laptops may only have a partial advantage over the paper workers if they work off-line, not connected to their information assets. This is often the case because of the struggles of connecting to corporate email or intranets while remote. Even mobile phone conversations are normally conducted in multiple parts. We all should have suspected something when the cell phones first introduced a new feature called "*redial.*" I thought this a good development but I certainly did not suspect at first how much this feature would need to be used. Can you hear me now?

I personally have been frustrated in just about every way possible trying to connect while on the road. I have heard many excuses for not being able to connect. Here are my favorites:

- My battery is dead;
- I forgot the cable;
- I could not get through from this "*blankety blank*" hotel room;
- I cannot find my VPN token;
- The dial up line is too slow to down load the needed files;
- It keeps saying my user name and password are incorrect;
- I left my glasses on the plane;
- I forgot my glasses in the taxi;
- The tech support person is not in today;
- I cannot remember the local number I am supposed to dial;
- I left my compute at the airport security check-in.

"*Just shoot me; I am too tired, this is the third city this week; I no longer care.*" I hope I am not the only one that can relate to these excuses and feelings. How many of you understand why the procedures to work while remote have to be so different from those used when working in your office? Why does the change, by the other region's tech support person, make your computer not work when you get home?

For those mobile workers that can connect, it is getting easier with Wi-Fi and other wireless technologies. The impact of time and geography are no longer inhibitors to remote work. The mobile information workers are primarily accessing emails and other materials to do individual work. In Stage Two we are still very much in the early or experimental phase of working in groups and using basic collaboration software tools. The ones using the tools today are the early adopters with great technical aptitudes or great need. This is changing very rapidly, are you?

New communications capabilities, supported by a wide variety of devices, have made voice, email, data, games, pictures and video exchanges very convenient for the mobile worker. In fact, the same devices are now used equally to support personal and work usage. We have nationwide walkie talkie, instant messaging and entertainment all on mobile phones. All of the individual device capabilities will soon be in one small device that can be carried in a pocket. Then the only thing carried in a briefcase will be personal items, snacks or medication.

I had an early mobile experience with using a cellular phone in 1990. I was the account executive handling a large team at a very large client. The client occupied many buildings spread across 60 miles. I bought a cell phone and got a very heated response from my boss challenging me to justify the use and the costs. He felt they were not necessary. How ironic, this same boss two years later was angry, when on a visit to the same client, discovered most of our consultants were not using cell phones and losing time while traveling between buildings. Mobile progress can be achieved rapidly but not necessarily without some challenges.

The innovation of these devices is only exceeded by the imagination of the people who use them. For example, I have seen a person snap a picture of a cluttered whiteboard and immediately send it to others, on the phone but not at the meeting, for clarification. In a meeting in Japan, a colleague took digital pictures of a whiteboard, and the group working the issues, and sent them to his management in the U.S. This allowed them to see who was participating and what had been discussed. This technology is absolutely necessary when working in a foreign culture and language. While visiting our son in Chicago, he got a call from friends at a bar; he asks, "*Who's there*" and instantly receives a picture of the group on his mobile phone. Did you know, if you have an automatic car locking system and you lock your keys in the car, you can unlock the door, using a second set of keys at home by transmitting the signal over a cell phone held near the car lock? These are just a few of the innovations enabled by mobile phones. You probably noticed the new picture phones are not even referred to as mobile or cell phones. It is just taken for granted.

Devices like the Blackberry have enabled real-time wireless email messaging as well as voice communications. Direct reports to senior executives and government leaders are being supplied these devices, making everyone available by email or voice at all times. The idea of being always on or connected is the reality for these mobile workers. One of my closest friends is a connected person involved in communications, and she feels one of the difficulties is that mobile workers are more responsive but less reflective.

These mobile workers need to acquire the skills for working real-time, thinking and responding while connected. This is where the younger people have an advantage because of the dexterity developed playing electronic games. Can you type 30 words a minute using only your thumbs on a tiny keyboard? Can you respond to a text message using only one thumb while driving? This may not be a good thing but if you answered yes, you are probably in your 20s or 30s.

There are whole new languages emerging within organizations. You need to be able to read and send messages using the abbreviations that have evolved within specific work groups. Most wireless email and text messaging is totally without capitalization, punctuation and very cryptic. We are reaching the point that encryption may not be necessary. I defy anyone to understand what has been communicated without being part of the knowledgeable inner circle.

In Stage Two most organizations have limited policies and procedures or none at all, with regard to mobile work. For those trusted employees actually working from home, there may even be less in the way of organization, technical or HR policies. Most everything being done is by exception or special circumstance. Only the most creative organizations have engaged large groups to work from mobile environments with appropriate technologies, even fewer have tracked and measured the results, and virtually none are utilizing this as a strategic advantage.

Mobile activities are taking place in all organizations, and in spite of some difficulties, they are proving to provide fantastic tangible benefits. I see an irony here. Many of the managers I have interviewed are encouraging or insisting on the extra mobile work efforts, are the same ones that when asked, are not in favor of employees working from home on a permanent basis.

There are others that believe there is a condition called *"infomania."* These are the people who find it hard to focus on the task at hand, because they're maintaining a permanent state of readiness to react to technological interruptions. These are the over the top *"always on folks."* Still others I have spoken to believe very strongly that mobile work is just not healthy for anyone. They are comfortable with maintaining the existing time boundaries between business and personal activities.

These attitudes will keep some from transitioning through Stage Two in a timely manner. Others will make the journey in a planned, effective way, tied closely to the technology introduction timeframes that enable Stage Two, not the preservation of the status quo. Nonetheless, information workers and organizations will make the transition because the benefits are too compelling to not do so.

Nissan is a great case study for mobile work that I will cover in detail in the chapter on Case Studies. In summary, they began to address their IT issues with moves calculated to reduce costs, streamline company operations, and improve worker productivity. They had no common platform across the company making connectivity a problem. Key to the improvement project was the provision of universal connectivity for Nissan employees, including full mobile access and the creation of a common employee portal. This provided the ability to provide anywhere, anytime access to their mobile workforce in a way that was almost identical to being in the office. Nissan expects to save at least $135 million over a few years thanks to the savings coming from increased productivity of their staff and at the same time they will spend less on technology, maintenance, travel, printing, telephone, and outsourcing.

Chapter Summary

- The Mobile Worker Stage begins the always connected life style of the future and the mobile capabilities that exploded during the 1990s and early 2000s.
- The normal time and location boundaries for work are now obsolete for mobile workers.
- The discipline and the ability to start and stop work while mobile is a key skill that must be learned—there is no transition time.
- Without the mobile workers enablement initiatives, organizations would not be successful with the "*doing more with less*" strategy employed by most.
- The impact of time and geography are no longer inhibitors to remote work.
- Mobile workers are more responsive but less reflective—the emphasis is definitely on speed.
- The innovation of the mobile devices is only exceeded by the imagination of the people who use them.
- Many of the managers I have talked to that are encouraging or insisting on the extra mobile work efforts are the same ones that when asked are not in favor of employees working from home on a permanent basis.
- In Stage Two most organizations have limited policies and procedures or none at all, with regard to mobile work. For those trusted employees actually working from home, there may even be less in the way of organization, technical or HR policies.
- Nissan expects to save at least $135 million over the next few years thanks to their national mobile implementation.

CHAPTER 5

STAGE THREE: "VIRTUAL WORKER"

It is in the Virtual Stage that collaboration is enabled across the organization and information workers and mobile workers work from home offices in virtual teams. The capture and personalization of knowledge are automated and readily available to team members. It is in the late 2000s through the 2020s that we will be enabling these capabilities for the *virtual worker.*

When I started working from home, I checked with colleagues to see what practices were in place and found most everyone was treated differently and had unique arrangements with their managers. What was covered through expenses and what was not varied greatly. Most of these arrangements never went through the executives, legal, finance, IT or HR before they were agreed to. Later in the book, I will present what should be covered in a policy for virtual workers. Initially for most organizations the justification for having information workers become virtual workers will be the facility cost savings.

Although, these savings can be harvested and measured through standard metrics, FTE (full-time equivalent) per square foot, $ per FTE and $ per square foot, in many cases they are not being realized by organizations. There are a variety of reasons for not eliminating the space for a virtual worker. I think the most common are:

- The employee is still working in the office part of the time.
- The employee is uncomfortable permanently releasing the space.
- Management and the employee are reluctant to break the connection.
- There are no policies, thus no one is confident in what to do.

The Virtual World of Work, pages 31–42
Copyright © 2008 by Information Age Publishing
All rights of reproduction in any form reserved.

- For each individual the savings are not that great.
- They do not want to make the change that obvious.
- It could impact someone's budget or headcount status negatively.
- There is a fear of starting something that could get out of control.

In most organizations there are workers who have traditionally worked out of the office: field workers, engineers, consultants, sales reps., pilots and flight attendants, to name a few. To not have an office in these positions is normal and accepted, so we know it is possible. In fact, according to government sources there are now 25 million or 16 percent of the information workers in America that have transitioned to working from home, at least on a part-time basis. I am one who moved to my home office when the local branch office was downsized. The early virtual employees are in their position because of special situations, enlightened managers, cost cutting measures or they have volunteered to be part of a pilot. They all have one thing in common; they are usually long-term, trusted and proven employees with good reputations.

In most organizations there will be a few trusted quiet employees working from home. Even with this early experience, the inhibitors to information workers working from home on a regular basis are the attitudes, habits and mental models that are pervasive in corporate America. Attendance and other Industrial Age thinking still are dominant with the baby boomer peer group. It is not because of age—it is because of how they think. This is fortunate because it is easier to change how people think than change their age, but not by much. A few years ago my boss lived on the west coast in the Bay Area and was named the President of the U.S. division. Since the CEO and many of the other senior executives worked out of the corporate office in New Jersey, she was expected to relocate to be able to do her job. She did not move to the east and thus had to fly there every Sunday night on the red eye and back home on Friday night. Can you imagine anything more disruptive to one's personal life? The ironic thing was that most people did not even see anything odd about this lifestyle; many were also doing weekly commutes from DC, Toronto and Atlanta.

Industrial Aged thinking does not take into account the needs of the employees nor is it open to more flexible ways to do work. After all, the thinking is based on the need for control. This practice has been dictated by past management practices for years without major challenges. During the Industrial Age it was the facilities that were the most expensive and important assets, thus there was a need to leverage them. Today most employees still go to the assets to work. But, in the new digital work world the information assets can come to the information workers through technology, thus changing the paradigm. Even though we can access the information assets from anywhere we can connect, many information workers I have talked to are so indoctrinated that they feel a need to go to the office to focus on work. Being comfortable in the workplace has much to do with habit not necessity. Do not underestimate the need for some to be connected to the office "*umbilical cord.*"

Most managers say the employees are the most critical part of an organization, but I really wonder why people say that and then act different. Actions are always a more accurate barometer of how people think than words. Most people do not even realize they have strong biases against people working from home until they are faced with the situation. These biases are very combative to employees balancing their work/life challenges and still having a productive career.

Here are a few examples of the prevailing management attitudes experienced during interviews:

- Employees cannot fully contribute if working from home.
- I will not be able to manage the employees if they are not at work.
- I will not be able to reach them quickly enough.
- Wanting to work from home is certainly not something I would expect from a fast tracker.
- Home workers are not team players.
- Homes can be too disruptive to work effectively.
- Face-to-face contact is what I am most comfortable with.
- We need to be able to rally quickly, brainstorm, solve problems, which can only be done together in the office.
- There is no way to know what they are really doing at home.

There is a strong underlying belief that employees need to be closely managed and monitored to get the expected and necessary performance. Managers are the ones that represent the interests of the business so they know best what to do. These attitudes foster the feeling that employees cannot be trusted on their own. People believe that to get the initiative needed, to work hard, to know what to do if unexpected things happen, are all best handle, "*in the office.*" Many existing managers just do not believe it will work for them so they are reluctant to have others try.

A lot of our attitudes, structures and practices have been derived from the old military paradigm of command-and-control. Today the modern military has changed considerably to an emphasis on Special Forces. Small teams that are trained to think and react on their own based on the circumstances and conditions they encounter. This thinking is portrayed in the slogan, "*an army of one.*" There are many new military strategies and battle field technologies being developed that business may what to modify for their own use. New capabilities to identify where everyone is, what technology they are using, what they are encountering and what they are doing. I understand this will be difficult because it might look too much like big brother, but it can be done and will be very beneficial particularly in a virtual world of work.

The technical infrastructure implemented to support effective and efficient mobile work is the baseline needed to support productive home offices. Organizations will need to set standards for acceptable home-based work space. I believe the organizations will need to control the technical environment and be assured that security controls protecting the corporate assets are sound, acceptable and at the same level required in the business office. Site visits are a good practice.

It is very probable that organizations will currently find themselves with activities in all of the first three Stages. I have included a few thoughts that describe Stage Three activities for your review. How many of these apply to you and your organization today?

- The HR department has established a complete range of policies and procedures with regard to employees working remotely, working from home and in collaborative teams.
- All necessary hardware, software, security, high speed communications, video conferencing and technical infrastructures are available to virtual workers.
- Organizations will provide incentive packages for current employees to change to a virtual worker status.
- Incentives will also be offered to retiring employees to stay on and work from home with a variety of employment options.
- Home office policies and procedures are amalgamated with corporate processes, guidelines and rules governing such areas as technology, communications, laptops, remote access, security, time keeping, attendance, expenses, meetings, availability, et cetera.
- Organizations will officially sanction home offices and will have defined a standard for what they will supply or pay for, and what they will not pay for in a home office. Do not expect to be treated with the same facility, supplies and equipment rules that apply to on-site workers.
- HR departments provide new flexibility to employees with regard to classifications, definitions for full and part-time employment, eligibility for benefits, expenses, and other unique work arrangements.
- New reward, evaluation and pay programs are in place for virtual workers based on productivity, not just time and attendance.
- Training for a variety of life and work issues will be available to help employees and management with the new virtual world of work.
- Integrated work management software is used to enable collaborative work. It will be capable of managing both individual and team work processes.

- Global collaboration between co-workers, contractors, suppliers, and partners is accepted as, "*the way we do things around here.*"
- Knowledge management practices (methods, techniques, tools and learning events) are deployed and used consistently group wide.
- Global resourcing, recruiting, and outsourcing are standard practices.
- All resources will maintain a virtual presence that indicates work status (e.g., available, online, busy, offline, etc.) to facilitate impromptu chats and work conversations.

For those workers considering retirement, there will be options to continue working from home, full or part-time, supporting the businesses processes they know and understand so well. The "*graying of the population,*" combined with a noticeable reduction in the available resource pool of qualified information workers, will make hiring and retaining employees difficult for businesses that have not made themselves an attractive employer to this demographic group. This will be especially true for those in large mature industries and the public sector. The number of retired workers is large and getting larger each year. According to the government statistics there are currently 35 million people more than 65 and that number will double by 2030. Of particular interest are the estimated 76 million baby boomers in this country that are just beginning to retire.

Other countries like those in Europe, Australia, Canada and Japan have an even bigger problem convincing their retiring workforces to continuing to work as they reach retirement. This is because these countries tend to have much more generous retirement and social benefits. We do not think of China having a shortage of workers but they have had a "*one child policy*" for many years, precipitating a potential workforce shortage in the future. In Australia the government is designing policies that will encourage business and mature employees to work beyond the retirement age. In the next decade Japan will have 26 percent of its population more than 65 according to work colleagues quoting their government statistics. This large increase in mature Japanese citizens, couple with one of the lowest birth rates in the world, will create a significant shortage in their labor pool. Their tradition of fewer women in the workforce also will have an impact.

These same trends affecting business will cause other social problems. Here in the U.S. there is a lot of focus and attention on the affordability of Social Security and the costs of medical assistance for retired seniors. Similar problems will also impact the other developed countries. With the percentage of retired workers dramatically rising, coupled with the tremendous increase in the life expectancy after retirement, we have a significantly different mix in the population that existed when these plans were conceived. Corporations that offered generous pension plans, (like the auto industry) never anticipated retired workers living so long. Many organizations will be unable to meet their commitments to their retired employees. My Father, for example, retired from Exxon and now at 91, he has been retired longer than he worked. These demographics will force changes to our current practices and expectations.

Just as serious is the loss of expertise and insights into customer, partner and supplier relationships. Without this experience dealing with the exceptions to key business processes, which are not typically documented, will cause business to repeat the problems of the past. Business will be increasingly faced with a multi-generational, multi-cultural workforce. A powerful practice is to put together workers that have great potential with those who have great experience. Those organizations that excel at handling the blending of these different work groups will have a definite edge in the virtual work world.

Redirecting recruiting efforts and budgets to retain mature workers through more flexible or alternative work arrangements might be a business saver. Avoiding the daily commutes and costs, political games, as well as the inevitable office pressures, may be a very powerful persuader for convincing the senior workers to continue working. With some training these veterans can continue to work from home, perhaps part-time, until replacements can acquire their knowledge. Successful organizations in the virtual world will focus on and become proficient at capturing, organizing and distributing this critical yet undervalued knowledge. To succeed in the Virtual Stage the practice of *knowledge reuse* must greatly outweigh the attitude of "not invented here" that has been so dominant.

Organizations need to evaluate collaborative software and choose a supplier they feel will have an all-encompassing solution that integrates with their infrastructure. There will need to be education and training programs in place to complement the deployment plans. I am a strong advocate for choosing a supplier that will over time provide a comprehensive integrated software platform that you can start with and grow with. Although the practice of technology insertion is starting to emerge, I think providing coaching for the deployment of sophisticated solutions is a good practice. I have seen organizations try to piece together a mix of software packages to inexpensively come up with solutions. Creating a working collaborative environment with the right methods, techniques, tools, learning events and support is too critical to risk with a *"plug and pray"* mentality. You cannot afford to be buying your future problems today.

The globalization of the resource pool and the demographics facing most nations will lead organizations to create and/or give more power to a *"resourcing function."* This function will be responsible for the acquisition of the best resources and the challenge of objectively assigning those resources where they can make the greatest contribution. The resource managers must look inside and outside to do their jobs. Being limited to only local, available employees will not be sufficient to compete in the future. I understand that this will cause some problems between resourcing and the local management that believe they own and control the resources. Critical resource assignment decisions need to be made with a combination of local knowledge and a wider organizational perspective. This does not mean somebody thousands of miles away should make the final decisions without understanding the local situation, circumstances or in fact the resources.

Working together in collaborative teams regardless of location, organization, position, all without moving, is a new skill that must be learned and practiced. Language and cultural differences will be complex issues we need to find solutions for. This practice is very different from utilizing the employees in a local single group or department to do the work. There will be many tradeoffs and issues that will arise, but the only way to maximize the make-up of a team will be through the concept of resourcing. This enables looking broader across multiple pools of resources and having the selection process balanced by evaluating the need, assessing current assignments and the preferences of the resources. This is a technique used very successfully by the consulting, engineering, film and legal industries for many years. The challenge is to find the best resources that may be well hidden by their local managers.

To allow the corporate files, processes or IP (intellectual property) to be used off-site by virtual teams, requires a more sophisticated security strategy. It is a delicate balance to protect the corporate assets while allowing easy remote access. With the heightened computer threads we need to be extra vigilant. Transparency into who is doing what, how, where, and when is very important for those monitoring the work efforts. Management will need to use new technology enabled techniques to have traceability with what is being done and to manage the resources, schedules and deliverables. We need an equivalent technology to that of the RFID (radio frequency identification) tags used with physical assets to track and locate important digital assets.

Current policies in many organizations control what has to be worked on premise and limits what can leave the physical location. The specific rules for privacy and security were most likely conceived with paper documents in mind, not electronic images. These policies still must be observed or modified where possible. Even exemptions to the rules may be difficult to obtain, because many corporate policies are implemented to meet government regulations and are very exacting as to who qualifies or is authorized for specific types of work and may carry large penalties if not abided by.

I worked in the aerospace industry where there are many ITAR regulations that control access, including nationality. As a Canadian I was limited to where I could go and what information I could see, until I became a U.S. citizen. These controls will need to be continually reviewed by the different government agencies requiring compliance. Over time this will happen but it will not be easy to get any government body to move quickly. Unfortunately, this will be one of the factors that will limit some organizations from moving forward quickly. The increased sophistication of biometrics screening is part of the answer. Leading edge uses of the new monitoring technology will need to evolve so we can trace the creation, movement, usage, modification and replication of information assets.

In Stage Three organizations will have completed the analysis and be ready to mandate what types of work, teams, groups or departments, will be eligible for virtual work. This is unlike Stage One and Two where it is primarily special circumstances or through personal initiative that brings employees to work from home. In my personal situation, I became a home worker because I used an office in a branch that was closed. From the corporate standpoint it was easy, my support and all direct reports were dispersed across many states and several countries. I was already a virtual manager in a special situation. Until the closure, the company was not receiving the benefit from a reduction of my facility costs. In fact, if I had asked to work from home it would not have been accepted without consequences. Conducting assessments and surveys to find the virtual workers like me, referred to as, *"finding low hanging fruit,"* or easily harvested benefits, will be common place.

Organizations need to establish or strengthen special interest communities so that the virtual workers can become part of and belong to something they value. Everyone has the need to feel comfortable, belonging to something that is work related, particularly if it is important to them. Virtual groups are required so workers can discuss issues, get advice and share discovered knowledge with others. At Fujitsu there was a lot of thinking that went into the creation of SIGs (special interest groups), COPs (communities of practice), and Councils. These membership associations were the responsibility of the senior consultants but funded by the corporation. The COPs had their own annual budgets to commission projects or studies that would contribute to the knowledge and skills of its members. They had a combination of mostly virtual but some face-to-face meetings. The communities gained status and respect as a valuable part of the corporation, independent of the typical organization structures. Representations from these groups were even included in the annual strategic direction setting meetings held by the CEO.

Organizations need support structures for the virtual workers and ideally will include access to education, tips or lessons learned, and counseling for those that require help. When you cannot go down the hall to get a technical issue quickly solved, you need a help desk or some form of real-time support for remote virtual workers. You do not want one person's technical problem impacting the working effort of a collaborative team. My experience shows that the agile techniques used in project management, work very well for collaborative teams. Keep the teams to 3–5 members, plus or minus one, for short periods of time. As dictated by the assignment, mix the members as often as possible.

Break up large assignments into smaller more manageable chunks. This allows much greater visibility for the team and management. It also allows the possibility to be more nimble and react more quickly. The size of the work assignments is in direct proportion with the ability to clearly define the requirements and get consensus on the outcome. Control and manage the outcomes of each team by deliverables, just like in any successful project. A smaller structure will reduce the inevitable wrangling that can appear in larger groups by making each individual contribution more visible.

I learned the hard way, when projects are managed by activities, instead of finite deliverables (work products), you never know exactly where things stand. At least when managing by deliverables and somebody says they have completed something, you can ask to review the deliverable. Even better, if there is a process that describes the input and output relationships with other deliverables, you can trace progress accurately. Most people I worked with were optimists and always thought they were on track until the schedule was at least 75 percent consumed. If you keep the estimated time to complete a deliverable to less than 10 days, then based on my observation you will not be more than 7 days into it before you really know where things stand. If the plans define four month deliverables you may waste lots of time and effort. This is a good reason for chunking the work efforts into smaller standardized deliverables. If this is not possible then question how well those involved understanding the assignment.

"*Hoteling*" facilities have become a common approach to accommodate employees for the time when they are required or choose to be in the office. This will allow them to feel more enabled and not totally cut off from the old environment and people they associated with. It is bad if employees need to scrounge space, inconvenience others or be asked to vacate a space when in the office. Remember how possessive people are, there are no squatter's rights for virtual workers in traditional offices.

Some trusted employees will be allowed to better balance their work days from home. This may involve the trading of typical work-time for non typical work-time, and may be permanent or temporary. Flexibility and trust are critical aspects of the virtual world of work. For example, parents with young children coming home from school may want to trade the 3:00 to 5:00 p.m. time slot for an equivalent time in the evening or early morning. This must be done with the approval of the work team and management.

Many enterprises are experiencing a major shift in thinking away from the Industrial Age beliefs that are holding change back, to proactive strategies to capitalize on the social and technology changes influencing work. In the Virtual Stage, very seldom would anybody try and win an argument with words like, *"that's the way we have always done things around here."* Many will recognize the need to create a new image or brand recognition that will enhance their likelihood to attract new young employees, retain the most knowledgeable ones and be acceptable to foreign workers.

Organizations will need to understand the social changes taking place and accept new flexibilities to accommodate employee needs and their desire to balance their lives and not sacrifice their careers. New visions will be established and used to create new organization structures, work teams, management practices, employee classifications, and work flexibility. These changes will require the dramatic reduction of organizational levels and the elimination of many middle management positions. The movement to a practice of using individual contractors, resourcing globally, organizing work around small agile teams and using new approaches to collaborative work supported by knowledge bases has definitely already started.

In Stage Three attitudes will shift and employees and management are comfortable with a mix of on-site and off-site workers. Experience shows that with the right encouragement, people get comfortable with the idea and the reality of virtual work. Group productivity can be achieved regardless of location. Increasingly, there becomes a level of acceptability or normality to hearing babies, children or pet noises, as well as other home generated temporary interruptions. Working from home should not become an alternative for daycare. I had one meeting interrupted when a person in Atlanta had a car crash into her front yard. Unexpected interruptions are not new; on several occasions I have had work sessions disturbed by a surprise fire drill or false alarm requiring everyone to evacuate the building.

Management's interest in having workers work from home is initially based on cost savings. This thinking will be expanded when productivity and quality are proven benefits of the virtual world of work. Once proven in an organization, very quickly new converts will appear and the movement will spread. Contractors and outsourcing will be part of the same overall business strategy that supports virtual work. The reality is new employee work arrangements will allow you to outsource to your own employees instead of third parties. There is definitely a shift to thinking more in terms of work products, trust and output verses attendance and payment for time; *"how warm is the seat compared to what is the productivity."*

The definition used for Stage Three is still viewed by many today as very uncomfortable, not clear and too risky, but this will change.

Management will base their virtual work decisions on opportunities to create enterprise value, not just cost savings. Over the next 5 to 10 years, new thinking, advanced technologies, positive experiences and social adjustment with the virtual world of work will prevail, and the ideas presented in this chapter will become commonplace. This future Virtual Worker Stage will gradually become the past and we will all need to fasten our seat belts, for from here we cannot see clearly what the virtual world of work will look like in the next stage. It took 30 years of my career to get through Stage One, then less than 15 years to progress through what I have envisioned as Stage Two and into Stage Three; so sit back, relax and together let's imagine what the future could be.

Chapter Summary
- It is in the late 2000s and the 2020s that organizations will encourage employees to work from home offices and enable collaborative strategies through new software environments that also emphasize the personalization of knowledge.
- Initially for most organizations the justification for having information workers become virtual workers will be the facility cost savings—although important this will prove to be less significant than the increases in productivity, morale, retention, and recruiting.
- The inhibitors to information workers working from home on a regular basis are the attitudes, habits and mental models that are pervasive in corporate America.
- Most managers and many information workers do not believe working from home will work for them so they are reluctant.
- A lot of our attitudes, structures and management practices have been derived from the military paradigm of command-and-control, and from the Industrial Age work habits derived over 200 years.
- Responsible organizations will provide the home technical environments assuring that security controls protecting the corporate assets are sound, acceptable and at the same level required in the business office.
- It is very probable that organizations will currently find themselves with activities in all of the first three Stages.
- Organizations will provide incentive packages for current and retiring employees to change to a flexible virtual worker status.
- The number of Baby Boomers starting to retire (76 million), the doubling in two decades of the population more than 65 years old and the decreasing birth rates are all demographic factors that will force changes to our current work practices and expectations.

- Retired workers often take with them the experience dealing with the exceptions to key business processes, suppliers and customers, which are not typically documented.
- A powerful practice is to put together workers that have great potential with those who have great experience by blending multi-generational and multi-cultural work teams.
- To succeed in the Virtual Worker Stage the practice of knowledge reuse must greatly outweigh the attitude of "*not invented here.*"
- Organizations need to evaluate collaborative software and choose a supplier they feel will have an all-encompassing solution that integrates best with their infrastructure.
- The globalization of the resource pool and the demographics facing most nations will lead organizations to create and/or give more power to a "*resourcing function.*"
- Organizations need to establish or strengthen special interest communities so that the virtual workers can become part of and belong to something they value.
- Trusted employees will be allowed to better balance their work days from home trading typical work-time for non-typical work-time.
- Organizations will need to understand the social changes taking place and accept new flexibilities to accommodate employee needs and their desire to balance their lives and not sacrifice their careers.
- Management will base their virtual work decisions on opportunities to create enterprise value, not just cost savings.

CHAPTER 6

STAGE FOUR: "KNOWLEDGE WORKER"

To imagine is to be human, and if what we imagine does not seem impossible, then it probably does not deserve the effort.

This is the point where we can really enjoy ourselves, free our minds and speculates on the future, 10 to 20 years out beyond the midpoint of Stage Three. We cannot see that far into the future but we can imagine what it "*could be.*" The future is the portion of the time line that is still to occur, i.e., the place in space-time where lie all events that still have not occurred—in this sense the future. The future will always be a surprise!

How would the scientific community, perhaps Stephen Hawking, tackle the problem of predicting the future virtual world of work and the capabilities of a *knowledge worker*? They are practiced at using solid theoretical and experimental techniques (observations and experiments) to understand how things work so they can predict the future. They have a lot of experience working on the really small (sub atomic) and extremely large (universe) problems. If we had a telescope and the knowledge of cosmologists, we could see way out into the universe to witness the past and see what has already happened on other worlds. That's how they know and predict what is in our celestial future. In the Appendix is presented a theoretical formula for possibly predicting the future world of work.

We do know at least one thing; the changes going forward will be more dramatic, faster and wilder to predict than the changes experienced during the past three Stages. What I imagine is based on my research, experience, thoughts, observations and dreams. But, what will really make the future, are the experiences, changing attitudes, technology, organizational

The Virtual World of Work, pages 43–53
Copyright © 2008 by Information Age Publishing

engineering, collaboration work experiences and knowledge gained in Stage Two and Stage Three. These are the factors that will influence the timing and make-up of the Knowledge Worker Stage.

The intention is to observe, discuss, identify and analyze what happened in the past, and what exists today, so we can better plan strategies and visions for our future world of work. We reviewed a glimpse of the past work environments. We discussed what is currently taking place and what we know is going to happen in the near future. Let's now take a moment and agree we will engage in some powerful *"imagineering"* as Walt Disney would say.

I use the term, *"imagine"* instead of *"vision"* in this chapter. Vision, for me, is a detailed, vivid description of what something will look like when you get there. It should be thought through and in sufficient detail, so the text, pictures and models will communicate an appreciation and understanding of what to expect. Others may think they have visions of the future that meet this definition, but I know I still do not have sufficient understanding to call this image of the future a *"vision."*

One of the key pillars to what our future work-enabled world can be is how well we capitalize on global knowledge. Another key pillar is collaboration progressing far beyond the individual team or organization until the approaches and movement reach a global scale. The utilization of global resources, community knowledge and the practice of contracting, will necessitate the formation of new resource-based entities. I imagine these organizations being created for and by the knowledge workers.

These entities or networks of knowledge workers will define how the work tasks are performed and the relationships that the knowledge workers will have with those buying their services. Services will progressively be priced by deliverables, eliminating the notion of pay for time. This will require a much more precise approach to defining, parsing and sequencing the work scope into standardized deliverables. There will be precise guidelines for each deliverable and the process to follow; only the specific content will vary by situation. Industries like health care, construction and many others have used this method for costing services.

We can establish standardized estimates for many common work packets, perhaps not all, but I hope most. The pace of change we face will dictate the movement to standardized approaches that will help facilitated more accurate estimates of work effort. These approaches need to be more structured while the content will be more creative. Just like in music we do not argue about the method of documenting the music. Experts devised a graphical scheme that transcends time, instrument and language, so people do not need to worry about the approach and can totally focus on what they are creating. The IT industry has made many attempts to create modeling approaches without sufficient acceptance to establish such a scheme for effective creativity, collaboration and communication.

My dream is for new technologies, employed by the knowledge workers that will enable advanced work techniques, connectivity and global leveraged knowledge. The following describes the progression I believe will lead us into this future Knowledge Worker Stage.

The corporate pressures brought about by quarterly performance expectations, globalization, exporting jobs offshore, the aging workforce, staff cuts (referred to as "*right-sizing*") and cut backs of employee benefits are creating increased uncertainty for all employees. No position, role or individual will enjoy job security. This in time will cause more and more employees and employers to seek new working arrangements. I see evidence in the recovery over the last few years that former employees are being brought back as contract resources, to ensure greater corporate flexibility. What has surprised me is not the fact that it is being done, but how positive many contract workers are about the new flexibility this gives them. There is a realization that virtual workers do not need to depend on permanent corporations, unions or governments to survive and prosper. In fact, just the opposite thoughts are dominating the thinking of the emerging knowledge workers.

In the Virtual Stage I see collaboration as one of the most significant advances in the effectiveness and efficiency of virtual work, but the capabilities are limited to reside primarily within single organizations. In the Knowledge Worker Stage global collaboration will reach every modern society and be deployed across most organizations. It will not matter where the competent resources live or whom they work for, as long as they have the tools, security, connectivity and experience necessary to perform at a competent level and at a competitive price.

The vast discrepancy in costs and labor rates will not survive in the future. The current experiences with "*off-shoring*" will continue, not because of cheap labor but because of the availability of skilled resources. The advantages of having work performed from around the globe will tremendously outweigh any disadvantages. The effect of time zones has already allowed organizations to double the work effort applied to tasks. For example, India, China and Russia work while we sleep here in North America and Sunday is a work day in Israel.

In Stage Four hand-offs of work between virtual resources will be simplified and managed by software technology, no matter where the resources reside. The benefits achieved through globalization of the knowledge worker will potentially triple the work performed because of the effect of time zones enabling 24 hour productivity. When getting things done faster is important, (and it just about always is), globalization will help make it possible. This will also be very helpful with the current practice of business offsets between cooperating countries and organizations.

Simply having international offices does not make an organization a global player in the new virtual world of work. If the control in the executive suite and board of directors is dominated by people from only one geographic region, culture, language, employment status, or background, the organization is not truly global. I believe this to be true even if the organization makes and sells its products and services around the world. Corporations will streamline their structure by focusing on what is essential for their survival and prosperity in a competitive global economy. They will view their common business processes as a burden and shed them to others that can execute better. I see a big future in BPO (business process outsourcing). The worth of a corporation will exist and its value measured in their ability to:

- Attract and retain the brightest minds.
- Reward new ideas.
- Foster great working relationships with employees, customers and suppliers.
- Develop deep understanding of their purpose, strategy and value.
- Relentless pursuit of continuous innovation.
- Master their core in-house critical business processes.
- Efficiently and effectively execute the processes.
- Agility to improve, react and adapt before others do.

Success is the ability to continually meet and exceed the immediate needs and desires of the customers, partners and employees while making sure things will integrate smoothly into the longer term plans. You will not survive as just a supplier; you will need to be strategic to your customers. Products provide at best a brief competitive advantage; it is the ability of people to adjust and innovate that will provide a more sustainable competitive advantage.

The global Knowledge Worker Stage will contribute to *"level the playing field"* for organizations and resources that understand and take advantage of the contributing factors. The coalescing of globalization, demographics, technology, attitudes, collaboration, security and global knowledge are the major factors that I believe will lead us into a better life.

To read about this concept in more detail please check out the book *The World is Flat,* a brief history of the twenty-first century by Thomas L. Friedman. Friedman presents compelling evidence of the events and technologies that level the playing field and bring the two largest countries in the world to be part of the global supply chain for products and services. He explains how the flattening of the world will impact individuals, companies, communities and countries, causing everything to change and adapt.

As a foreign affairs journalist he cuts through the complex foreign policies and issues in explaining globalization and defines its successes and the discontents it is creating.

Globalization is brought about by the exchange of goods and services, intellect, ideas, knowledge, the free movement of capital and immigration in a secure, safe environment. I add resources and their expertise to this list of items contributing to globalization and suggest they will be the most critical items of globalization in the future world economy. Other authors have also added to the list, for example *"security"* is added by Thomas Barnett, in his book *The Pentagon's New Map*, globalization or what he calls *"connectedness"* and that global security can be the U.S.'s gift to the world. He explains why security of not only America but the entire connected world is critical to economic globalization.

He describes an increasingly expanding *"Functioning Core"* of economically developed, politically stable countries integrated into global systems, and a *"Non-Integrating Gap,"* the most likely source of threats to U.S. and international security. His position is that without security none of the other global factor will prevail. Our focus in this book is not the political or social impacts of a changing world but simply how the work world is changing from the worker and organizational perspectives and how this will drive global changes into our lives.

We can see a change of terms used to describe the workers. The term *"employee"* will shift to *"resource"* to reflect the fact that many will actually stop being full-time employees, as we know them today. New arrangements and classifications will be created to accommodate how resources are contracted, paid, and what rights and benefits they will retain. The contact channel for assigning and negotiating with resources and their services will be the *"resourcing function."* They will be the ones to work the new global resource supply chain to acquire resources and services and their assignments.

There is a definite evolution of terms used in a purposeful way to identify the type of resources associated with different competency levels and how, where and when they perform their work tasks. Consider the term *"worker"* as the base definition of a person providing labor or a service. The worker is redefined as an *"information worker"* when their work processes and tasks are performed using a computer to create, analyze, communicate and use information every day. Next, the information worker takes the additional designation of a *"mobile worker"* when they use laptops, cell phones and other portable devices to stay connected and perform individual tasks while traveling or remote from their business office. The information and mobile workers are known as *"virtual workers"* when the majority have the capability and technology to work in collaborative teams, accessing global knowledge, with other remote resources from their home offices. Yet another progression is registered when the virtual worker earns the right to be recognized as a *"knowledge worker."*

A knowledge worker has personally gained in-depth experience and expertise in doing many jobs and can readily access other global digital stores of knowledge and know-how, specific to a process or task. They have the necessary understanding and context to make decisions, ask the right questions and alter course to recover any problem in the performance of complex tasks. They have the confidence to identify difficulties early in the work cycle and the ability to call on others to quickly solve surprises. The person with the highest level of knowledge and leadership capabilities that can guide others with their advice and teaching is thought of as a *"wise"* person. Those that can provide this leadership consistently, under tremendous pressure and tension, have proven themselves to be looked up to and to be called a knowledge worker of *"wisdom."*

In the future, knowledge workers will be too valuable to only apply their skills, for an entire career, for a single organization. They will have the experience to lead information, mobile and virtual workers in performing tasks. In our imagineering they will be responsible for building and provide quantum advances in technology infrastructures to optimize work. They will enable the capture, retention and personalized dissemination of global knowledge from secure stores. They will create knowledge software to enable coordination and management of these processes. They will have the industry specific process knowledge necessary to perform and lead others in being personally productive and effective in delivering work commitments. The senior knowledge worker with wisdom will provide overall mentoring and leadership, so that the organizations they lead will perform at a superior, predictable, and trustworthy level. They will be the magnetic force that attracts, organizes, protects and leads information, mobile, virtual and knowledge workers from all corners of the globe.

Imagine a small number of large independent service organizations emerging, called *"Service Guilds,"* that will dominate the global services market. As a pool of highly skilled virtual knowledge resources, each will start with the best software engineers joining together with innovative thinking that will enable new secure capabilities in the use of knowledge, holograms, language and collaboration. Once they integrate this incredible software with the best-of-the-best communication, hardware platform and system software, they will rapidly gain international respectability.

They will receive so much media attention that many independent contractors, most top graduates, the best of the dissatisfied corporate virtual workers and even many of the most knowledgeable retired or partially retired resources will be clamoring to join these guilds. The service guilds will grow so fast they will cause a great disruption in the status quo (you thought I was going to say *"the force"*). The key to their success will be the worker related knowledge technology. The hype this will generate will in turn attract many of the remaining (smartest and brightest) global resources, all working from virtual environments. Over a relatively short period of time (5–10 years) these entities will mature their management and financial structures and through mergers and acquisitions will take over other research and services related organizations. The capital to back this kind of unprecedented explosive growth will present a challenge and those with sufficient financial backing will acquire most of the remaining Guilds.

This growth combined with their global reach, membership, knowledge, expertise and influence will enable them to acquire massive political power at the same level enjoyed by countries. If you want to get any complex project done successfully, you will increasingly need to use the services of one of these Guilds. There will be many small service providers but none of them will have the propriety suite of technology that the Guilds control and provide to their members. The Guilds sell and negotiate all contracts globally, provide issue resolution, establish secure communications and implement their technology on corporate facilities for their members to use. Because of their power, the world governments will have to negotiate favorable terms, treatment, legislation and tax rulings for their members. They fund and work with selected universities and other education entities to assure themselves a steady supply of the best and brightest entry level resources.

They have classification levels, internal education and personal development programs, job training and provide career enrichment programs for their members and their families. The Guilds will provide a competitive environment, with specialized technology and knowledge repositories for use by their members, enabling incredible personal productivity and quality.

The Guilds possess specialized technology that will seamlessly integrate with all private and public platforms. They have highly sophisticated language processors to enable all resources to work in a language of their choice, without the current problems associated with text, voice and culture. Members will be connected and enabled to work from home anywhere in the world they choose to live. They will have the ability to stay put and still attend meetings and engage in collaborative work sessions. The Guilds will be able to equip meeting rooms so members can visually occupy a chair at a meeting in the form of a realistic functioning personal hologram. The hologram will represent the knowledge worker real-time through a fully realistic live virtual image. The knowledge workers have the same ability in reverse through the hologram to interface, see and fully experience the other members whether real or also digital. This technology and the communication capabilities will be controlled and provided as part of the Guild's service contracts. It will simulate personal contact while allowing the knowledge worker to be in multiple locations at the same time.

All technology will have voice interfaces and communicate verbally or digitally for ease of use. Members will be personally equipped with biotechnologies and in constant contact with the technology infrastructure, and others that are similarly equipped. Access can be with other member but progressively the interchanges will be with computer hologram and their global knowledge stores in a simulated human form. The technology will know who you are, exactly what you have been working on and with whom, while connecting you to everyone and everything you will need to continue your tasks. It will know how you prefer to work, who the team members are, and the preferences of the client you are interfacing with. The software understands if this is the first time you will be doing a particular task and will adjust the level of support. It checks real-time to make sure what you are doing will properly integrate with the tasks being worked by other team members. The functions of scheduling, security, quality assurance, usability, traceability, work breakdown structures, process management, testing, project management and reporting will all be automated by the work management software (WMS) infrastructure.

The Guilds' members will reshape our thinking about what it means to be human; we are facing another frontier that involves dramatically enhancing ourselves, not just the tools we use and environment we work and live in. The Guilds will have the equivalent of enhanced Special Forces for the most difficult jobs. We are evolving into a society that will contain two species of humans—those that are *natural* and those that are *enhanced*. This should not come as a shock with all the coverage of the steroid use by athletes. The problem they are causing is to do enhancement drugs in secret, giving them an unfair advantage over those that remain natural. But, what is a surprise is the gap between what scientists and engineers are researching today and what the public finds believable. We have already started down the path of genetic engineering and embedded technologies. Just think of the possibilities of an enhanced specialized workforce working for you. They would be able to:

- Think much faster and be more creative.
- Devour a book like document in minutes and have total recall.
- Silently communicate with team members.
- Download vast amounts of information directly into their brains wirelessly.
- Work around the clock for days without sleep, rest or degradation.

The gap between what is real and credible will cause us to rethink how we feel about being enhanced. The relationship between humans and technology will dramatically change within the time frame laid out for this

Fourth Stage. You may be born homo-sapiens but you will surely die robo-sapiens. If you doubt me then please read Joel Garreau's book, *Radical Evolution* and what he has to say about DARPA (Defense Advanced Research Agency and GRIN (Genetics, Robotics, Information and Nano-processes).

I will stop before we are all assimilated by other biotechnological development and for the moment leave going any further into the future to the science fiction writers and the neuro-engineers. I am not a psychologist, so I will leave the social and behavioral experts to deal with how humans will cope and adjust to these changes. I am also not a lawyer, politician or expert in foreign policy, so how all this will work will be a major challenge for others to solve. What I do know is that what has been described is currently feasible. These technologies will be available and in use during the careers of most of the information worker employed today.

"HOW WE WORK IS CHANGING AND THIS WILL CHANGE EVERYTHING"

I hope you enjoyed as much as I, this very brief walk into the future. Although we do not know precisely what will take place, or the time frames for these changes; I do believe there is a strong probability most of these events will come true faster than can be imagined today. After all, the possibilities are infinite.

If this chapter has inspired your imagination to freely think of the innovations and changes that could quickly take place, then I have achieved part of the objective in writing this book. The goal for the remainder of the book, is to provide some further understanding, tips, lessons learned, guidance and advice that will be of value to you in your transformation to the virtual world of work. We will cover in a practical way what you should be doing today and planning for tomorrow to benefit from the coming global economy. By the time most organizations are functioning at Stage Three we will have a better idea of how to prepare for the next step of the journey into the future virtual world of work.

I believe that if enough people imagine the future then they will impact the present, which in turn will influence that future to come true. So be thoughtful with your imagination and with whom you share your ideas, because they just might come true.

Chapter Summary
- To imagine is to be human, and if what we imagine does not seem impossible, then it probably does not deserve the effort.
- We cannot see 10 to 30 years into the future at this time but we can imagine what it *"could be."*

- The pace of change we face will dictate the movement to standardized approaches that will help facilitated more accurate estimates of work deliverables.
- The corporate pressures brought about by quarterly performance expectations, globalization, exporting jobs offshore, the aging workforce, staff cuts (*"right-sizing"*) and cut backs of employee benefits are creating increased uncertainty for all employees.
- The lack of job security in time will cause more and more employees and employers to seek new working arrangements.
- The current experiences with *"off-shoring"* will continue, not because of cheap labor but because of the availability of skilled resources.
- When getting things done faster is important, (and it just about always is), having people working around the globe will help make it possible.
- International offices do not make an organization a global player—if the control in the executive suite and board of directors is dominated by people from only one geographic region, culture, language, employment status or background then the organization is not truly global.
- Organizations will streamline their structure by focusing on only what is essential for their survival and prosperity in a competitive global economy. They will view their common business processes as a burden and shed them to others that can execute better.
- Success is the ability to continually meet and exceed the immediate needs and desires of the customers, partners and employees while making sure things will integrate smoothly into the longer term plan.
- The coalescing of globalization, demographics, technology, attitudes, collaboration, security and global knowledge are the major factors that I believe will lead us into a better life.
- Thomas Freidman explains in his book, *The World is Flat*, how the flattening of the world will impact individuals, companies, communities and countries, causing everything to need to change and adapt.
- A knowledge worker has personally gained in-depth experience and expertise in doing many jobs and can readily access other global digital stores of knowledge and know-how, specific to a process or task.
- In the future, knowledge workers will be too valuable to only apply their skills, for an entire career, for a single organization.
- I imagine a small number of large independent service organizations emerging, called *"Service Guilds,"* that will dominate the global services market.
- All technology will have voice interfaces and communicate verbally or digitally for ease of use.

- The functions of scheduling, security, quality assurance, usability, traceability, work breakdown structures, process management, testing, project management and reporting will all be automated by the work management software (WMS) infrastructure.
- The relationship between humans and technology will dramatically change within the time frame laid out in this book.
- How we work is changing and this will change everything.
- I believe that if enough people imagine the future then they will impact the present, which in turn will influence that future to come true.

Section Two

WHAT FACTORS HAVE ENABLED
THE VIRTUAL WORLD OF WORK?

CHAPTER 7

SECTION INTRODUCTION

The virtual world of work is enabled and made possible by *technology* and our *attitudes* that cause us to devour the technology and seek out new possibilities. It is *demographics* and *globalization* that drive us and make the emerging virtual world of work necessary. These factors are fundamental to the creation of the virtual world of work.

A mobile and virtual work environment, enabled by technology, is new over the last ten to twenty years, but the process to develop tools and become proficient with them is not. Thinking, evolving, adapting, and mastering tools are the basic attributes of what makes us human and why we have successfully become the dominant species on this planet. It is our well-developed brain that enables us to innovate, change, survive and prosper. We develop technologies to make our lives easier, safer and better. Our evolution was spurred along in significant leaps caused by major events, such as the ice ages or collisions with asteroids. These events challenged our early ancestors to learn, change, adapt, or disappear. Today our challenges are different; they involve keeping up with the pace of the technology developments, handling the social changes happening around the globe, and not destroying ourselves in the process.

Our development of tools has continuously enabled us over tens of thousands of years to completely change how, where and for how long we live our lives. We have developed more new tools in the last century than in the rest of human history. Take a moment and think of some of the technology developments that have taken place and how these have changed our lives. The invention of the automobile has changed the design of our cities. TV has changed how we receive much of our news

The Virtual World of Work, pages 57–61
Copyright © 2008 by Information Age Publishing

and entertainment. Electricity and gas provide us with the power to run our modern tools.

The advent of innovative tools like computers, software and communications has enabled us to work in new ways and has created an environment in which we are poised for a major step forward in how we do our jobs and live our lives. The impact on how we learn, communicate, work and play will forever be changed by these technologies. Connectivity is continuing to make the world smaller and more familiar by enabling global communications. It is amazing, the faster we develop new technologies, the faster we become totally dependent on them in both our personal and professional life.

The most significant difference from past advances is the pace at which change is now taking place. These changes are not small improvements or simple upgrades to existing tools but new breakthroughs that open new doors, allowing us totally new capabilities. The changes are causing disparities and taxing people to keep up. Many are being left behind and the inequalities between people are something that our society needs to address. The majority is being pushed or pulled along by the innovations of a few.

If you accept this evolutionary hypothesis of tools, then you will probably agree that the imagination, innovations, and advances in the tools we use, and become dependent on, will not stop anytime soon. The work environments we have today, with computers, the Internet, airplanes and mobile phones represent the tools modern information workers use to improve their productivity and their lives every bit as much as the printing press, steam engine and the wheel did for our ancestors. Humans did not stop when they learned to control fire and we will surely not stop now. Just like fire, these new tools and the associated capabilities they provide will require people to change how they think and adapt to new ways of doing things. Our abilities to think, imagine, innovate and adapt are what will enable a new virtual world of work and beyond.

There are many factors that can influence a major change. Some are easy to identify and some can be very subtle. I have chosen to focus on the obvious factors that I believe are the most instrumental in enabling—who, how, when and where we do our jobs. They are the amazing enabling technologies and the changing attitudes, habits and mental models of the information workers. In this Section, I will examine the different attitudes and thinking that I have encountered and their roles in contributing or hindering our change to a virtual world of work. There are a few other key factors that will strongly influence a permanent change in the future work world. They are *globalization* and *demographics*, and they will be dealt with in later chapters along with *knowledge* and *collaboration*. These are the factors that are fundamental to the formation of our virtual world of work.

The premise I believe in is very simple—technology is changing social behaviors and personal beliefs which in turn are influencing how people think about work and life. We have those that are leading the change and there are those that want to maintain the status quo. Always in the past, those that try to stop progress will eventually lose their control, and their influence will diminish until they are irrelevant. The information workers that want to preserve the attitudes and habits of how things worked in the past are slowing the change in many organizations. This is annoying but temporary, and it will not stop the change to a virtual world of work, in fact, the movement is picking up huge numbers of new supporters daily.

The U.S. Census data indicates that there are already 25 million U.S. virtual information workers working from home, at least part of each month, and that does not include home-based self-employed people. I believe in the next 5 to 10 years this number will triple or quadruple, forcing organizations to rethink their workforce strategies. There will also be a significant increase in the number of days the people work from home with many becoming full-time virtual employees. So do not despair, if you are thinking of working from home you are not alone, you are in good company and part of a significant change taking place in the workforce.

Let's look at the U.S. Census data. Despite the Bureau's conservative method of counting at-home workers, the 1990 census showed a 56 percent increase in the number of Americans who worked from home in just 10 years. This represented a dramatic reversal of the previous twenty year trend. Between 1960 and 1980, the decline in the number of family farms and the growing tendency of doctors and lawyers to leave home offices and join group practices seems to have contributed to the decrease. In a private survey for Telecommute America, estimates for the number of telecommuters rose from 4 million in 1990 to approximately 11 million in 1997. In yet another separate survey, *"Characteristics of Business Owners,"* the Census Bureau reports that in addition to the above numbers, nearly half of the 17 million small businesses (self employed) were home based. These are large numbers and cannot be dismissed even by the most avid opponent to virtual work.

The changes taking place in how we think about work and the enabling technology advances are beginning to change everything about our current world of work. As more and more workers become comfortable with working from home we will see changes in the designs of a typical home. Real estate ads in a few years may read—3 bedrooms, $2\frac{1}{2}$ baths, 2 private offices, 1 classroom, and bla-bla-bla. Where people live will not be tied to where the traditional office is located.

As a result of the virtual change to work we will see a dramatic increase in home schooling (currently 7 percent growth per year), which will slowly lead to a much needed transformation of the education system. A typical home classroom could accommodate from 1–3 students and be digitally connected to your chosen tutors, virtual class mates and learning curriculums.

I would like to do another related book titled, *The Virtual World of Learning*. I think the current education system will drastically change over the coming decades, heavily influenced by the same pressures that are changing business. This possible education paradigm could evolve from the current home schooling industry, continuing education (the fastest growing educational segment) and corporate learning and development. Like the business campuses many of the education facilities could be transformed to a community center culture for specialized learning and the social development of the learners.

Technology is enabling the virtual world of work and will enable a new learning paradigm.

The same companies developing the business software today will work with the best educators to produce thousands of learning events that can be combined into learning networks and delivered digitally to learners anywhere. Parents and the independent learning agents (qualified teachers) will provide the facilities, administration, tutoring, and adherence to the standards, all in a new technological enabled virtual world of learning. The current education environments are one of the last remaining examples of Industrial Age thinking. The large schools, like the large factory complexes will gradually fade away as will the huge bureaucracies.

The pressures to provide virtual worker flexibility in who, how, when and where we do work will be relentless as new technologies are introduced and old attitudes are retired or changed. The technologies needed to function as a mobile worker already exist and the technologies to support the enhanced virtual workers are currently in R&D and limited use. What exists to support collaboration and knowledge management is immature with many integration limitations. Microsoft, IBM, HP, Oracle, Apple, SAP, and many specialty players are busy building out their platforms and trying to fill the gaps. The "*how,*" or technology issues, will be explored in more detail in Section Four. In this Section, I will present ideas and answer the following questions—what people related factors will influence the change to a virtual world of work and why some information workers will or won't make this change quickly, smoothly and completely?

Section Introduction Summary
- Our challenge is trying to keep up with the pace of the technology developments, handling the associated social changes happening around the globe and not destroy ourselves in the process.
- Our development of tools has continuously enabled us over tens of thousands of years to completely change how, where and for how long we live our lives.

- The faster we develop new technologies the faster we become totally dependent on them in both our personal and professional life.
- Our abilities to think, imagine, innovate and adapt are what will enable a new virtual world of work and beyond.
- In this Section, I will examine the different attitudes and thinking that I have encountered and their roles in contributing or hindering our change to a virtual world of work.
- Technology is changing social behaviors and personal beliefs which in turn are influencing how people think about work and life.
- The 25 million virtual information workers who work part of their time from home will triple or quadruple in the next 5–10 years.
- Where people live will not be tied to where the traditional office is located.
- As a result of the virtual change to work I believe we will see a dramatic increase in home schooling (currently 7 percent growth per year) which will slowly lead to a much needed transformation of the education system.
- The pressures to provide virtual worker flexibility in who, how, when and where we do work will be relentlessly propelled as new technologies are introduced and old attitudes are retired or changed.
- In this Section, I will present my ideas and answer the following questions—what people related factors will influence the change to a virtual world of work and why some information workers will or won't make this change quickly, smoothly and completely?

CHAPTER 8

ATTITUDES

Let's examine the business, social, and personal attitudes, habits, and mental models that are impacting this movement to a new virtual world of work. The change in attitude required for the acceptance of the Mobile Worker Stage, has already taken place but the same cannot be said for the Virtual Worker Stage. Not to say everyone agrees with the mobile work schedules or are doing it themselves, but if they do not think this shift is permanent or believe it will not affect them, they are in for a big surprise.

This shift in attitude toward work is persistent and the momentum is becoming explosive. If your company has not equipped your employees to effectively and efficiently work while out of their business offices, you are seriously falling behind. If you are not already planning to support work-at-home employees, you will not be competitive in the rapidly emerging global resource market.

Everyone I interviewed had a quick, strong reaction to the virtual home office; this tells me that their beliefs are associated with strong personal convictions like—"*good and bad or right and wrong.*" Based on these very basic feelings, a change to doing work in a virtual home setting will cause many individuals and organizations to struggle. The strategic event enabling the necessary change in attitude will be the retirement of the baby boomer generation. The younger workers will adapt to the change by blending this new work reality with the other changes they are initiating with social and family roles.

Management Challenges for the 21st Century, Peter Drucker's book, looks at the profound social and economic changes occurring today. Prior to Drucker's death in 2005 he discussed the changes in the concept and structure of organizations from command-and-control to information-based.

The Virtual World of Work, pages 63–75
Copyright © 2008 by Information Age Publishing
All rights of reproduction in any form reserved.

According to the pre-eminent expert, "The job of building the information-based organization is the managerial challenge of the future." He forecasts that in twenty years the typical large business will have half the levels of management and one-third the managers of its counterpart. I would add to that my estimate; that they will also have less than half the number of information workers employed. Drucker believes work will be done by specialists brought together in task forces that cut across traditional departments. Coordination and control will depend largely on the employees' willingness to discipline themselves. Behind these changes lies the incredible enabling information technology.

In Drucker's book he presents how to create knowledge worker productivity and the practice of starving the problems and feeding the opportunities. Change before the change, this is the key to success. Drucker made a prediction,

> In the next century, the productivity of the knowledge worker will be increased fifty-fold, which is the increase in the productivity of the manual worker during the Industrial Revolution. For this to happen, knowledge workers will be essentially self-managed. They will be responsible for their own contributions, they will be continuously innovating, and they will be continuously learning, capturing knowledge and teaching.

He follows up with his perspective on the increase in available information, which he says was paralleled by Gutenberg's invention of the printing press. He urges that the focus of IT be on the information, not on the technology.

The *business attitudes* referred to are those held by information workers, not just management, but at all organizational levels. These attitudes were introduced and matured over the last two hundred years, during the Industrial Age. They have been integrated with a military management style based on command-and-control. These approaches have been exercised over many years and are well entrenched. They have changed some over the last half century as we started our transition to the Digital Age, but many of the practices are still part of the mental models held by the management generation in control of most organizations.

A *mental model* for me is a picture, image or description we individually create for later reference of what things should look like or how things should function; it is part of our memory. We can instantly take in new inputs, through any of our senses, and compare how the inputs fit with the corresponding mental models we have stored. The process takes a fraction of a second for simple inputs, complex comparisons may require a series of questions and dialog to validate our understanding of the input and make sure we are using the right models. A puzzled look or a gesturing of the head is an indication that what was just experienced may not fit nicely into any of the existing models. The models provide us a context for evaluating what we experience. They help us identify, compare and react quickly.

We create a vast number of models over our lifetime to help us have a context in which we can try to understand the world and communicate what we experience. The models are very helpful in keeping us comfortable and stable in environments where we need to handle a tremendous amount of varied and unpredictable input. Models can vary from very simple mental model of the image and smell of a ripe yellow banana, if it is green then we know without thinking it is not ripe. Much more complex models also exist, involving family, children, religion, politics, processes, work, et cetera. Comparisons to these models may engender feelings that produce responses that may start with, "*I believe—in my opinion—I doubt—I think—I do not agree—no way*," and definitely can evoke a tremendous amount of emotion.

I have a personal example of a powerful stored memory. I severed my left Achilles tendon playing tennis. I had unfortunately had the same accident on the right tendon, doing the same thing, one year earlier. The instant the sound and pain registered in my brain and compared to the mental model I stored from the previous accident, I knew exactly what happened. This was unlike the first time when I had no idea what I had done because I did not have a mental model of such an event. The comparison was so quick, I knew before I hit the ground what terrible damage I had done and what I would be in for.

Mental models can be learned from our experiences or learned from others. We constantly evolve and build new mental models all the time. Those that contribute to our belief or value system are more difficult to alter and pose a dilemma if they are proven to be incorrect. The models involving what is acceptable in the work environment are important because we depend on them every day to make evaluations, judgments, or to take action and make decisions. What are the mental models of your workforce and how have they evolved in recent years are questions you will need to answer? Will they be a benefit or an obstacle to the transformation to the virtual work environment? Assessments will allow you to better understand your workforce and plan appropriately.

We also develop and store in memory *habits*. These are made up of behaviors or patterns that assist us in performing known or routine tasks without using a lot of mental energy. Habits are very necessary in going about our daily rituals. They allow us to do things without focusing or thinking about them. They guide us, so much so that when we cannot use them we tend to get uncomfortable, irritable, or stressed. These habits are very beneficial, but sometimes they can activate automatic actions that keep us from thinking about what we are doing. For example, I left my office to attend a late afternoon meeting in a different part of town, while thinking about the meeting, I actually drove home. I will not tell you how many times I have done this, but it is more than once. Talk about being on auto pilot.

Once you have performed a job function many times and dealt with most of the exceptions, you will store this behavior associated with the task in memory. You then can work productively without getting as tired, because you do not need to think through the patterns and steps to perform the task. These work related habits and mental models are an accumulation of experience and knowledge of how your work world really works. They vary from or are additive to the official documented work processes and represent the worker's contribution to our knowledge stores. Turnover causes seepage of this knowledge and causes organizations to re-experience past problems.

There are many examples of Industrial Age and military thinking that exist in many businesses today. Let's look at some examples of the attitudes that we may all have experienced in our careers:

- These facilities have been provided so workers can effectively do their jobs.
- The workers must come to the facilities to do their work.
- Attendance is critical to managing and paying for work performed.
- Managers should be proficient at the work to be able to manage it.
- There are limits to how much you can trust an employee.
- Time boundaries are provided for work and must be followed.
- HR policies and procedures must be strictly enforced.
- Organization structures and hierarchies are designed for span of control.
- Never confuse work and play.
- Productivity has to be managed to be attained.
- Careers, classifications, pay and promotions are achieved through seniority.
- Employee flexibility must be limited.
- Work is optimized for the benefit of the business, not the workers.
- Employees need to locate and organize their lives around the work location.

We are social beings, we live and exist inside of an organized society, thus social attitudes play an import role in how we perceive ourselves and the world we are part of. There are differences between *social* and individual *personal attitudes*, but for this book we are grouping them together and are not worrying about any differentiation or which one may have the greatest influence on the other, or which has the greatest impact on our feeling.

Interviews showed me that many people, particularly young people, have little confidence in corporations, unions, world bodies and governments to make decisions that take their needs into account. It appears that self interest and greed is the standard that is rampant today. The United Nations, for example, is one of the most prestigious organizations, yet they are setting new thresholds for deniability and not taking responsibility for their actions, no matter how blatant and corrupt they may be. We are all bombarded by the media trying to find bad things to report. Events that shake our trust in others are regularly reinforced again and again on the daily news reports. I would never have believed it possible that powerful organizations like Enron, Arthur Anderson and WorldCom could be destroyed, in such a very short period of time, obliterating so much value and trust.

Is it any wonder that there is a lack of trust today? Employers do not trust their employees and the employees do not trust their employers. It seems we are following the same path our favorite players and sport teams are exercising, changing teams regularly. Do you think loyalty has a place in today's workplace? The aging population is very concerned by examples like recent court decisions that have given large corporations permission to take away part of the pensions and roll back salaries and benefits. Many information workers have had salaries, bonuses or benefits cut which is better than those that had their jobs downsized or outsourced.

Trust and sharing are the attitudes that enable true collaboration in the workplace. We can supply the technology for collaboration, but for this advance in work performance to succeed we will need to worry about the attitudes of both the managers and the workers. It is trust and not a policy or procedure that will enable the key attributes of a high performing team. Collaborative work groups need an environment which promotes shared goals and interpersonal skills, (a *"working together"* philosophy), as well as the freedom and confidence to innovate and self-manage personal productivity.

Workers today that have pensions are worried about them; most people, who have the option, are taking pension payouts to make certain they and their families get their money. It is ironic, these facts and the attitudes they create are prevalent in a time when most information workers are better off financially than any time in the past. Perception is reality, but it is hard to tell if the news reports are true or just cheap sensationalism, or are politically motivated. A friend speaks of *"facts vs. truth"* and *"perception vs. reality."* What we want is truth and reality but what we get feed is facts and perception.

I believe our inability to relate to each other is causing a lack of compassion in the work place; have you heard, *"These actions are required by the business."* How impersonal, it is as if the business is making the decisions not a person. Have you used or heard this expression, *"Don't take it personal but your position has been eliminated,"* well it is very personal to the worker losing their job. Lawyers have all of us convinced that they can always find somebody else who is responsible and can be blamed for your actions. There are ads all the time on TV that state, *"for little or no money down you can have an aggressive attorney—."* What attitudes are these creating? What about personal responsibility?

The amount and pace of business change is hard to keep up with. There is a cute story about a colleague attending a meeting when they were interrupted by a co-worker who entered the conference room and said, *"It is your boss on the line,"* and the reply was, *"Good get their name and number and I will call them right back."* Changes are constant, rapid and allow little time for adjustment. It seems most companies have reorganizations as part of their annual or semiannual operating plans. This might be appropriate if the changes were capable of making the organization more nimble or competitive. Usually they entail some cost cutting measures and some shuffling of the same personnel. They tend to cause management to focus on internal matters and not the market, innovation, productivity, suppliers, competition, or customers.

Information overload is another factor confronting most information workers today and it is impacting their attitude toward work. How much information does one need to make a decision? This question is dangerous because it seems apparent that if you wait a few more days there will certainly be more information to apply to the decision. It is quite difficult to make a decision, without enough information, especially if you suspect additional information could make the decision obvious. We also have more information available on individuals, products, trends, industries, companies, and their positions on major issues and important topics, et cetera. This can help tremendously when preparing for a meeting or a proposal but remember there are very few secrets in the wired community.

A successful transition to a home office environment will take more than the physical trappings of a workable office. It requires handling the intellectual and emotional aspects of the change. Intellectually you can discover all the issues, think them through and use logic to make sure everything is OK, but remember change will be emotional and the adjustments may be difficult. Logical arguments do not work on emotional issues and each individual may find different issues that create different levels of emotion.

These are examples of a few of the issues you will deal with in transitioning to a home office:

- Was the change initiated for a good reason?
- What do I tell my family, friends, and colleagues?

- Where should I set up my workspace?
- What if there are too many interruptions?
- Will people think I work for a rinky-dink outfit?
- Is the organization going to cover the expenses?
- How will functions like technical support work?
- Who arranges the high speed cable and phone lines?
- What software will I need?
- How will security be dealt with?
- What will I put on my business card?
- Who helps set up the workplace?
- How will I stay in touch with co-workers?
- Where will I work when in the business office?
- What will happen to my career?
- What if it does not work out?
- Should I look for a new job?

There are a myriad of things that can be dealt with logically, so get them done so you can deal effectively with the emotional things. Getting everything done will be a lot of work; think of it as opening a new mini branch office and then you will put it in the right perspective. If you have been as lucky as me, having great support, you will find it scary the first time you look around, and it sinks in, you are really alone. In fact, the first time I moved to a home office in 1992 my assistant came with me. Don't try that, it didn't work.

I must admit I had no idea it took so long to mail documents from a busy post office, or pick up some supplies from a retail store. Some tasks took longer and some were new, but they were all offset by the productivity gained by being able to work without the normal office interruptions. There are many things we have to do ourselves. Pumping your own gas, checking into airports, banking at a kiosk, checking out of a grocery store, paying bills on-line, we have adjusted to doing these things just fine so we can also adjust to working from home.

The emotional side of the change I found the most difficult to deal with. As said earlier, logic is a poor tool to combating emotion, so do not treat logical and emotional issues the same way. The items in the list above can all become emotional issues, so be careful. When working from home you will confront feelings that are different than those encountered when you worked in the business offices. Do not expect everyone to treat you the same when you work from home. You will find that spouses, children, family, friends, business associates, clients may treat you different without even realizing. Here is a typical situation that happened to a good friend. She moved back to the Northwest and started to work from a home office. One night her partner came home and inquired if the laundry was done? The assumption was that she was home all day so why wouldn't she have time? Even in good open relationships people will say things without thinking based on certain old perceptions or expectations. Another friend has worked from home for several years, yet her father still calls out for her as he enters her home office, even if she is on a conference call. Be warned; prepare yourself and put a shield on your sensitivity for a while until you and the people around you adjusts.

This will be especially noticeable if you are struggling with your own mental models and feelings. I did a little research and asked many people to explain how they felt about people working from home. The differences were dramatic between age groups. The more senior responses were represented by comments like, *"That can't be good for your career, you will be isolated, you will be forgot or passed over, this is the last step, your career is now behind you, or the dreaded frown and shoulder shrug."* The younger people reacted very different with responses like, *"That's fantastic, I envy you, you must be well thought of, and you must be trusted."* I am not sure what this proves but if you are having a bad day adjusting to being a virtual worker talk to somebody who is younger.

I think I am fairly open to change, or at least I have gone through many changes, but like most my age (60s), I found I had lots of traditional mental models of how the work world should work. Some of my models were definitely challenged and really needed to be replaced or seriously modified. I supported my direct reports in working from home but when it was my turn, I still felt awkward for several months. Once the brief honeymoon with the home office was over, I found myself caught in an emotional spiral. Where I worked, my office and all the artifacts accumulated over a career were part of who I was and how I felt about myself. You do not even think about these things until you face them. My organizational status was visible in the business office surroundings and they contributed to my personal self image (it sounds so shallow—but—).

We were building a new home when I first started to work at home. Thus, I started working at the kitchen table of a condo. Although this was for a short period of time, this impacted how I felt about what I was doing and my value. My attitude, habits and mental models impacted my work. I got past this with some helpful support from my wife and friends but it will be something you may need to deal with. If you think this will be important to you, then if at all possible, try to duplicate your previous business workspace at home. Convert a bedroom, dining room or den into a private office (one with a door and a window). Over time with wireless technologies you will adjust and enjoy the new flexibility enabled by your new work environment.

Just after I started working from our new home I found myself doing things I did not do in the business office. If I was in the kitchen or somewhere else and my office phone rang, I would sprint through the house to get it. After all I did not want anyone thinking I was watching TV, in the pool or goofing off. I soon found it was me that needed to deal with those perceptions; the majority of my contacts did not care. But, watch closely for offhand remarks, things said in jest usually contains the greatest truth. Make sure you understand how others feel about your new work arrangement and operate appropriately.

It took a while for me to adjust my routine and work habits to the new environment. Even though I usually worked late at the office and even later at home, there was something different when I worked permanently from home and worked late. At home it was definitely much more convenient to accommodate extra hours of work, so I did. I had more flexibility and became a more dependable dinner partner. Even if you lived next to your office building you will not have the same level of flexibility as working from home. With this newly found flexibility you can achieve a better balance between family-time and work-time that is just not possible when you commute to an office.

I gradually reshaped my workday and my attitude to become comfortable working a longer daily schedule but taking breaks during the day. A new routine set-in after 2–3 months that worked much better considering I interfaced daily with people spread across, not only the U.S. time zones but with other countries as well. I was proud of the fact that I was available when people needed to make a decision or talk through issues, but still had more time for myself. I felt better about my job and was a better manager for my direct reports. It took me a while to adjust and get comfortable, but once I did I became more productive and I believe delivered greater value.

To adjust and have the right attitude you need to create an office environment that works for you. You will become less dependent on other people and more dependent on yourself and your technology. Make sure you have adequate furniture, hardware, software and communications that work efficiently and effectively for you. A dial up line might be OK for your retired grandparents but it is not acceptable for a virtual worker working from home. A home high speed connection might even be faster than what you had through the office server. I know it was for me. Never work from your home telephone line; you need at least one separate business line. Obviously the more like a business office you can equip your home office the better. You need to take into account lighting, comfort, privacy, ergonomics, convenience and many other factors.

I have a chapter on lessons learned that will deal with the home office in more detail. I gained some valuable insight by visiting with colleagues and friends to see where and how they set up their home workplaces. There is a much greater variety than you will find at a "*properly*" design modern office complex. One friend has her office in a converted closet and another works from a small desk in a spare bedroom. Some others have better facilities than they did at the traditional office.

Another friend has a very clever, unique set-up. He lives in a two-bedroom condo with his wife, a senior executive at a university, and a daughter in high school. He thought through the challenge and then for little money converted a large hutch into his office. It now sits nicely in the dining room and when the doors are shut you would never guess it was his office. But, as soon as he swings open the two doors, there it is. It contains a server, two computers, printer, multiple phone lines, headset, modem, shredder, files, a bit of storage and a small surface to work on. He is just as proud of his new office as he was of the huge one he had before—very impressive, yet practical. I would not suggest that working from the corner of the kitchen table with young kids at home is an acceptable work environment, but maybe there is some innovative way to improvise.

It is important to start the transition to working from home with expectations that are reasonable. First, do not expect that everything will be the same as they were at the business office. You can make it better, but it will be different. Do not expect to be treated by the organization, colleagues, customers or friends in the same ways as in the past. Some will be very supportive but some will do and say things, usually without thinking, that you will not expect. The challenge will be to handle those incidents without overreacting and try to minimize the impact they have on you. Take the opportunity to educating them with some facts about what it is like to work from home. Do not forget they may also go through the same change to where they work in the future and need help.

In fact, according to the last U.S. Census Bureau the number of home workers is dramatically rising. The Bureau segments home workers into different categories; the one that makes up the largest population of virtual workers is "*management, professional or related occupations.*" They report that the majority have bachelor degrees and are employed by, for profit corporations. There are more females working from home but only by a few percentage points.

Make sure you understand or have an agreement with your boss, finance, IT, and HR, as to what costs will be covered by your organization and what will not. A seemingly small thing like whose name is on the business phone bill or cable contract is important. Understand how bills will be paid. Do you submit the invoices for direct payment or do you pay them and submit expenses? Make sure the invoice payments do not fall through the cracks. If you have your phone line or cable connection cutoff it will reflect on you, even if it is not your fault. It may even affect your personal credit record. It is unfair so watch for these types of situations.

Find out if there is a corporate contract with an office supply company. Make sure this new employment arrangement has no personal tax consequences. Even small unexpected surprises will impact your attitude. An information worker working from home will feel less emotionally connected with the organization or the department they report to. The reverse may also be true.

Let's look at the same situation from the employer's perspective. It is important for organizations to foster multiple connections with the virtual employee, encouraging and allowing them to feel they belong and are part of something they care about. Many organizations develop a variety of special interest groups, professional and learning programs or other activities that are of interest to the virtual worker. It is also important to have a mix of virtual and face-to-face sessions between virtual workers and the management, if possible. The most important point is to have regular communications with the work-at-home employees.

Weekly, monthly and quarterly scheduled updates will help offset the reduction in hallway gossip and the ever present, unofficial internal network. These communications should be delivered by individuals from different levels in the organization and focus on what is happening throughout the organization. They should not be long or overly polished; they should simulate an impromptu chat between the employee and a manager. Keep them short but regular, so the virtual worker can depend on them, even if the employee initially does not seem interested. To make a short unsolicited call to check how things are going can provide considerable motivation, greatly out weighting the minimal investment in time. This is the equivalent of walking the halls. If an organization did just these suggestions, the virtual worker may know more about what is important to the company and feel more informed than they did working on-site. A person's attitude directly influences their motivation, which in turn impacts their personal performance.

I strongly recommend that each organization do assessments on the management and staff when planning for the virtual world of work. There are several companies that provide instruments for discovering personality traits, work tendencies and attitudes. I am currently working with one of the most successful companies to specialize their assessments to focus on the attributes of successful virtual home workers and management. Having the knowledge to understand why people do what they do, what their capabilities are, and how they work, will be of tremendous help in planning the transition to a virtual work environment.

Chapter Summary
- The attitude change required for the acceptance of the mobile worker has already taken place but for the virtual worker we are just starting to change.
- Peter Drucker's advice is "change before the change" and predicts "In the next century, the productivity of the knowledge worker will be increased fifty-fold, which is the increase in the productivity of the manual worker during the Industrial Revolution."
- The current business attitudes have been exercised over many years and thus are well entrenched.
- We depend on attitudes, habits and mental models to help us have a context in which we can try to understand the world and communicate what we experience.
- Work related habits and mental models are an accumulation of experience and knowledge and are additive to the official documented work processes and represent the worker's contribution to our knowledge stores—Turnover causes seepage of this knowledge.
- We are social beings and live and exist inside of an organized society, thus social attitudes play an import role in how we perceive ourselves and the world we are part of.
- I would never have believed it possible that powerful organizations like Enron, Arthur Anderson and WorldCom could be destroyed, in such a very short period of time, obliterating so much value and trust.
- It is trust and not a policies or procedures that will enable the key attributes of a high performing team.
- A friend speaks of "*facts vs. truth*" and "*perception vs. reality.*" What we want is truth and reality but what we get feed is facts and perception.
- Business changes are constant, rapid and allow little time for adjustment; this causes management to focus on internal matters and not the market, innovation, competition, customers or productivity.
- Information over load is another factor confronting most information workers today and it is impacting their attitude toward work.
- A successful transition to a home office environment requires handling the logical and emotional aspects of the change—I found the emotions the most difficult to deal with.
- I asked many people to explain how they felt about people working from home and the differences were dramatic between age groups—older people were generally negative and younger people positive.
- Watch closely for offhand remarks, things said in jest usually contains the greatest truth. And make sure you understand how others feel about your new work arrangement and operate appropriately.

- Working from home was definitely much more convenient to accommodate extra hours of work and I enjoyed having more flexibility.
- To adjust and have the right attitude you need to create an office environment that works for you.
- It is important to start the transition to working from home with expectations that are reasonable.
- From the employer's perspective, it is important for organizations to foster multiple connections with a mix of virtual and face-to-face sessions—the most important point is to have regular communications with the work-at-home employees.
- A person's attitude directly influences their motivation which in turn determines their personal performance.
- I strongly recommend that each organization do assessments on the management and staff when planning for the virtual world of work.

CHAPTER 9

NEW GENERATION
OF WORKERS

There are many factors influencing how the new generations (X, Y, or N) of workers think and act. The term N generation was used by Don Tapscott in his book, *Growing up Digital: The Rise of the Net Generation,* in which he gives us a glimpse as to how the N-Geners use of digital technology is changing human interactions and impacting our future. Although the book was written in 1998, his 300 interviews and his observations remain one of the best accounts of this new generation. The Net-Gens are currently between the age of 9 and 29 years of age and because they are born with technology, they assimilate it, rather than accommodate it. There are more than 88 million and they represent the largest demographic group in North America. They know more about technology than their predecessors. Tapscott mentions that they are learning, developing, and thriving in the digital world and in the workplace, they will function better in a decentralized, independent, collaborative, and innovative environment.

These youngest information workers have adjusted to and enjoyed the digital world for their entire life. Here are a few of the critical factors that I believe have influenced their lives and how they think about work:

- Faster paced lives with continuous change.
- More scheduled lives to deal with complexity.
- A greater variety and number of choices.
- Comfort, dexterity and familiarity with technology.
- On-line interactive games, news, entertainment and relationships.
- More money and credit availability.

The Virtual World of Work, pages 77–83

- Second generation of working parents.
- More uncertainty, less employment stability.
- Lack of loyalty and trust for the establishment.
- Evolving family responsibilities and duties.
- Less intimidated by things they do not know.
- More interest in a blended life, better balance between work and personal goals.

I have a simple story that helped me identify how much technology is changing our children. On a visit to a good friend's home their teenage son asked if he could go hang out with his friends. He had finished his school assignments, so his parents said yes. He then proceeded to his bedroom and signed onto an Internet game site where he and his friends congregate. I used to go to the ball field or over to a friend's house to hang out. Times have definitely changed!

The youngsters have incredible computer skills and have adapted to being virtual with their friends, all with no formal training. They learn through trial and error and from each other. Parents are having a difficult time knowing how to prepare their children for the future, let alone understand what they are doing today. Most of the youngsters have sufficient knowledge that the new wireless technologies, Internet, software, computer games, picture phones, iPods, or other handheld devices can all be used without education, training or implementation planning. This is a very important point I will explore in the Technology Insertion chapter.

The young workers are learning and taking technologies for granted that the mature workforces have not yet mastered. Our youngest son is a teacher at North Shore Country Day, a private school in the northern suburbs of Chicago. They participated in a North American trial of a new software package. Each grade 4 student logs onto a special Internet site, with their wireless laptops (the campus was equipped with Wi-Fi in 2003), where they can work individually or on teams to complete assignments. They are learning the value of community knowledge and how through collaboration they can build greater knowledge. They use a scaffolding technique (where each student has their own level) to store their work and it can be combined into the class community data base. The teacher has complete access and can monitor from their wireless laptop, having access to each student's work and their contribution to the community. The teacher can collect the work into a secure space for grading.

In a recent assignment the grade 4 students were asked, *"What makes a civilization?"* The students worked together to produce a shared work deliverable, creating collaborative knowledge. Our son loves to observe the students to see how they participate and how this computerized work environment differs from face-to-face interaction. You can see the fantastic possibilities this technology enables and how they are preparing this generation to be ready to take their role as Stage Three collaborative virtual workers. They are learning and getting comfortable with technology that is changing how they learn and work. This is a great example of preparing the young students for the future virtual world of work. It also makes obvious the discrepancies that exist in our schools. In our son's school they have invested in wireless laptops while other schools need to invest in metal detectors. A key question is where will the new generation of workers come from?

In a sobering discussion in Friedman's book, *The World is Flat*, he elaborates on Bill Gates' statement,

> When I compare our high schools to what I see when I'm traveling abroad, I am terrified for our work force of tomorrow. In math and science, our fourth graders are among the top students in the world. By eighth grade, they're in the middle of the pack. By 12th grade, U.S. students are scoring near the bottom of all industrialized nations.... The percentage of a population with a college degree is important, but so are sheer numbers. In 2001, India graduated almost a million more students from college than the United States did. China graduates twice as many students with bachelor's degrees as the U.S. and they have six times as many graduates majoring in engineering. In the international competition to have the biggest and best supply of knowledge workers, America is falling behind.

I think the education institutes are the most endearing artifacts of the Industrial Age structures and philosophy. The facilities are large and very expensive. Students need to come to these facilities and be regimented with precise rules involving attendance, schedules, work assignments, roles, et cetera. Even a well known international business school here in Phoenix surprised me a couple of years ago. On a visit I discovered they had yet to install a complete campus wide Wi-Fi environment.

Much to my amazement some professors do not allow laptops to be open and used by the students during lectures. This must be a control thing designed to accommodate the professors and not the students. It is not indicative of the work world and how they will need to perform to compete in their careers. It is the equivalent of not allowing my generation to use pencils and paper because we may doodle and not pay attention. How do they think people work, learn and keep notes in today's technological world? If we can lead the world in utilizing the new technology tools in our learning environments, perhaps we can help improve how our students rank in the world.

The greatest legacy of each generation may be how well they prepared the next generation for their future world. The post-World War II baby boomers and their children, the echo boomers, are different and think differently. My hope is that the teaching emphasis taught during the baby boomers will dramatically change to collaborative learning through the use of technology for the future generations. For us to be productive when working, over the next 10 to 20 years, collaboration must become the reality of how we work.

"The demographic changes at work across the globe will dramatically change the workforce," according to Peter Drucker. There are 76 million baby boomers and the first of them have started to retire. A baby boomer is someone born in a period of increased birth rates, such as those during the economic prosperity following World War II. In the U.S., demographers have put this generation's birth years from 1946 to 1964, despite the fact that the U.S. birth rate actually began to decline after 1957. Many references to this generation think of them as being born between 1946 and 1958. This generation brought the computer to the world. The generation that followed the baby boomers (those 25 to 45 years of age) led the explosion in computing technology devices, software and how they can be used to improve business and personal lives. The workforce that is under 30 expects and demands the latest technology and they are totally influenced by it.

I attended a large meeting where Phil Condit, ex-CEO of Boeing, talked about globalization, education, and how best to prepare incoming employees. If he could choose the ideal education program to prepare future employees, it would involve attending classes offered by many different universities from around the world in order to get the best instruction possible. A problem with this reality is who would provide the degree? Globalization is a lot more than where to sell products; it will include where to best learn and find the knowledge workers of the future, even if they do not want to immigrate.

In 1997 I sponsored a knowledge workplace prototype, developed jointly by Boeing, Microsoft and Fujitsu. The prototype's purpose was to demonstrate a quantum improvement in personal productivity for new workers using a software development methodology. The key was the support that can be enabled through a fully knowledgeable workplace. It was built on an EPSS (electronic performance support system) approach and new leading edge techniques for dealing with knowledge. Fujitsu pioneered the techniques for capturing, organizing, and distributing knowledge and contributed these knowledge resources and the methodology to the prototype. Microsoft supplied the software platform and technology expertise, and Boeing offered the hardware, space and the project workers using the methodology knowledge.

Once the user and their work assignments were entered into the system, the knowledge system coordinated a personalized view of what they needed to perform their tasks. The methods, techniques, tools, deliverables, learning events, templates, samples, help desk, re-use library, reviewers and approvers were all coordinated specifically for the individual worker. They continuously had available the exact information they needed to perform their tasks and no more. As they changed what they worked on the knowledge system would automatically refresh a new personalized view. Each time they signed on they could immediately pick up where they left off. We used the terms, *"Just in time, just enough, and just in place."*

For a prototype it worked pretty well but seemed to be ahead of its time based on the reactions we received. One comment received during a critical review with some senior executives was priceless. One of the executives said, "He only went to a state school and thus could not understand how it would work but did acknowledge that it must be really important based on how excited a lot of clever people were." That was the end to a very promising project in how captured knowledge could enhance personal productivity for on-the-job learning while performing new tasks.

The National Home Education Research Institute, founded by Brian D. Ray, estimates that there was 1.7 to 2.1 million K–12 home school students in the U.S. during 2002 to 2003. They report that home schooling has grown about 7 percent per year during the past 4 years. If these students are becoming more familiar with technology and the practice of learning while virtual, they will be more prepared for the future work world. Schools like the University of Phoenix and other similar distance learning institutions can help students not only learn and earn degrees, but become comfortable with learning and working in a virtual environment.

Many of the new generation of workers may not be all that new. Corporations will need to explore a variety of sources to meet their requirements in an expanding economy. This will include hiring contract workers, outsourcing work and establishing alternate employment arrangements to retain those retiring. For the organizations that have adopted a virtual work strategy, the span of their resource search can be global. This will allow them access to not only the largest pool of resources but the best resources.

They can contract to re-employ former employees, outsource to existing employees and retain retiring employees, all helping to gain experienced workers through more flexible virtual work environments. I am aware of several companies that are targeting their ex-employees for rehiring, not as full time employees but with a "1099" (tax category) employee arrangement. The reduced requirement for training, orientation and start-up will make many of these known resources very attractive. Some industries such as entertainment take advantage of contracting, building diverse teams and structuring their working environments as projects.

India has been readying itself for the future over the last 2 decades. Government and private interests have built a thriving business center called Bangalore as a great example. The high tech park is huge and has been built to exacting international standards and is supported by a state-of-the-art infrastructure to support a global reach. It is home to more than 250 high-tech companies. To prepare the required future workforce for virtual work the government created Bangalore. It is now the best education center in India with many colleges, university and research campuses. From this location they can connect to anywhere and anyone in the world. It is no wonder that homegrown IT giants like Wipro and Infosys have emerged as dominant global players. If any country in the world wants to compete with India they will need to accomplish what India has, integrating the combined efforts of the governments, business, education and their people to be successful. It takes insight, leadership, passion and persistence along with capital to make it happen. India made their mark based on low prices and high quality, but will continue to be successful based on quality and resource availability.

Chapter Summary

- The N-geners are currently between the age of 9 and 29 years of age and because they are born with technology, they assimilate it, rather than accommodate it.
- The youngest generation of information workers have adjusted to and enjoyed the digital world for their entire life.
- Most of the youngsters have adjusted to being virtual with their friends and have enough knowledge that the new wireless technologies can all be used without education, training or implementation planning.
- Our youngest son is a grade 4 teacher at a private school and his students have wireless laptops and are learning the value of community knowledge and how through collaboration they can build greater knowledge.
- In Friedman's new book, *The World is Flat,* he elaborates on Bill Gates' statement about our public schools, "When I compare our high schools to what I see when I'm traveling abroad, I am terrified for our work force of tomorrow. In math and science, our fourth graders are among the top students in the world. By eighth grade, they're in the middle of the pack. By 12th grade, U.S. students are scoring near the bottom of all industrialized nations."
- "The demographic changes at work across the globe will dramatically change the workforce," according to Peter Drucker.

- Globalization is a lot more than where to sell products; it will include where to find the knowledge workers of the future, even if they do not want to immigrate.
- In 1997 I sponsored a knowledge workplace prototype which pioneered new techniques for capturing, organizing, and distributing knowledge. The system continuously made available the exact information workers needed to perform their tasks and no more, and as they changed what they worked on the knowledge system would automatically refresh a new personalized view.
- Many of the new generation of workers may not be all that new— they will include hiring contract workers, outsourcing work and establishing alternate employment arrangements to retain those retiring.
- India has been readying itself for the future virtual world creating over the last 2 decades more international capabilities and information workers than any other nation.

CHAPTER 10

BALANCING LIFESTYLES

According to the *Families and Work Institute,* Americans spend more hours at work than people in any other part of the world. In one of their studies, "*Overwork in America: When the Way We Work Becomes Too Much,*" reports that one in three American employees are chronically overworked. The study states that, "Being interrupted frequently during work time and working during non-work times, such as while on vacation, are also contributing factors for feeling overworked." Employees who are work-centric are more likely to overwork than those who maintain a dual-centric lifestyle, giving equivalent priority to their lives on and off the job.

Possibly contrary to expectation, employees with greater family responsibilities and those without these responsibilities were equal when it came to feeling overworked. There are a few simple signs to watch for with overworked employees. They are more likely to make mistakes at work, to be angry with their employers for expecting them to do so much, to believe a lot of what they do is a waste of time and to resent co-workers who do not work as hard as they do. To be effective these people need better balance in their lives.

Another sign is to identify who is not taking all their vacation time or holidays. According to the study more than one-third of employees had not and were not planning to take their full vacation. American workers take an estimated 14.6 vacation days annually. Since it takes three days on average to begin to relax, the data shows that the longer employees take off at any one time, the more likely they are to return to work feeling more relaxed and energized. But, the statistics show most employees take short vacations, with 37 percent taking fewer than seven days at a time. Only 14 percent of employees take vacations of two weeks or more. Many say they

The Virtual World of Work, pages 85–91
Copyright © 2008 by Information Age Publishing
All rights of reproduction in any form reserved.

do not take longer vacations because they want to avoid a pileup of work on their return. Being truly away from work is becoming harder because technology makes it convenient to connect from nearly anywhere.

In a study commissioned by ABC (American Business Collaboration) and conducted by the Families and Work Institute (FWI) with nationally representative samples of the U.S. workforce, found that younger workers (Gen-Y and Gen-X) are more likely to be "*family-centric*" or "*dual-centric*" (with equal priorities on both career and family) and less "*work-centric*" (putting higher priority on their jobs verses family) compared to members of the Boomer generation. Ellen Galinsky, president of Families and Work Institute. "What we found was striking—specifically because it uncovers a marked shift in the attitudes of both women and men who are redefining their priorities in life and in work."

Some of the ABC member company reported,

> What they found is that it's not your father's workplace any more. A very compelling trend among the younger generations is that they favor family time over the rewards that usually accompany increased job responsibility. This poses a new challenge to managers responsible for growth within their companies since this is clearly a gap between how we currently work and what the next generations of employees want.

Flexibility is a critical ingredient in creating an effective workplace that is acceptable to the new generations. The study results showed a significant change:

- Today's economy is far different from the economy of the past.
- It is increasingly knowledge and service-based and technology-driven. It is more ethnically diverse—21 percent are people of color today versus 12 percent in 1977.
- It includes almost equal numbers of men and women—51 percent men and 49 percent women.
- It has also aged as the Baby Boom generation has moved through the ranks-with fewer young employees (22 percent under 30 today versus 37 percent in 1977) and older employees (56 percent are 40 or older today versus 38 percent in 1977).
- This is not your father's workforce.
- In fact, far fewer fathers are the only ones bringing home the bacon—one in three (33 percent) today, compared with just more than one in two (51 percent) 25 years ago.
- The job-for-life has been replaced with growing job mobility and job insecurity-only 36 percent feel truly secure in their jobs (or report that it is not at all likely that they will lose their jobs in the next two years) versus 45 percent 25 years ago.

- Employees no longer work from 9 to 5—men now work 48.2 hours per week on average while women (including the 24 percent who work part-time) average 41.4 hours. And just more than one in four (26 percent) U.S. employees work at least one weekend day.

Though their focus may have shifted, the study refutes an often-held assumption that Gen-Y and Gen-X employees are *"slackers."* The study found that in 2002 Gen-X employees actually worked more than 8 percent more paid and unpaid hours per week than employees of comparable ages in 1977. This information can help create a workplace that is more effective in attracting and retaining top talent both now and in the future.

Even those who are workaholics would like to strike a healthier balance in their lives. The issue for most career minded information workers is how? The long days make striking a balance between the demands of work, home, community and personal goals a real challenge. Information workers must come up with a solution to the *"work/life"* balance or should we say imbalance issue. The new technologies have extended the possibility of doing work anywhere, anytime, and it is working. This has made it easy to do extra work answering emails, reviewing deliverables and exchanging thoughts well outside the traditional work week. For many it is an obsession to respond at odd hours to prove their work ethic. I even became aware of one young sales exec. setting his system to send emails late at night while he was sound asleep.

Making things even more difficult is the fact that the same technology is used for both work and pleasure. Some of our friends and colleagues have been known to have a few beers or a bottle of wine in the evening. This would not be acceptable in the office while working but if you are always working when is this behavior acceptable for virtual workers? I can think of several situations where emails were sent, outside of normal working hours, while having a glass or two, that caused the senders a great deal of embarrassment at best, and one a much more damaging result. How would your HR department and management handle this type of situation?

The challenge facing all successful workers is achieving the right balance in their life. Technology allows you to think about family while you are at work and think about your work when with your family. Without some level of healthy balance, difficulties will emerge in at least some part of their life. Research from the *Families and Work Institute* reports that Americans are chronically overworked in part because of the access technology provides. In fact, 1 in 3 employees are in contact with work every week outside traditional working hours. Lisa J. Whaley, the Connecticut author writes, *Prisoners of Technology* says, "It's up to each individual to set the boundaries—companies will get as much as they can from you—set boundaries—most workplaces have a modicum of respect for personal needs and issues." Work is important but so is your personal life. The same technology that is enabling the *"always connected"* society will also be the solution to better balancing one's life.

Time, technology, decisions and discipline are the necessary elements of healthy balance. The most obvious way to free up some time can be achieved by eliminating non-productive time; like travel, unnecessary meetings, lunches, interruptions and excessive socializing during work. I believe that because we can easily extend the work day, we have a tendency to be sloppy with our time, thus contributing to work creep and an imbalance.

Kathie Lingle, Director of the Alliance for Work-Life Progress,

> believes that success needs to be measured in terms of creativity and making your deliverables, not just counted in hours. We need to reward people for productivity not just effort. In fact, hours and productivity have been shown by research to be negatively correlated. Employers recognize that nearly everyone in the workplace is actively working two agendas, one personal and one professional.

Remember the saying, "if you want something done give it to the busiest person you know."

Many employers try to help their employees balance the competing demands of work, family and social commitments, through flexible work arrangements, paid time-off, health and well-being counseling, caring for dependents, financial support, community involvement and cultural change efforts. In fact they may need to do more. Gayle Porter at Rutgers University School of Business suggests employers may need to warn employees or be liable for the effects of work addiction. I believe the establishment of work-from-home initiatives, if done with some thought, will enable the largest potential improvement in the struggle for work/life balance.

To achieve success when working from home will require improved communication and organizational skills. Self motivation and a strong desire to perform are attributes of a successful virtual worker. A lack of these traits will make success difficult. Most will be nervous at first because of the lack of training in how to be a virtual worker or how to be the manager of a virtual worker. But when it works well, the benefits will be measurable. Workers report fewer interruptions, hence greater concentration for those who work in the virtual world. If only half of the time saved from not commuting to an office is reinvested, productivity will be increased by a significant amount. Most studies show a marked improvement in productivity for those that work from home.

Balancing lifestyles will involve effort on the part of everyone in the family. We have a good example of this in our own family. Our middle son in Montana is a Life Flight paramedic and works a 24-hour shift, a 12-hour shift and is on call for a 3rd 12-hour shift approximately every week. Our daughter-in-law is an X-ray technician. She would like to work part-time so they can coordinate their schedules with their daughter's schedule. Their goal is to maximize their work hours while having one of them at home so their daughter's time at a daycare is reduced. This is balancing work/life needs at the family level. I heard a statistic during a discussion, without the source, that among dual-working couples with children less than 6 years old, 41 percent rely entirely or mostly on parental care for their children while they are working, and 64 percent of these parents have specifically arranged their schedules to make this possible.

Young parents today are much more protective and involved in their children's lives. Most organized children activities require money and somebody always needs to drive them there and back. Never before in history has so much effort been put into scheduling the children into programmed activities where they are taught everything by trained staff. With today's much smaller families there is much greater focus given to the offspring. Consensus is that this is necessary in today's society, but I also believe a big part of this feeling is that parents are much more involved in protecting their children from any risk. I believe because of the smaller number of offspring, families are continually trying to manage and monitor all potential risks. In the past large families required parents to spread their attention among many children, but today the scarce asset needs to be scheduled as well as better protected.

Decisions with regard to balancing our lives will impact other decisions with regard to work. There are many things to consider when making work/life decisions, and as always the consequences must be clearly understood. Each decision is unique and to most people it may not be obvious what balance is appropriate, wanted, or achievable. The desired balance will also be different at different times. In many cases people try to gain short term balance by stealing time from other parts of their lives to get everything accomplished. Unfortunately, sleep time or vacation time is the easiest place to steal from. This may appear to work when you are young but the consequences will be noticed in the long-term. As they say, *"pay me now or pay me later."* According to an email set to me, men that take less than their full vacation die much earlier than those who take their allotted time-off. I was not able to validate this data but it just may cause you to reconsider some of your decisions with regard to holidays and vacations.

Even those who feel they do not have a work/life balance problem understand that to advance up the corporate chain takes increased commitment to the job. The commitment is shown in more work time, increased travel, greater responsibly and stress. This is the rat race that many information and mobile workers live. Certainly across all of my interviews, it appears that everyone feels their lives are moving faster and faster.

I worked for one corporate president who felt that everyone was running at a rate that he determined was too slow. He felt his task was to get us all sprinting faster and faster. No corporate athlete can sprint forever, you need to take breaks. The more virtual you become, the more important it is to take advantage of small pauses between tasks. A colleague uses the concept of "*holi-hours*" for his breaks. You may want to ask yourself, do you have a job or does a job have you?

Men clearly are having a harder time of this, because our society in general and the corporate world in particular have old-fashioned mental models about parental roles. We probably all know of situations in which both couples have professional careers and it is the wife that earns more and/or travels more. With children in daycare, who gets the emergency calls? If it is the husband, you just know that somebody at work is saying, "*In my family it is the wife that takes care of those situations.*" There are double standards and it is still more acceptable for women to work part-time or full-time from home and be the ones having more flexibility to deal with the family.

Chapter Summary

- According to the Families and Work Institute, Americans spend more hours at work than people in any other part of the world and as many as one in three American employees are chronically overworked, and one-third of employees had not and were not planning to take their full vacation.
- To be effective these overworked employees need better balance in their lives.
- Only 14 percent of employees take vacations of two weeks or more and since it takes three days on average to begin to relax, the data shows that the longer employees take off at any one time, the more likely they are to return to work feeling more relaxed and energized.
- Another study by the American Business Collaboration found that younger workers (Gen-Y and Gen-X) are more likely to be "family-centric" or "dual-centric" and less "work-centric" compared to members of the Boomer generation.
- What was found is that it's not your father's workplace anymore. A very compelling trend among the younger generations is that they favor family time over the rewards that usually accompany increased job responsibility.
- Flexibility is a critical ingredient in creating an effective workplace that is acceptable to the new generations.
- The study results showed a significant change in the economy and the workforce by showing some amazing statistics.
- The fact that the same technology is used for both work and pleasure make work/life balance more difficult for virtual workers.

- Lisa J. Whaley says, "It's up to each individual to set the boundaries—companies will get as much as they can from you—set boundaries—most workplaces have a modicum of respect for personal needs and issues."
- Kathie Lingle, believes that success needs to be measured in terms of creativity and making your deliverables, not just counted in hours.
- I believe the establishment of work-from-home initiatives will enable the largest potential improvement in the struggle for work/life balance.
- To achieve success when working from home will require improved communication, organizational skills, self motivation and a strong desire to perform.
- Balancing lifestyles will involve effort on the part of everyone in the family—and with today's much smaller families there is much greater focus given to the scheduling and protection of offspring.
- There are many things to consider when making work/life decisions, and as always the consequences must be clearly understood.
- Men clearly are having a harder time with work/life balance because our society in general and the corporate world in particular have old-fashioned mental models about parental roles.

CHAPTER 11

PACE OF CHANGE

We all know that technology is changing, and changing fast, but if these next few pages do not make you a little nervous, then you are not paying attention to just how fast. A good place to start when trying to understand the pace of technology change and how this will impact our lives is the pre-eminent technology historian, Thomas P. Hughes. His theory about the relationship between society and technology is called *technological momentum*. The term was a synthesis of two separate models for how technology and society interact. One is *technological determinism*, also known as technology-push or technology imperative. This theory claims that society itself is modified by the introduction of new technology in an irreversible and irreparable way. A good example is the automobile which has altered the manner in which cities are designed, a change that can clearly be seen when comparing the older cities of the world, which evolved prior to the automobile, and new cities designed to accommodate the automobile.

There are many other examples of new factories, office buildings, and communities designed with technology in mind. A fairly new example is the proliferation of cell towers of which we obviously still do not have enough. Robotics is a technology that is just starting to be visible to the general public and is evolving millions of times faster than humans evolved, so you can be assured we will see these technologies changing our lives over the next short while. Technology, under the technological determinism model, self-propagates itself and once adopted there is no turning back. We very quickly become totally dependent on the new developments. The very existence of the technology means that it will continue to exist and evolve in the future.

The Virtual World of Work, pages 93–99

The other model, *social determinism*, claims that society controls how a technology is used and when it is developed. This is referred to as demand-pull and relates to ideas from the social construction of technology. There are examples where specific government leaders and religions have actually stopped technology evolution and usage for periods of time. Some examples would be radical religious movements such as the Taliban in Afghanistan or the rejection of new nuclear power generation plants in the U.S. based on public fears. Hughes has a compromise approach, which states that technologies start out in a position of social construction, but become eventually integrated to a more driving or technological deterministic role.

The rapid rate of technology evolution is an issue that impacts our whole planet; even if there is not equal global access to technology, no individual will be unaffected by the changes. Technology and the required social changes are evolving much more quickly, and with each new generation, societies, individuals and organizations that are not keeping up will increasingly have a harder time catching up.

Change is difficult and too big a change, in too short a time, will require an effort that is overwhelming for many people. The reality is that each of us will become technologically obsolete more quickly than our parents. The faster we change the faster we need to change. It is like a technology birthday party; every time we open a new gift we discover new technologies that are ever smaller, cheaper and faster. They continue to be more complex, while easier to use, and they use less energy.

Moore's Law is attributed to Gordon E. Moore, a cofounder of Intel. He first presented his thoughts in the form of an empirical observation; that based on the complexity and capacity of the integrated circuit, the rate of technological development would double in about every 24 months. The observation became a prediction and then quickly became widely accepted as the goal for the semiconductor industry. Moore's Law, has taken on a mythical status and is now most often thought of as referring to a doubling every 18 months.

Moore's law is like a yardstick that measures the phenomenal progress technology has achieved in recent years. This equates to an average performance improvement of more than 1 percent a week. Ray Kurzweil developed a *Law of Accelerating Returns* that extends Moore's Law to a wider perspective of future forms of technology. He believes that the exponential growth of Moore's law will continue beyond the use of integrated circuits into technologies that will lead to a technological change so rapid and profound it represents a rupture in the fabric of human history. The law described by Kurzweil has in many ways altered the public's perception of Moore's law. It is common for most to incorrectly believe that Moore's law makes predictions regarding all forms of technology, when really it only concerned semiconductor circuits.

Here is an excerpt from Kurzweil's thoughts:

> An analysis of the history of technology shows that technological change is exponential, contrary to the commonsense "intuitive linear" view. So we won't experience 100 years of progress in the 21st century—it will be more like 20,000 years of progress at today's rate. The "returns," such as chip speed and cost-effectiveness, also increase exponentially. There's even exponential growth in the rate of exponential growth. Within a few decades, machine or artificial intelligence will surpass human intelligence, leading to *The Singularity*. The implications include the merger of biological and nonbiological or artificial intelligence, immortal software-based humans, and ultrahigh levels of intelligence that expand outward in the universe at the speed of light.

Even if we take a more conservation position than Kurzweil on the technology progress that will be achieved in the 21st century, it will be way beyond what any of us can comprehend. A technological singularity, based on Moore's Law, is a predicted point in time when technology accelerates beyond the ability of humans to fully comprehend or predict it. The term, singularity, refers to both the advances in technology and its impact on human society. Actually, the term was chosen as a metaphor from physics— models of the future become less reliable, just as conventional models of physics break down as one approaches a gravitational singularity represented by the "*big bang*." This feedback loop of self-improving intelligence is expected to cause unimaginable large amounts of technological progress within this century.

Current technology roadmaps predict that the current rate of acceleration will continue for at least several future technology generations. Depending on the doubling time used (greater than 3 years to less than 18 months) in the calculations, this will mean from a 10 to a 100-fold increase in just the next decade. Within a couple of decades we will have computers that have greater capacity than the human brain and within a few more decades we will have computers that will have more capacity than all the humans on earth.

These theories by the experts, about the evolution of technology, put into perspective the daunting task to be leading edge. To understand and be in a position to take advantage of what this means to the new world of work, we need to focus on enabling the work processes and the readiness of the workers, not just the technology. Remember what Drucker said, "One cannot manage change only try and stay ahead of it." Are you and your organization willing to take the risks? Are you ready to change before the change? Will you be a winner? Will you survive?

The majority of sociologists and anthropologists believe that technology influences social change, and for many it is the measure of social change. Let's take a look at what some of the experts are predicting and how they have created various timelines for the evolution of societies, based on the evolution of technology. Radovan Richta coined the term *technological evolution*. The term is used in the theory about society's replacement of physical labor with mental labor. According to Richta, technology, which he defines as "a material entity created by the application of mental and physical effort to nature in order to achieve some value," evolved in three distinct stages: *tools, machines,* and *automaton.*

The emergence of technology, made possible by the development of the brain, paved the way for the first stage: the *tool.* The first tools were material objects such as spears, arrows, cutting edges or clubs that augment physical labor or effort to more efficiently achieve a specific objective. Tools allow us to do things impossible to accomplish with our body alone. Modern tools allow us new capabilities, such as seeing minute visual detail with a magnifying glass, manipulating heavy objects with a pulley, or binoculars for seeing distant objects.

The second technological stage was the creation of the *machine.* A machine is a tool that substitutes the element of human physical effort, and requires the operator to control its functions. Examples of this include cars, boats and airplanes. Machines allow humans to tremendously exceed the limitations of their bodies but require a human to run them.

The third and final stage of technological evolution according to Richta is *automaton.* Automaton is a machine that removes the element of human control with an automatic capability to execute commands and tasks. Examples of machines that exhibit this intellectual characteristic are robotic equipment, automatic telephone switches, pacemakers, and computer programs. An implication of the above idea is that intellectual labor—and thus intellectual property, will become increasingly more important relative to material labor and physical goods. The creation of markets for intellectual property will be an indication that a society is transforming into this stage of technological evolution. We are definitely at this point and moving well beyond Richta's model.

I believe some time ago we reached a level of dependence on technologic automation. Humans no longer make many of the products that are produced and used. We actually make the technology that in turn makes the products for us. Thus, we have become one step removed in the process. The next step will remove us one more step, developing the technology that will make the technology that will make the automated processes to produce the products that we cannot build ourselves.

We long ago reached the point at which an individual cannot know everything about one area of knowledge. The extent of our information is so wide and deep on most subjects that a single individual can only truly be an expert in a very narrow cut through the information. Take for example, *The Standard Model of Elementary Particles* or just *The Standard Model.* According to Robert Oerter in his book, *The Theory of Almost Everything,* he describes the Standard Model as the greatest accomplishment of twentieth-century science and the most important theory in modern physics. It explains, at the deepest level, a picture of the basic building blocks from which everything is made. The Model explains how computers are made of wires, integrated circuits, power supply and all that is really happening is that little bunches of electrons are being shuffled around through these circuits. Oerter explains that The Standard Model has a surprisingly low profile for such an important work. It is understood and can be explained by only a small number of people in the scientific field and a relatively small number of people on this planet have even heard of it. My point is that we are actually closer to the singularity than we want to admit.

The very concept of evolution has made some scientists try to analyze various trends and predict the future development of societies. They have created theories of post-industrial societies, arguing that services and information are becoming more important than industry and goods. Leslie White defined technology progress by plotting society's ability to create and utilize energy. Gerhard Lenski views the technological progress as the most basic factor in the evolution of societies and cultures. Lenski focuses on information—its amount and uses. The more information and knowledge a given society has, the more advanced it is. In 1974, Daniel Bell, divided the history of humanity into three eras: pre-industrial, industrial and post-industrial.

Alvin Toffler, author of *Future Shock* and John Naisbitt, author of *Megatrends* have followed in Bell's footsteps and created similar theories. No serious sociologist would argue it is possible to predict the future, but only that such theories allow us to gain a better understanding of the changes taking place in the modern world.

Vernor Vinge is a professor and science fiction author who is best known for his novel *A Fire Upon the Deep,* and for his works on *The Technological Singularity,* in which he argues that exponential growth in technology will reach a point beyond which we cannot even speculate about the consequences. The simplest categorization for society I have seen is to think in terms of pre-singularity and post-singularity.

Virtually all anthropologists and sociologists agree that human beings have natural social tendencies and that particular social behaviors are learned in a social environment and through social interaction. Societies exist in both social and technological environments, and adapt themselves to these environments. It is thus inevitable that all societies change.

For more information on singularity and the evolution of technology/ society contact the Singularity Institute for Artificial Intelligence, a non-profit research think tank and public interest institute for the study and advancement of beneficial artificial intelligence and ethical cognitive enhancement. They focus on Friendly Artificial Intelligence (AI), as they believe strong AI will enhance cognition before human cognition can be enhanced by biotechnologies or gene therapy. The Acceleration Studies Foundation is also an educational nonprofit. They produce Accelerating Change, an annual conference on multidisciplinary insights in accelerating technological change at Stanford University, and maintain Acceleration Watch, an educational site discussing accelerating technological change.

My purpose for including this chapter is to convince you that the pace of change is real and accelerating. Like the experts you can choose to be a pessimist or an optimist on the impact of wildly accelerating technological development. I choose to be an optimist. The question to you is what will you do about these facts—be proactive, reactive or hope that somebody else will figure out how the pace of change will impact you and the new virtual world of work?

Chapter Summary

- Technological determinism, also known as technology-push—under this model technology self-propagates itself and once adopted there is no turning back.
- Social determinism, is referred to as demand-pull—relates to ideas from the social construction of technology and claims that society controls how a technology is used and when it is developed.
- Technology and the required social changes are evolving much more quickly, and with each new generation, societies, individuals and organizations that are not keeping up will increasingly have a harder time catching up.
- Moore's Law, attributed to Gordon E. Moore a cofounder of Intel, has taken on a mythical status and is now most often thought of as referring to an integrated circuit capabilities doubling every 18 months.
- Ray Kurzweil developed a Law of Accelerating Returns that extends Moore's Law to a wider perspective of future forms of technology. He believes that the exponential growth of Moore's law will continue beyond the use of integrated circuits into technologies that will lead to a technological change so rapid and profound it represents a rupture in the fabric of human history.
- A technological singularity, based on Moore's Law, is a predicted point in time when technology accelerates beyond the ability of humans to fully comprehend or predict it.

- These theories by the experts, about the evolution of technology, put into perspective the daunting task of what it will mean to be leading edge.
- Drucker said, "One cannot manage change only try and stay ahead of it."
- Technology influences social change—many sociologists and anthropologists believe it is the measure of social change.
- I believe some time ago we reached a level of dependence on technologic automation.
- We long ago reached the point at which an individual cannot know everything about one area of knowledge.
- It is inevitable that all societies change—they exist in both social and technological environments, and adapt themselves to these environments.

CHAPTER 12

TECHNOLOGY INSERTION

The obvious question, if we believe the chapter on the pace of change, is how do we keep up with the technology change? Technology Insertion (TI) may be part of the answer; it is a relatively new implementation strategy that will become the most used deployment practice as the rate of change becomes overwhelming for those responsible for the planning, selecting, and implementing technology. Organizations can no longer live with the time required by strategic planning methods or start with a green field approach (from scratch). Even traditional delivery methods and in-depth cost justification case studies are too slow. The incredible pressure to demonstrate profitability, growth and innovation will force organizations to react quicker and take more risks. Organizations will need to adopt the TI approach already used in our personal lives—we hear about something, briefly check it out and buy it. To make the best selection we watch what our friends and what others do, and then we buy the same, similar or a better product and insert them into our life. There are many examples of this behavior, one most can relate to is the continuous changing of mobile phones. How many times have you changed your cell phone and plan in the last decade?

TI emerged in the 1990s in response to the increasing success of COTS (commercial off the shelf) software and the military need for the latest technology improvements in their systems. It will continue to be adopted by organizations as a means of copping with the speed of change. The TI term is used in various ways to describe a wide spectrum of usage. I found several descriptions of TI that I combined and added to for our use in this book. Most definitions involved definitions of processes for managing

The Virtual World of Work, pages 101–106
Copyright © 2008 by Information Age Publishing
All rights of reproduction in any form reserved.

101

information pertaining to new and emerging technologies and integrating them into an existing enterprise or operations.

Once an accepted industry standard definition is available, I will use it. But for now here is the definition I use: TI is a rapid response practice used for acquiring or developing hardware and software capabilities that are inserted into existing systems and products to effectively meet immediate and future viability requirements. Viability is a measure of many of the "*abilities*," like affordability, producability, supportability, evolvability and usability of a system and these "*abilities*" are the metric for assessing technology insertion opportunities. Technology and requirements keep changing at an ever increasing pace. This is today's reality and we all live with it. TI is a means of continually adjusting to the changing environment with small and immediate performance improvements as quickly as they become available. The alternative is waiting, studying and initiating more major changes less frequently. Maintaining the status quo drives up costs, erodes competitive position and does not meet today's changing needs.

Compliance to industry standards and using suppliers that adhere to those standards will help in enabling TI. To successfully deploy TI as a practice across an organization it must first be dealt with at the architecture and strategic levels. If not, it will add to the complexity of the environment and lead to future failures. Not purchasing tomorrow's problems today is a considerable challenge. All computing environments are extremely complex, being composed of a wide mix of elements: legacy and new applications, COTS, systems software, hardware, learning and development, suppliers, partners and contractors. Most organizations will have hundreds of variables making it difficult to have a consistent architecture, thus making the possibilities for TI less than optimal.

TI will be used mostly at the project level but the greatest benefits will be achieved at a higher portfolio or enterprise level. For best results and to be able to measure the benefits, the implementation of projects should be managed as program level initiatives. Although TI is increasingly used to solve immediate needs or take advantage of opportunities, you must be targeting both short term and long term value from TI.

I highly recommend doing a review of the complete IT environment before making any overall TI decision. I have used tools like Visio and Pro-Sight's tools to plot the results of such reviews for easy communication and evaluation. A useful graph of the application portfolio would be complexity and sustaining costs shown through the size and color of a circle representing the individual application. Place the circles on an X Y axis diagram with one axis being criticality to the business and the other axis being adherence to the architecture or standard, and you will have a useful picture for analysis. You can use the same technique for system software, tools, hardware, even suppliers. You could also display additional attributes, like age of the system, replacement or retirement schedules, technology assets not covered by warranty, assets by location, impact to the organization of a failure, et cetera.

This type of graph will help with understanding some of the ramifications of using TI and how it can help enable your transformation to the virtual world of work.

All organizations can buy process best practices embedded in technology or COTS applications. A small company can have the same technology solution deployed at a huge global organization. Competitive advantage will be enjoyed by those that make the best use of the systems, not the ones that simple purchase the latest technology. Although technology is often the focus, what is really important is how it will improve the organization and contribute to the organization's goals, competitive position and value.

Competitive advantage may be accomplished for a short period of time by successfully implementing first, but sustained competitive advantage is achieved by continually improving the systems to meet changing performance requirements. Most organizations are not ready to abandon traditional strategic planning, methodological approaches and structured analysis. But, it is what they will be pressured to do, except for the most critical systems. The requirement for change is relentless and the outcome is that every aspect of business will continue to speed up. TI practices will cause people to deploy technology first, and with the early experience gained, make informed adjustments using some of the TI techniques. Rapidly delivering smaller amounts of functionality and continuously making adjustments to the systems and the strategy, based on performance results, will be the normal operating procedure.

This will place tremendous pressure on organizations to be nimble and responsive beyond anything experienced to-date. For teams to work at this pace we need new practices like TI, everyone involved must be continually connected and available virtually to react to the changing demands. The new virtual world is changing our lives and our abilities; it will be up to all of us to discover the opportunities it will create.

Architecture adherence, commercial specifications and standards, as well as configuration management are all necessary to preserve the integrity of the systems as they absorb TI efforts. The concept of TI is straightforward, but in practice it is risky and very complex. Because of the higher potential risks, a risk mitigation process will need to be established. There will be some situations that the rapid TI approach is not suited. Program offices, with user management involvement, will need to establish an ongoing series of performance objectives that will allow TI teams to explore incremental solutions that can be implemented monthly, weekly or perhaps in some cases daily. TI solutions will be evaluated against these performance goals and consistent with the funding which should be negotiated, using portfolio management techniques, at the highest levels of the organization. Every level in the organizational chain needs to understand the purpose, approach, schedule, risks, and value in relationship to their personal participation.

Proven practices need to be in place to impact how the performance needs are defined at any given point in time. The performance objectives will be fluid and thus defined only in specific detail as they move forward on the schedule for short term response. The objectives should be defined independent of possible solutions. This will dictate a need for requirement-design-delivery teams to be highly collaborative. One team may be implementing a small upgrade one week that will be replaced by a larger upgrade a few weeks later by another team.

The program offices will need to establish repeatable TI processes and evaluate potential vendors based on their TI expertise. The business will need to continually evaluate performance enhancement candidates and schedule them appropriately. These performance candidates must drive the business in the direction set by those navigating the organization. The program management office will need to maintain an architecture that meets the needs of the business, short and longer term, while carefully monitoring and understand the direction of the IT industry. They will need to negotiate with the delivery teams and the business teams to establish the release schedule of the TI improvements. The priority of the items on the schedule will be in constant negotiation.

A large number of small integrated teams will be required. Each team will be independent but part of the larger TI initiative. They may work on different candidate domains but the entire outcome must be orchestrated. For example the teams will focus on requirements, applications, tools, training, hardware, vendors, architecture, et cetera. They may be assigned a future candidate and work with it as it moves forward on the schedule. These teams will be small and comprise 3–5 members, plus or minus 1, with people skilled in performing the range of project skills necessary.

Many members will play multiple roles on the team and the teams will work in a collaborative virtual relationship. This will make it difficult to coordinate and integrate with traditional approaches. We will require new methods, techniques, tools and training for managing the collaboration and knowledge management aspects of TI. It will take new skills supported by work management software that is still not available to successfully manage and coordinate a proven TI practice. The goals and boundaries must be clear and established up front. Without this clarity and scope definition the TI initiatives can spin out of control.

Organizations must continually investigate totally new technology solutions and recognize that eventually systems will require more than incremental changes and be scrapped in favor of new viability solutions.

Successful technology insertion efforts must ensure interoperability between applications and systems over time. As the pace of business accelerates, TI practices amalgamated with the virtual work approach will be how the future world of work will unfold. The TI process is all about being leading edge, understanding what this means, and being willing to take the risk. We need to focus on enabling advanced work processes and how they are changing, not just new technologies. But remember, one cannot manage change only try and stay ahead of it. TI can help you change before the change and win.

Chapter Summary
- Technology Insertion (TI) may be part of the answer to the pace of change; it is a relatively new implementation strategy that will become the most used deployment practice as the rate of change becomes overwhelming for those responsible for the planning, selection, and implementation of technology.
- The incredible pressure to demonstrate profitability, growth and innovation will force organizations to react quicker and take more risks.
- TI is a rapid response practice used for acquiring or developing hardware and software capabilities that are inserted into existing systems and products to effectively meet immediate and future viability requirements.
- TI is a means of continually adjusting to the changing environment with small and immediate performance improvements as quickly as they become available.
- I highly recommend doing a review of the complete IT environment before making any overall TI decision.
- Competitive advantage will be enjoyed by those that make the best use of the systems not the ones that can purchase the latest technology.
- Architecture adherence, commercial specifications and standards, as well as configuration management are all necessary to preserve the integrity of the systems as they absorb TI efforts.
- The program offices will need to establish repeatable TI processes and evaluate potential vendors based on their TI expertise.
- The program management office will need to maintain an architecture that meets the need of the business, short and longer term, while carefully monitoring and understand the direction of the IT industry.
- A large number of small integrated teams will be required—each team will be independent but be part of the larger orchestrated TI initiative.

- We will require new methods, techniques, tools and training for managing the collaboration and knowledge management aspects of TI.
- The TI process is all about being leading edge, understanding what this means and being willing to take the risk.

CHAPTER 13

ECONOMIC PRESSURE

We have discussed the major forces influencing the future virtual world of work: attitudes, technology, demographics, and globalization. Let's now look at what financial pressures are influencing our virtual world of work. Both family and business economic pressures are contributing to our struggle to find new ways of running our businesses and our lives. We are consumed by our desire to consume. Thus, there are tremendous consequences to our financial decisions. We are a driven society, our need to succeed, our passion to acquire, our fear of failure, or even our ability to opt out of the race are pressures that influence our daily lives. It seems to be the intoxication of the all mighty buck that is the real driver, pushing us along into positions with which we are not totally comfortable.

The large public organizations receive the bulk of the continuous economic media coverage. For them the game of forecasting quarterly earnings, whether by executives, analysts, or the infamous *"street,"* can be devastating to the value of any public company that misses their forecasts. The markets were made by stock promoters, brokers and company disclosures. But, today I think the market moves on what the media says or doesn't say about current events, industry analysis reactions and interpretations of what the Fed. or other government statements mean. If you try and play the game conservatively, the market will punish you. If you choose to be optimistic and fall just slightly short, your shares will drop dramatically. If you have a couple of good quarters, the expectations will soar.

If you provide less than stellar guidance about some future quarter, management will be made to look like they are incompetent. If the numbers are not great, it appears the only move management can depend on to produce a short term jump in the stock price is to announce costs cutting

The Virtual World of Work, pages 107–115
Copyright © 2008 by Information Age Publishing
All rights of reproduction in any form reserved.

schemes. Since most organization's costs are committed to labor, we all know what that means. It is much more difficult to understand and believe a plan that will drive a larger top number to get the right bottom number. It is usually suicide to propose a strategy based on raising prices; thus, the simplest solution seems to be the cut strategy. But, what does this do to the business and its workers? This is the essence of the main economic pressure faced by most organizations.

Other pressures are coming from the cost of health care and other social programs. Benefits in general are receiving an increased focus but it is health costs and options that are presenting all businesses with future concerns. Also, as the resource market tightens the cost of retaining, acquiring and training new resources will become significant cost items.

Another option in improving the bottom line is to increase productivity. This strategy is what many companies would like to demonstrate, but it is not an easy one to measure or successfully execute. Technology and/or automation usually are the enablers we depend on to improve business processes and somehow deliver on the promise of greater throughput with less labor costs. Gains in productivity with lower costs can often be achieved through an outsourcing strategy. Here you contract out all or a part of a process to somebody else who can do it more efficiently through better processes, greater volume or lower labor costs.

Outsourcing and contracting are strategies that tend to be more under the radar or less visible because they can be controversial. A CIO we were selling to very clearly stated, "If I don't offshore our software maintenance to dramatically lower our costs, and our competitors do, then I would be hurting my corporation's ability to compete!" This seems to sum up the thinking of most management in most large organizations.

Another tactic to meet the growing economic pressure is the very controversial move taken by the airlines and the auto industry; use the courts to take on the unions and cut salaries, benefits and pensions. Cuts of whatever kind provide a short term partial survival solution but are not the moves that will produce a great organization. They buy time and may deflect the media's attention to other prey. In severe economic times the organizations depend more heavily on the Chief Financial Officers (CFOs) for right sizing, transparency and greater controls. The approach is usually to analyze the financial spreadsheets, ask the business managers to derive schemes to cut 5 percent, 10 percent, 20 percent, 30 percent or such numbers, and listen to the strength and believability of the noisy feedback. The exercise is to set cost budgets that will result in an acceptable profit and profitability of the middle and bottom lines. Cost cutting is what you do when you do not know what else to do. My own experience is that cuts alone most often result in further cuts.

Let's look at some economic successes from the early adopters of a virtual world of work. From the organization's perspective, going virtual with many of the information workers is a possible solution that can save money, save jobs, increase productivity and give the workers more flexibility and a better chance to get more balance in their personal lives. Kathie Lingle, Director of the Alliance for Work-Life Progress, commented in *USA Today*; "Studies have shown tele-commuting to increase productivity 10–35 percent. There are fewer interruptions, hence greater concentration for those who work out of the office."

The experience of *Crawford Beveridge*, Chief Human Resources Officer and Executive Vice President in charge of people and places for Sun Microsystems, Inc.; provides us quantitative results. He states, "Few of us recognize just how much the workplace has changed—and fewer still have done much about it. Your workforce is already more mobile than you think. Sun's experience showed that 30–35 percent of their people are not in the office on any given day and with a large, globally dispersed workforce, typically they have a 10–15 percent vacancy rate in their buildings."

Sun implemented their "*iWork*" program, which is a system of workplaces, work practices and technology designed to support an increasingly mobile workforce. It has dramatically reduced Sun's facility and related costs. Beveridge reports, "The iWork program has already helped Sun reduce real-estate holdings and lower operating costs by $50 million a year, and we believe it has the potential, through cost savings and cost avoidance, to have a bottom-line impact of $140 million a year when fully implemented."

In addition to the above cost savings the program has contributed to overall productivity through the reduction of commute time for the virtual workers. Sun found that, "Work-from-home participants save 12.4 hours a month (and give 8 of them to Sun). Those working part-time from home gave Sun an even higher percentage of their saved commute time."

In another significant internal study, Intel wanted to understand the business value of going wireless and what the benefits would be for the employees. They found some stunning results:

> Wireless mobility changes the way employees work. Employees perceived a benefit: time shifting, location flexibility, time slicing, and greater availability. The wireless notebook became like a cell phone, watch or wallet—always with you (don't leave home without it). The results showed a significant impact on productivity: 2hours and eight minute, or 5 percent, or 100 hours per employee per year improvement—across 25 thousand employees this is like adding 1,250 experienced employees or approximately $5K per employee in savings; that covers the additional costs. The big surprise was that the improvements start in days of the beginning of the study.

The study showed if you can accommodate increased mobility and virtual work programs in your organization, the cost savings can be considerable, productivity will be increased and you will have happier employees.

A critical component in meeting the business economic pressure is the increased responsiveness afforded by the new technologies and work habits. Information workers can simply access everything digitally and respond more quickly to problems or opportunities. Connectivity allows workers to test their ideas with other trusted confidants, check the information against the sources, and provide the backup data to decisions, which enables more confidence in decisions and responses. Simulation and scenario planning techniques, better enabled by technology, can help in making better decisions, with better information, faster. It is difficult to judge these new approaches against a scale of creativity, innovation or clever metrics, but they will allow the enterprises to be more competitive, agile and more professional in their responses.

There continues to be business cycles that repeat themselves. When corporations, industries or governments try to maintain the status quo longer than is justifiable, the consequences get bigger. Look at the UK during the Industrial Age, the northern region was the center for worldwide manufacturing. Due to its location Glasgow was well positioned to build and send ships to the West Indies and America. Many merchants acquired great wealth by importing sugar, rum and tobacco. Tobacco was the primary product that funded the Industrial Revolution. Technological advances by Clydeside inventors such as James Watt, allowed railway locomotives manufacturing and shipbuilding to flourish. "*Clyde-Built*" became synonymous with quality and reliability. The launch of the three "*Queens*"—luxury passenger liners—was the pinnacle of Glasgow's shipbuilding achievement.

Belfast became the center of the power production of yarn. Although linen mills flourished in the region, Ireland did not industrialize. The Industrial Age required investment in machinery that required steam power which in turn required rivers, coal and iron ore. Liverpool, Manchester, Leeds and Birmingham all flourished with steel production that was used to manufacture machines, railways, ships and factories. This is where the working class was born. Sadly, the changing pattern of industry means that the region no longer employs the vast throngs of workers in what was the "workshop of the world." Once the area's costs and productivity got out of line with alternatives, the capabilities of the area became irrelevant to the world and they were no longer able to hold onto their manufacturing monopoly. This is an important globalization lesson.

The U.S., in the earlier days, leveraged its lower cost position to become an alternative to more expensive European countries. We went into the two World Wars a debtor nation and exited a world power, creditor nation. We have seen a similar yet shorter economic development cycle with Japan.

They initially became known as a cheap alternative on the world market from a perspective of price and quality. They were smart enough to realize that to become a successful supplier of products to the world they needed to study what the world wanted. From the early 1960s it became apparent that they knew better than many domestic manufactures what the consumers wanted. Today they have come full circle and are known for innovation, quality, and as a leader in the use of technology. Today India, China, Russia, Korea, and many others are at the early part of the same economic cycle.

In the present economic environment, everything is changing faster. We unfortunately must not fall in the trap of protecting industries that need to be released to other parts of the globe. This is the inevitable consequences of globalization, but there is a silver lining, many new opportunities will be enabled that can be realized through technology. We see this with natural resources, ship building, computer components, steel, cars and even services. It is not just dramatically lower labor rates that will win these industries over; like in the UK and America it takes enormous investment, commitment and infrastructure to compete. This may not be the case for all products; cut flowers for example are flown into the U.S. daily from Africa and South America capturing this market.

For nations that put up protectionists boundaries to protect their workers, are trading a short term political gain for a bigger loss in the future. In my view protectionism will produce isolationism which is a terrible strategy in a time of globalization. This may cut you off from accessing the global human resources pool. Resources will be the key to the future virtual global economy. Even in an open society it is hard enough to find, train, retain and motive the top global skills. The future successes will be determined by those having the best virtual resources. Pressures to gain improved productivity are being met through innovations like these examples:

- Technology—WiFi, mass storage, execution speeds, compact circuitry, and unbelievable connectivity speeds.
- Software—CATIA, messaging, project management, security, email, Internet.
- Processes—just-in-time inventory, supply chain, portals, simulation.
- Decision Making—value management, portfolio management, scenario planning.
- Focus—choosing what parts of the business are strategic, and exploring what can be acquired.
- Shared Services—creating a model that can deliver common services to a wide range for business units, divisions or owned enterprises.

There is tremendous pressure to be successful, regardless of your metrics that drive business constantly forward. One metric or economic pressure point that gets limited attention is turnover. It affects both business and the employees. Turnover is very costly, and managing unwanted turnover may become one of the most important business issue over the next decade. If turnover is bad business why would an employee leave an organization when they get the chance. According to the CWP (Center for Workforce Preparation), an affiliate of the U.S. Chamber of Commerce, a lack of flexibility may be a major contributing factor. They report that flexibility needs to be a business improvement strategy, not an employee compromise. Flexibility is a way of defining who, when and where people work and how careers are managed for the benefit of both employees and employers. When considering direct and indirect costs, the impact of unwanted turnover can reach one to two times the persons annual salary. Flexibility is a retention strategy and must be viewed as such.

From the individual's perspective the economic pressures can be just as great. Over the last couple of years costs have risen dramatically for such things as gas, day care, education, health care, mortgages, food, brand named clothing, insurance, to name a few. In fact, there are financial pressures involving the debt most families carry and concerns relating to their future needs. Most workers do not have company pensions or confidence in the long term viability of Social Security.

Let's look at some of the related cost details. Gas and diesel costs have risen from $2.00 per gallon to well over $3.00 in the past year. Oil prices, exceeding $70, $80, $90 a barrel will surely mean more money is spent to fuel commuters' cars each month than to make their monthly car payments.

Of all the costs associated with childrearing, childcare for those that use it must now be the largest expense. The following statistics are from a wide variety of sources. Most of the statistics were provided from friends. While costs can vary greatly, by region and type of care, the average cost of childcare is $500 to $800 per month per child, while topnotch care can cost $1,200 or more per month per child. The yearly cost per child for a K–12 education varied greatly, by the size of the enrollment per school and the region of the country. The median costs to run a school can vary from approximately $6,000 to $11,500 per student, per year. Now parents do not pay this amount directly but you certainly do indirectly through property taxes. Over the past 20 years higher education costs have doubled. The costs for state colleges and universities, for tuition, room and board, are approximately $11,500, and for private schools the cost for tuition would be roughly 4 times as much. Even taking these costs into consideration, more Americans than ever think that having a college degree is important to getting ahead; in fact, a college education has become as important as a high school diploma used to be!

The increased costs of medical expenses are caused by many factors. Twenty percent of the costs can be attributed to increases in prescription drugs because of the huge increase in sales and marketing costs of the pharmaceutical companies. Another twenty is made necessary because of the use of new technology. The new diagnosis and procedure technologies allow doctors to find problems earlier, patients to recovery better and improve their quality of life, but at a high cost. Already the nation is spending about $1.65 trillion a year on healthcare. That represents 15 percent of gross domestic product of America. Also impacting the costs, we find higher insurance premiums due to the increase in legal cases.

We all have seen the multi year increase in what it costs to purchase a home, but did you know that the cost of maintaining the average household has risen substantially? Food costs have risen according to the U.S. Dept. of Agriculture. The largest contributing component is marketing costs, which includes labor. These labor costs have risen primarily because of the increased number of workers and the high cost of benefits. In the south-west there are concerns about the supply of migrant workers.

Marketing costs have risen to approximately three quarters of the total cost of food over the last decade. Clothing costs have also risen. We could all save money on clothing if we were prepared to buy non brand named clothing. Whether it is baby clothing, kid's wear, children's wear, teen age or adult apparel, we all could save more than two-thirds of the cost if we were not so interested in wearing the latest cuts and brands. I do not believe for a moment that this will change so we just need to chalk this up to the cost of living in our society. Insurance coverage for life, health, auto, home, riders, dental, drugs, extended life, liability, business, etc. all seem to be costing more. There are so many types of insurance with so many different options, I found it too difficult to analyze.

Economists are constantly warning us about the rising ratio of household debt to income and the decline in the household saving. Both homeowners and renters have seen an increase in the share of income used to cover adjustable mortgages and credit card payments over the past decade. There are pockets of severe stress within the household sector that are a concern and most experts agree the mortgage default statistics are rising.

According to consumer credit reports, our debt position has risen to $1.842 trillion in 2001 to $2.170 trillion in April of 2006. Financial stress felt in the households is not new and the virtual world of work is not going to change things dramatically. However, the reduction of commuting costs, the additional freedom in where one lives and how one conducts their life, can make an economic difference worth striving for. The real value to the virtual worker is in non-financial benefits. I believe the government should look into awarding organizations and individuals a financial benefit for not commuting to work each day. This would be a partial fix for the crowded highways, polluted atmosphere and help reduce our consumption and dependence on oil and gas.

Chapter Summary

- It seems to be the intoxication of the all mighty buck that is the real driver, pushing us along into positions with which we are not totally comfortable.
- Large public organizations receive the bulk of the continuous economic media attention involving quarterly forecasts, disclosures and future guidance.
- Organizations are pressured to produce strategies to increase productivity or cut costs to improve performance.
- Going virtual with many of the information workers is a possible solution that can save money, save jobs, increase productivity and give the workers a better chance to get more balance in their personal lives.
- Kathie Lingle, "Studies have shown tele-commuting to increase productivity 10–35 percent."
- Sun Microsystems, one of the pioneers of the virtual world through their iWorks program, will provide a bottom-line savings of $140 million a year when fully implemented.
- Sun found that—work-from-home participants save 12.4 hours a month and give 8 of them to Sun.
- In another significant internal study, Intel found wireless mobility changes the way employees work.
- The Intel study showed employees perceived a benefit: time shifting, location flexibility, time slicing, and greater availability—quantitatively productivity improved by 2hours and eight minute, or 5 percent, or 100 hours per employee per year improvement—across 25 thousand employees this is like adding 1,250 experienced employees or approximately $5K per employee in savings.
- A critical component in meeting the business economic pressures is the increased responsiveness afforded by the new technologies and work habits.
- Nations that put up protectionists boundaries for specific workers are trading a short term political gain for a bigger loss in the future.
- The global human resources pool will be the key to the future virtual global economy.
- Turnover is very costly and managing unwanted turnover may become the most important business issue over the next decade.
- A U.S. Chamber of Commerce report shows that employee flexibility needs to be a business improvement strategy not an employee compromise.
- From the individual's perspective the economic pressures can be just as great as those faced by organizations.
- More money is spent to fuel commuters' cars each month than to make their monthly car payments.

- Of all the costs associated with childrearing, childcare is now the most expensive.
- The ratio of household debt to disposable income has risen especially steeply over the past five years and is at a record high.
- The reduction of commuting costs, the additional freedom in where one lives and how one conducts their life can make an economic difference worth striving for.
- I believe the government should look into the possibility of awarding organizations and individuals a financial benefit for not commuting to work each day.

Section Three

WILL THE VIRTUAL WORLD OF WORK CONTINUE?

CHAPTER 14

SECTION INTRODUCTION

Is working in a virtual environment a passing phase? In my opinion it is definitely not. Our lives are becoming too integrated with the capabilities enabled by the new technologies to ever willingly give them up. We use this new found ability to function virtually while working, playing, learning, communicating, as well as establishing and enhancing relationships. The major forces presented in earlier chapters have enabled the movement to a virtual work, and they will continue to contribute to the movement to an even more virtual world in the future. The current technology has more than influenced the possibility of doing work virtually; it has made it possible to live our lives in a digital world. As newer, cheaper and more comprehensive technologies are available, the possibilities offered by a virtual environment are becoming more and more compelling to a much broader spectrum of people.

Earlier technical developments like hearing aids, glasses and false teeth helped enhance people's lives. Today it is common to have pace makers, drugs, new hips and knees to improve our quality of life. Tomorrow there will be even more amazing advances to supplement our bodies and our abilities. People will not stop using these life changing technologies and they will not stop using the even more advanced computing and communication technologies that are enabling our virtual world of work. Those having trouble with the new technologies are being left behind; those embracing and connecting to the technological world will prosper. It would take an unbelievable event or series of events to plunge us back into a pre-connected, non-digital world.

Our civilization was transformed by the Industrial Revolution from an agrarian, rural society to an industrial, urban society. Now we have the pos-

The Virtual World of Work, pages 119–126
Copyright © 2008 by Information Age Publishing
All rights of reproduction in any form reserved.

sibility to move away from an urban, industrial society to a flexible connected global society. The virtual world of work is beginning to transform us in a major way. Here is a great example of what I see happening in the work world. Boeing designed their Joint Strike Fighter demonstrator in St. Louis and Seattle, and in Gloucester and Bristol, England. All the pieces fit together when they were assembled in Palmdale, CA. Hardware, software and communication technology allowed them to be connected and to work together as a team from many different places of the globe where the best expertise existed.

Looking into the future we must remember the wise words associated with Darwin, "it is not the strongest of the species that survives, or the most intelligent, it is the ones that are most adaptable to change." We can survive by adapting and taking advantage of the great technology that is available to us. The U.S. can lead the way in this transformation to a virtual world of work and maintain our position as the leader of the global economy. Let's not miss the opportunity.

As information workers increasingly do work while on-the-go, they are building a familiarity with the convenience. This will continue until mobile workers and our global economy are totally dependent on the availability. The dependence on technology has become so comfortable for most that it is now just how we do things. We do not even think about it. This scenario will be played out again and again until making a trip to the office will be a real inconvenience or even a disruption to getting work done. Once people stop noticing or caring that workers are not at the office, the evolution to a trusted virtual workforce will be irreversible.

The workforce will continue to evolve until the majority of us are operating as part of virtual organizations. Being a successful virtual worker requires several very necessary attributes or I have often heard these referred to as "*abilities.*" The most obvious is availability; it may not be fair but if you are not in the office with the others, you better be connected and ready to respond without delay. This always connected means you are dependable. Flexibility is the virtual trait that will contribute to our changing work patterns. Once a critical mass (more than 50 million workers in the U.S.) has reached the trusted virtual worker state, then the virtual work world will be here to stay. The dominant organization structure will be virtual, first on a national level and later on a global level.

There are many examples of new technology that will extend the possibility of doing work in additional environments. Two that I am familiar with are the following.

Telematics

A complete Internet, voice activated, connected work environment built into vehicles. Much of the following information has been adapted from a

Wikipedia contribution. The term used for this is *Telematics* or more specifically Vehicle Telematics. Telematics is the use of GPS (Global Positioning System) technology integrated with the Internet and mobile communications technologies.

Today it is already used for a number of practical purposes; one common application is providing driving directions based on the shortest distance or fastest route to a specific destination. Other useful applications include collecting road tolls, managing road usage, tracking fleet vehicle locations, recovering stolen vehicles, providing automatic collision notification, and specialized location-driven driver information services (where is the hotel?).

Vehicle telematics systems are also increasingly being used to provide remote diagnostics; a vehicle's inbuilt systems will identify a mechanical or electronic problem, and the telematics package will automatically make this information known to the driver, vehicle manufacturer and a service organization of choice. More work related capabilities and usage will be forth coming but not until the voice command and recognition systems can be made robust enough.

Current software providers like ESITrack are providing GPS data telematics, General Motor's familiar OnStar system, and ATX, in partnership with Vodafone, provide the systems for Mercedes-Benz and BMW. The initial capabilities represent the basic steps in making cars a more intelligent platform more usable and preparing the public for a virtual vehicle work environment.

There are projects and prototypes available for vehicle telematic experimentation today. It will not take long for the voice recognition software to become sophisticated enough to be completely useful. When this happens, it is then just a matter of time until it becomes cost effective, dependable and accepted by the busy mobile workforce. Just because you are driving in a vehicle does not mean that you need to be disconnected from the Internet and non-productive.

We have evolved to the point where nearly everyone has a powerful technical environment in their office. Many have duplicated those environments in their homes. I predict it is inevitable that cars and trucks will be next in-line to enable virtual work. The only question in my mind is whether the development of personal devices that we wear will win over the market before the vehicle telematics is used as a common mobile workplace.

Powering the Tools

When flying many virtual workers use their computers, but are frustrated to only be able to work off-line, and only as long as their battery lasts. One colleague always traveled with 3 two-hour battery packs for those long flights. Why can't the airlines provide a power source for each seat?

While I am on this topic, airports used to provide banks of pay phones at many gates. Remember rushing off the plane to get to the nearest pay phone. Many have been removed and those left are not widely used compared to mobile phones. It used to be a bit of an oddity to see people walking along talking to themselves, but not anymore, there are an amazing variety of headsets, Bluetooth ear pieces or lapel microphones.

I do not understand why the banks of pay phones were not converted to standing laptop workspaces, with power. Now you see travelers squatting or sitting on the floor to get a power source in every corner of every airport gate. Why can't they provide power in a convenient place with a ledge so one can connect without sitting on the floor?

There are now Internet enabled work environments built into the back of the seat on some commercial jets. Connexion by Boeing^{SM} is an example of a mobile information services provider that was designed to deliver real-time, high-speed connectivity to airline passengers, affording them personalized access to the Internet, firewall protected corporate intranets, and personal or business email accounts (including attachments). There are other players emerging in this market.

The access is just as usable as passengers have in a home or office environment. It allows travelers to use their own devices to connect to the Internet either wirelessly or through a standard connection.

If you work while driving or flying then perhaps you can spend more time with family and friends when you are not. Eliminating dead time is a relatively easy way to add flexibility in the effort to find better opportunities for work/life balance.

The number of workers doing work virtually is growing exponentially (more than 25 million in the U.S. according to the Census Bureau) thus assuring organizations will transition through Stage Two and into Stage Three. The benefits of a virtual work environment are compelling and inevitable. The exact timing to realize these benefits is difficult to predict for many organizations because it depends on attitudes, habits and mental models changing. The continued movement to a virtual world of work will happen more quickly for some organizations than expected and more slowly for others. Any delay or difficulty in transitioning will be at the peril of the organization and its workers to be competitive with those that are successfully changing.

There are other logical reasons for moving to a Stage Three model. The threat of catastrophic events inflicted by nature, terrorist attacks or pandemic medical outbreaks may just speed the process. The reason is quite simple; the very existence of a national or global virtual capability enhances the probability that most people can keep working during a disaster. The distributed workforce is subject to a wider variety of different risks. Our economic future is strengthened by having our workforce spread across a country or around the globe. This means that all our eggs are not in one basket or more precisely one location or even one building. The more dispersed we are, the less we can be impacted by any single risk. Once an organization is truly virtual and global, it may be harder to protect it from all risks, but the likelihood of any one event impacting the whole organization is much less probable.

I recall many references to these quotes; *"survival of the fittest"* or *"the strong will survive."* I believe the more accurate statement is, *"survival of the most adaptive"* or *"those that change will survive."* What we are going through is a very basic change and those organizations that adapt to the new technological environment will survive and prosper. The virtual world of work is an evolutionary path that has a future and not a dead end. This is just as true for individuals as it is for organizations, countries and the global economy. To better our way of life and that of future generations is the desired outcome of a transformation to a more virtual world. I can envision a day when everyone can connect and communicate in their own language, from within their own culture, to others anywhere in the world.

The impact of going global is very powerful for economic advancement. Globalization is the force impacting the virtual world of work that has the greatest number of variables and thus the hardest to predict with any certainty. Of the four forces emphasized in this book, I believe technology and demographics are the most predictable. Attitudes are harder to understand but it is the factors influencing globalization that are the most variable. Knowledge and collaboration will result from progress made with the initial four forces. Globalization will be selective globalization, not truly all encompassing globalization.

Thomas Barnett has written a fascinating account of globalization, *The Pentagon's New Map*. Until I read his book I naïvely thought that technology and business could successfully drive the global economy, but he taught me that Wall Street and the Pentagon will need to work closely together with politicians and technology leaders for globalization to succeed. This working together model needs to happen in each of the participating countries so that security and rule sets (the rules that govern how we operate) can be established to manage our integrated economies and protect us from bad guys, religious radicals and rouge nations that are trying to stop our drive to improve lives.

Barnett speaks of the *"Core and the Gap,"* the Core being the connected parts of the world and the Gap being the disconnected parts of the globe. The end goal must be to economically and intellectually connect the entire world by extending the Core and reducing the Gap. Today many do not want to be part of the Core, making an all encompassing global economy just not possible in the short-term. Connectivity is very powerful and given a chance will weaken the grip of those ruling the bad neighborhoods of the Gap.

Globalization involves the integration of economic, political, personal and cultural aspects of our nations. Many resist the integration of the cultural aspects the most. Connectivity is very threatening to many, and this will cause some to fight the transition by any means and make progress difficult in the Gap. We need to recognize that there will be differences in the rule sets for dealings within the Core and those needed to deal with the Gap. I will cover this in detail in a chapter dedicated to globalization.

Knowledge is another critical factor in enabling and extending human capabilities that I will cover in this section. As I see it, we have evolved three distinct libraries of knowledge. The first is contained in our gene library, where billions of instructions are contained in our DNA and reside in every cell, giving us the ability to initiate life and automatically function at a basic level. The second store of knowledge is our brain library, where the cerebral cortex is our own personal repository that contains one hundred thousand times as much information and knowledge as our gene library. The third and most recent library is a result of humans developing a written language coupled with technology. This library was stored in books, now it is increasingly contained and replicated through technology and is called the digital library. It has no physical limitations and as such will provide the ability to contain all the information generated on this planet. Technology is making it easier and easier to create, store and share this human generated digital information library.

We literally have the capability to connect every person on the planet to all available knowledge. This is not being done currently but we have the capability. We are currently doubling the amount of information contained in the digital library every seven years. Connectivity allows us to leverage this library in every aspect of our life. All the knowledge that ever existed or will exist can be available to those who know how to access it. This will contribute to a quantum improvement in how we do things. Just imagine if we had access to the best information or global experts when making decisions, think of the possibilities. Leveraged digital knowledge is extending our human capabilities similar to the improvements gained when we evolved from our DNA library of knowledge to our cerebral cortex library of knowledge.

The transformation to the virtual world of work has started, are you part of this movement? I have searched for great examples of business cases and lessons learned that experienced individuals and organizations are willing to share. This is a practical way for those that have gone down a path to demonstrate the new knowledge they have learned and to create an image that just may attract the next brilliant recruit to pursue them. We will review both quantitative and qualitative experiences in the last chapter of this section.

Section Introduction Summary

- Our lives are becoming too integrated with the capabilities enabled by the new technologies to ever willingly give them up.
- The current technology has more than influenced the possibility of doing work virtually; it has made it possible to live our lives in a digital world.
- Those having trouble with the new technologies are being left behind; those embracing and connecting to the technological world will prosper.
- The workforce will continue to evolve until the majority of us are operating as part of virtual organizations.
- *Telematics* or more specifically vehicle telematics will provide a complete Internet, voice activated, connected work environment built into vehicles.
- Connexion by Boeing^{SM} designed to provide mobile information services that deliver real-time, high-speed connectivity to an Internet enabled work environment built into the back of commercial jets seats.
- The benefits of a virtual work environment are compelling and inevitable.
- The threat of catastrophic events inflicted by nature, terrorist attacks or pandemic medical outbreaks are speeding the transition to a virtual model.
- The virtual world of work is an evolutionary path that has a future and not a dead end.
- I can envision a day when everyone can connect and communicate in their own language from within their own culture to others anywhere in the world.
- Of the four forces emphasized in this book, I believe technology and demographics are the most predictable. Attitudes are harder to understand but it is the factors influencing globalization that are the most unpredictable.
- Working together needs to be an accepted practice in each of the countries of the global economy so that security and rule sets can be established to manage our integrated economies and protect us from bad guys, religious radicals and rouge nations that will try to stop our drive to improve lives.
- Humans have evolved three distinct knowledge libraries—the gene library, the cerebral cortex library and the digital library and we are doubling the information in the digital library every seven years.

- All the knowledge that ever existed or will exist can be available to those who know how to access it.
- The transformation to the virtual world of work has started, are you part of this movement?

CHAPTER 15

VIRTUAL EXPERIENCE

The prevalent attitudes and habits of the older working generation are well formed into tested, and in some cases hardened mental models. These models represent our experience and are what guides us in what is acceptable and not acceptable for performing work. I feel my experience is fairly typical of both the pre-baby boomers and the early boomers—at least those I have encountered doing my research. I tried working from home in 1992, but it just did not work for me. I was not ready and the change was too great. To show how sensitive I was to the whole idea, I was sure people would look at the address on my business card and know it was a residential location. Somehow I knew people would care and this would have a negative effect on my ability to be successful. I did not have any friends working from home at that time and thus no examples to relate to. My mental models needed to be softened or smashed before this was going to work for me. I quickly did what many in this situation would do; I rented an executive office.

For the next ten years I would not choose to work from home. My failed experience was less than positive, in fact, the situation re-enforced my attitude and mental models about working from home. These models were not challenged again until I was forced into working from home four years ago. By this time the business environment had changed dramatically and I had also changed, a bit. Over the last seven years many organizations have gone through major cut backs and are still going through regular reorganizations. During this timeframe I had an increasing number of friends and associates start working from home. The majority of my direct reports worked from home. With the closing of the local office, I was forced to work from home, move or quit. This definitely influenced my thinking and

The Virtual World of Work, pages 127–134

I was much more amenable to the opportunity to become a work-from-home virtual worker. Besides most of our friends are retired, so many of them were focused on the challenges of being home. Knowing this I made my situation sound like this was an interim step to retirement, this way nobody would question me too closely. This worked well with friends but not so well with my business colleagues.

The timing was ideal; at the same time we were completing construction of a new home. I was able to make a few minor changes and had a fully equipped private office to work from. I was not encroaching on any existing territory or forcing a change to any routine already established. I was very lucky; I had a good excuse for working at home; I was well positioned with friends and fine within the organization. I had a great work environment. All in all, it was a near-perfect situation.

Then, why was it so tough to change my habits and routines? The first huge difference I experienced was I no longer had the benefit of an excellent assistant helping me. Over my career I was blessed with great support. I was spoiled and now suddenly I felt completely on my own and isolated. In this situation there are a lot of things that can make you will feel like a complete moron. How quickly these feeling pass will depend on how often they are reinforced per day. The little things you took for granted at the office will occupy more of your time than you expect. All that said, after one or two months I got comfortable with my situation and gradually became confident in my new work routine.

To work from home successfully there are some important new disciplines you will need to learn. One of the most frustrating for me was the proximity of the fridge. I never snacked in the office but at home I would visit the fridge for my favorite things to nibble on. Weight gain may be an unwelcome side effect of working from home. This was gradually controlled and I even substituted exercise for eating, after all I now walked to work. Later I will cover in detail, lessons learned from a variety of virtual workers and experts.

Somewhere around 4 months I became so completely acclimated that I could never again see myself going back to an office environment full-time. I can't seriously think of a good reason to justify such a move. At home I had many fewer interruptions; I also interrupted others less often. I was much more productive. I worked more hours, but they were spread across a much larger portion of the day, and I still had more time for personal things. I could conveniently make conference calls, conduct reviews, do presentations, and discuss strategies with those in any time zone in the world. I had more flexibility in my time, so I could accommodate others more conveniently considering their time constraints. It was simply a work environment that was better for me in nearly all respects. Once one works from home through their adjustment period, they will appreciate the increased flexibility and the organization will appreciate the increased hours worked, contributing to an increase in productivity.

Through technology we have the ability to connect with any individual or group in the world. This idea of connecting people anywhere in the world is still amazing to me. This is the realization of intellectual globalization. Organizations now have the ability to create thinking, working, global communities of virtual workers. Tapping the potential knowledge, experience and capabilities of such a workforce is what the virtual world of work is all about. Computers and communication devices have enabled our global economy and soon will make possible a true global village.

I have included a questionnaire that I send to a wide cross section of people and their responses have been reflected in the answers below and in the chapter on lessons learned.

Subjective Questionnaire
- **What were the circumstances that caused you to become a work-from-home virtual worker?** The answers were centered on two themes—changing business circumstances or personal decisions, none were the result of an organization strategy or planned workforce change.
- **Explain your initial feeling and attitudes toward this change?** About twenty-five percent immediately loved the freedom and productivity. The majority increasingly enjoyed the virtual environment although some came to feel left out and missed the work interaction. Most initially felt awkward and it took time to feel comfortable with the constant conference calls and Web casts from home. Nearly half reported a period of adjustment to being at home during the traditional workday, with their eyes and body telling them that they were at home and their mind trying to convince them that they were at work.
- **Did you need to change or adjust?** Most felt they needed to work harder at self discipline and being more aggressive with scheduling. The responders that were the most independent and did not miss the office chats and colleague visits needed the least adjustment. One perceptive response focused on team building and how it happens more naturally in face-to-face meetings but is not a natural byproduct of Web casts and conference call. Another had an interesting perspective, when she first started working from home she felt that during Web casts it was as if people were visiting her in her home. Most work longer hours because it is so convenient to do so.
- **What was the transition like for you?** The responses covered the whole spectrum with 1/3 feeling the transition was easy (a couple of days to 2 weeks) and 1/3 finding it difficult (4 to 6 months) with the

remainder spread in the middle. One described the actual stages they went through—they are "*awkward*," "*really productive*," "*a bit impersonal*," "*isolated*" and finally "*normal*." Several feel more comfortable if they work from the business office 1 to 2 days per week. One respondent made a most clever observation—there was no transition time between work and family time to either wind up or wind down.

- **Describe your physical workplace and if it has changed over time?** One person has changed their home office location 3 times in four years and wishes she had stepped up to remodeling the formal dining room into an office in the beginning. Most have an office, den or converted bedroom for their workplace. A few feel they only need a laptop, wireless connectivity, cell phone and headset to work, because everyone they work with is spread out across the country and they travel most of the time.

- **Were there any incidents, situations or funny stories that arose?— (family, friends, colleagues, clients, etc.)** It seems those without children or dogs at home have the fewest incidents. Most reported funny incidents related to family members forgetting that although they are at home they are working. Several with small children are sure their colleagues believe they must beat their children nearly every day because of the screams during conference calls. One person after 7 months still finds it helpful to dress and wear their corporate badge to simulate that it is work time to themselves and their family. One reported that she felt it more difficult to supervise office-based colleagues when she worked from home. One experienced an earthquake while on a customer call.

- **Do you still have a business office to go to and if so how often do you visit it?** Surprising to me was that nearly half the respondents still have business offices to go to, with some still going in 3 to 4 days per week but the majority visit their offices just 1 to 2 days per week.

- **What was your former commute like and what did you do with the savings?** The commuting times for the responders varied from 10 minutes to 1.5 hours per direction. One pointed out that their commute time would vary widely causing great frustration. Others felt the stress of their commutes were more important to eliminate than the time. Some used the time savings to sleep later, others to get more done around the house, but all recognized that much of the saving was invested in work. Some pointed out that eliminating the getting ready time was as significant as the commute time.

- **Have you achieved greater flexibility in your life?—(work/life balance).** A few feel they have not added greater flexibility because of the "*always on*" situation, they work much longer hours, not giving them any extra time. The majority find the increased flexibility a real bonus in their lives.

- **Do you feel less stress, are you more relaxed, and are you happier?** No one felt a significant benefit from any reduction in stress; in fact most felt the self-imposed stress levels were higher because of the hours and the pressure to immediately respond to requests. All felt more comfortable and good about their increased productivity and quality of work. They reported more feelings of satisfaction being able to be at home and contribute more both to work and home. Some felt the stress less because they could choose to work at home or go to the office.
- **Were you experiencing work creep (ever increasing number of hours worked) and did the change impact the amount of work creep?** Absolutely, the response was overwhelming that the virtual work environment has caused a large increase in the number of hours worked and that those hours are spread over a greater portion of the day. Most feel that the work hours are a problem because it is so convenient to work and harder to get away from working.
- **What are the implications for you of increased connectivity to work?** The responses were direct, here are a few samples—blurred work/personal distinction, you are always tempted to work, makes work constant, I am always closer to my work, I can never get away from work, the home computer used to be for fun, more responsive, more likely to check emails at night and on weekends.
- **Are you more productive and has anyone commented on your work hours?** Everyone responded that they definitely are more productive. Some feel they are concerned with how they are perceived, so work harder. Others feel there is a silent competition for how accessible and how responsive each is. Many use a new greeting—the language is "are you online?"—"are you working?" One respondent noted that—the more technically competent one is the less frustrating the new virtual world is. If you are down you are truly disconnected and isolated.
- **Has the company saved money because of you being virtual, explain?** Many felt that in the virtual environment there is much less overhead, less wasted time and people are more responsive. Most think the company must be saving on the physical infrastructure but all agreed that the main benefit for their company is more work being done by fewer people through more hours of work.
- **Have you saved any money, explain?** No one had tried to track the actual increase in house costs against reduced commute, parking, dry cleaning, and other miscellaneous costs like clothing, breakfasts, lunches and coffees. Even with this lack of data they felt the cost sav-

ing must be significant. Some that are paid hourly are making more money with the increased hours worked and those that do consulting both them and their companies are making more money. Only one mentioned a tax write-off as a saving to them.

- **Is your company moving to a formal virtual model strategy?** None of the companies represented by the respondents have any official strategy or plan for the virtual work model. Because of the increasing numbers of virtual workers, some of the companies have increased their communication efforts to accommodate this model. No one has received any training, orientation or counseling.
- **How have you been affected in relationship to: career, compensation, reviews, assignments?** None of the respondents feel these items have been negatively affected but do feel that these items now all take more effort.
- **Do you feel more isolated with regard to knowing what is happening in your company, status, friendships, relationships and work?** Most feel more isolated and miss some of the social aspects of going to the office but not the constant interruptions. One observed that more managers are working virtual and because of this there is less opportunity of having a chance conversation to learn what's up.
- **Did your organization have formal documented policies or guidelines for: HR, technical/work environments, security, expense compensation, facility compensation, new agreements you needed to sign, training, counseling, or other guidelines to help you in your transition?** Only a small percentage had some guidelines for some items but none had anything for the transition itself. All felt the support was minimal, you were definitely on your own and the companies could do a lot better.
- **Are there limitations to how and what you can do because of being outside the company?** There appears to be no obstacles reported to being virtual with the new security systems. Some of those in the aerospace and government sectors have restrictions as to accessing certain documents from outside the offices but you were never allowed to take these documents off-site. Several expressed that the opposite is true, they now have great flexibility to listen to music, dress the way they like and have pets or other familiar things that positively impact their mood.
- **How do you get tech support, supplies, etc.?** Technical support seems to be a huge problem for those that struggle doing it themselves. No one responded with a proven solution. Several indicated frustration with India based technical support.
- **What does a normal work day look like; do you have separation between work and personal time during the work day?** Generally

those that are the most organized and disciplined take breaks and try not to have their whole day blend together. Most take some personal time and are more likely to run errands, others go to the local Starbucks to work for a few hours and be around other people. One very innovative person has invented the "*holi-hour*" which is exactly what you would imagine—an abbreviated holiday, a time to relax, listen to some music or play his guitar.

- **What skills do you think you need to improve and succeed as a virtual worker?** Above average verbal, written and presentation communication skills are a must. Other attributes include confidence, technology competence, organized, ability to structure your time, when working on the phone you must maximize your time, discipline, focus, self-control, self-starter, independent worker, ability to minimize distraction in the home, control over work creep, ability to transition quickly. These are the words most used by the responders.
- **What techniques and technologies have helped you the most?** There was a complete list but most mentioned high-speed connectivity, separate phone line, good printer and scanner (separate units), good headset or speaker phone, Blackberry, large screen, etc. Several felt that creating daily to-do lists were more important than when in the office. Being considerate and efficient with other people's time was important. Several want inexpensive broadband wireless access from a laptop and some mentioned that unified voice and data messaging would boost productivity.
- **Has your technical environment changed?** The most common answer was the move to wireless capabilities, PDAs and Blackberries for travel but few have experienced much change in the last couple of years to their technology.
- **Summarize your overall experience and feelings, the best things and the worst things about working from home?** To summarize the best things about working virtual the responders used these words—I get to enjoy my home, more freedom, there is no commute, no time getting ready for work, far more productive, with fewer distractions, work/life balance, being virtual is a very important perk. The worst things are—loss of hall way chats, loss of information exchange, the work hours have increased considerably, less of an opportunity to get away from work, miss human contact, loss of espirt de corps, feelings of being left out and self-imposed stress. Overall, the experience has been very positive for those that responded to the questionnaire.
- **What are your lessons learned, hints and suggestions for others?** Any small business should be completely virtual; to have an office is no longer necessary. If you want to interest someone like me to work for your company you must offer a virtual work environment. I would

suggest having a training course on what to expect when going virtual and definitely a communication hotline for support. Start by allowing people to do the virtual work part time. People need to go into this virtual work environment understanding they will work much longer hours. Definitely you must understand how you work and what works best for you. Make sure you do not have distractions and buy the best equipment possible. Become fluent in using Web conferencing, email, instant messaging, phone conferencing and anything else that helps connect you to others.

- **Would you willingly move back to a business office environment?** A few have moved back but the consensus is a resounding no to moving back to a traditional office environment full-time. Most would consider part-time as long as it was flexible.

Chapter Summary
- The prevalent attitudes and habits of the older working generation are well formed into tested and in some cases hardened mental models.
- Somewhere around 4 months I became so completely acclimated that I could never again see myself going back to an office environment full-time.
- At home I had many fewer interruptions; I also interrupted others less often—I was much more productive.
- I worked more hours, but they were spread across a much larger portion of the day, and I still had more time for personal things.
- Tapping the potential knowledge, experience and capabilities of a global workforce is what the virtual world of work is all about.
- The questionnaire is already a summary.

CHAPTER 16

WHAT ARE OTHERS DOING?

Why should we care what others are doing with regard to virtual strategies? We must care because this is not something happening to one worker, one organization, one industry, or one country—it is a horizontal change happening globally and as such it is impacting everyone. People on every continent are connecting and engaging in new virtual abilities enabling them to work anyplace at anytime. Since we can all be connected, what happens to one will impact others.

Our planet is becoming smaller; I believe we will eventually move from "*six degrees of separation*" to four or five degrees of separation, because of the extent of interconnected networks. In 1967, American social psychologist Stanley Milgram's hypothesis was that anyone on Earth can be connected to any other person on the planet through a chain of acquaintances with a limited number of intermediaries. This is something that most people are not thinking through, thus they do not understand the implications. It will be very difficult to isolate yourself in a globally connected community. Sure there are people who can't participate or won't participate but they will not impede our future in creating a connected virtual world of work.

If we are potentially all going to work together, we must understand more about the members of our working community. When I say all, I am referring to a selected group of co-operating countries, organizations and individuals capitalizing on their combined abilities to better their lives. To do this we must be more understanding and caring. Tolerance to other cultures, habits, language, customs and thinking will in the end allow us all to leverage the power of a global capability. There will be prerequisites to participation in the global economy, this will eliminate those who can-

The Virtual World of Work, pages 135–139
Copyright © 2008 by Information Age Publishing
All rights of reproduction in any form reserved.

not be trusted, oppose the idea, or are just not ready for such an incredible change.

If we look at past experience with new technologies, it is my observation that once introduced; we very quickly become totally dependent on them. The global working community will become dependent on each other and the technologies that enable them to work effectively. For some time now we have had the ability to communicate with each other around the globe, but now we have the ability to truly work together in ways not possible earlier. This working together is collaboration and increasingly we will work in small dynamic teams to increase innovation, productivity and quality.

Of course there will still be competition between workers, it has always existed, but it will be through team collaboration that we will accomplish most work in the future. The prospect of sharing global information will enable significant performance improvements. Sharing proprietary knowledge and processes is scary and risky, but it will be the combination of global best practices that will provide outstanding outcomes. To be able to take advantage of the power of global thinking will accelerate the creation, storage and access to our planet's best knowledge. This will not happen without tremendous obstacles and setbacks, but the rewards for those that lead the way will be well worth the risks and effort.

Technology today moves from concept to commodity faster than any time in the past. From introduction of new technologies, to taking the technologies for granted, can happen overnight. At one point in time we think something is impossible, the next minute we celebrate that we can now do it, and the next minute we consider it trivial. There have been many examples of this over the last few decades. Those that were working 20 plus years ago will relate to my experience with the portable telephone. For those just entering the workforce, this quick visit into the past will help you realize how quickly things have changed.

In the late 1970s, I had two business partners install car phones; these were heavy, very expensive and in the trunk of the cars they had a transmitter/receiver that was as large as a pull-along briefcase. I could not get one because I had a sports car at the time and my trunk was not large enough. In 1988 we moved to Boston and because we did not know the area, my wife and I bought car phones that were still heavy with large antennas, but there was no equipment in the trunk. The phone's batteries weighed so much you needed to regularly change hands during a call.

In 1990 we moved to Seattle and I got a much better cell phone, still analog, to use for business for the first time. It was lighter but still large enough to be nicknamed *"the brick."* It was very expensive to use, so much so my employer would not pay for personal calls. They did not have *"in network,"* *"evenings and weekend,"* *"unlimited calling"* or anything like the current plans. You paid per minute per call.

Seventeen years later it seems that everyone has mobile phones. They are small, cheap and absolutely necessary. The same device is used interchangeably for personal and business discussions, checking stock reports, connecting to ESPN, playing games, instant messaging, or listening to your favorite music. In fact, they can even be a status symbol or a fashion statement for some. Like so many young people today, our youngest son and his friends in Chicago do not have land line phones, they simply are no longer necessary.

They use all the new features, particularly the picture capability on their mobile phone in some very innovative ways—while visiting, our son's friends called for them to join the others at a bar. He asked who was there, and they instantly sent a picture. During a different visit we followed a Cubs game on the cell phone while driving.

In basically a few short years, everyone from grade school students, to people in retirement homes, have become completely dependent on the mobile technology. Most are encouraged to use it because friends or families are using them. They have changed how we do things, how we think, how we work, even how we live our lives. Our grand children will laugh at the idea that we phoned a physical location to see if the person we wanted to talk to was there, instead of just phoning the person. Also, image how they will look at us when we tell them we used to answer the phone without knowing who was calling.

We are spoiled and expect continual rapid improvement of costs, features, usability, etc. in the new technologies. Some are moving from expecting great technology to thinking it is their right to have it. I understand that in some cites the iPod is the number one stolen item. The best way to select technology is to observe what others are doing and follow. The information available from early adopters of technology is easy to get and can supplement the advertising and sales pitches.

Using the same devices for both business and pleasure has caused an exponential growth in technology. Once enough early adopters have experienced innovative and improved ways to use technology, the masses will purchase them and there will be no going back. Organizations will not be able to control or stifle these new found capabilities. Those organizations that are laggards will be viewed as obsolete and an obstacle to the new generation of workers.

It is critical to understand what your competitors, suppliers and others are doing with the technologic advances. To remain competitive you cannot afford all new technology, all the time, but on the other hand you can't fall behind. I was once told an interesting story about how technology is adopted; it is very similar to how a zebra herd functions. The herd has no leader but each animal watches each other very closely. It is very important for survival; they must stay together in a herd. When the zebras stand together the lions have difficulty identifying a single animal to attack. But, if one zebra was to get too far out front, fall behind or wonder too far to the side, they will be easily killed and eaten by the lions. Thus, their actions are to continually observe each other. If one sees another move, they will immediately move. If others are staying still then they will all stay. If one starts running, they will all run without knowing why or where they are going. This is a tried and true survival strategy. We must observe and hopefully understand what others are doing to know what we should do and not be eaten by the lions.

It should be easy to find out what others are doing and the pace at which they are doing it, because most organizations are not currently looking at virtual work as strategic to how they compete. Once you understand what others are doing, then with an assessment of your own organization, you should be able to predict the appropriate pace of change and to evolve your own adoption strategy. Perhaps an assessment will open enough eyes that your organization will look at this as a strategic opportunity for competing for business and resources. Hiring and retaining the best resources through an attractive virtual work image will become increasingly important.

Although this movement to a virtual work environment for large numbers of your workers will take place over multiple years, it will still take many managers by surprise. Many of today's top executives and managers will not agree with a significant movement to Stage Three. Remember attitudes, habits and existing mental models will change slowly. I would think that reducing facility costs, extending their employee's ability to work more hours and be more productive, would be a "*no brainer*"; even if providing greater flexibility to balance their lives was not an organizational objective. There are legitimate obstacles to overcome, security and attitudes being the main ones. These can be successfully worked, but not by organizations that don't see the necessity to equip their employees with mobile phones, Blackberries, laptops, conferencing techniques and other technologies that enable virtual work. Do you know what the others are doing?

Chapter Summary
- We must care because the virtual movement is not something happening to one worker, one organization, one industry, or one country—it is a horizontal change happening globally and as such it is impacting everyone.
- Since we can all be connected, what happens to one will impact others.
- It will be very difficult to isolate yourself in a globally connected community.
- Tolerance to other cultures, habits, language, customs and thinking will in the end allow us all to leverage the power of a global capability.

- For some time now we have had the ability to communicate with each other around the globe, but now we have the ability to truly work together in ways not possible earlier.
- the power of global thinking will accelerate the creation, storage and access to our planet's best knowledge.
- Technology today moves from concept to commodity faster than any time in the past.
- Using the same devices for both business and pleasure has caused an exponential growth in technology.
- To remain competitive you cannot afford all new technology, all the time, but on the other hand you can't fall behind.
- Once you understand what others are doing, with an assessment of your own organization it should be an easy job of predicting the necessary pace of change and to evolve your own adoption strategy.
- Although this movement to a virtual work environment for large numbers of your workers will take place over multiple years, it will still take many managers by surprise.

CHAPTER 17

BENEFITS, OUTCOMES, AND VALUE

If an organization could create an environment where employees worked longer, performance better, produce greater quality, all at less cost—you would think it sounds too good to be true. Let's examine the business case for the new virtual world of work and you can decide if you believe it is viable. Let's start by looking at the viability from the virtual worker's point of view.

I attended a presentation quite a few years back where the CIO of a large cellular company was laying out their pitch for using cellular phones. I still remember one of his statistics because I was living the situation he described. He stated that the work year had actually expanded by 1 month (160+ hours) over the previous 15 years. Although I could not find any similar statistics for the last few years, we all know that work creep is still alive and well. With no clear beginning or end to the workday, the 24/7 online culture has dramatically accelerated work creep.

In a series of interviews I conducted it became obvious that the majority of respondents feel work creep is affecting people in all walks of life. They felt that they, and those they know, work way more than 40 hours a week, take less than their allotted vacation and are nervous about staff cuts or downsizing; the old "*doing more with less*" strategy. Nearly half of those surveyed were considering a job or career change because of the pressures.

The new technology makes employees more productive and produces better quality work but at a potentially high price. Employers may be held responsible for the effects of the always on connectivity of their employees. Gayle Porter and N. K Kakabadse have studied the advent of addiction to technology and suggest that employers need to warn their employees

The Virtual World of Work, pages 141–148
Copyright © 2008 by Information Age Publishing
All rights of reproduction in any form reserved.

about being always connected and force employees to disconnect while on vacation. Eric Lesser, from IBM, in his research, *"The mobile working experience: A European perspective,"* provides an in-depth study of the difficulties, dangers and challenges facing mobile workers.

Expectations generated by management, technology convenience and employee pressure are causing work creep. So what can we do? Obviously just working longer is not the solution, nor is rejecting technology between 5 p.m. and 8 a.m. Turning off technology does not stop it! We first need to understand the situation we are in and be smarter about utilizing our time. We treat time like so many have treated the oceans, air and our rivers; there will always be more than we need so don't worry about it. We have to understand that there are limits to how much time we have and how much we can misuse it. Time is the most perishable commodity we have. Stealing from vacation or sleep time will provide a false, short term benefit.

Let's analyze the average information worker's day at a traditional office. I have been involved in several internal and client studies that showed the average employee was working on tasks, at best, 4–5 hours per day. That means that nearly half of the average work day is spent doing things that are not directly contributing to work production. This shows that the office is a not a productive place to do work. So where can you work that would be less disruptive. Yes, you know what I am going to say, a well-equipped home office will allow the average employee to get more done, in a shorter period of time, with fewer distractions. So the same technology that is enabling the work creep can be deployed to contribute to a solution, but it will take personal discipline.

The single greatest time saving for most employees can be achieved by eliminating the normal daily commute. Statistics show that approximately half of the time saving is retained by the employee, and the other half is invested in work. Based on a conservative estimate of the average commute this will give you 25–60 minute a day to be used for yourself or work. Additional saving can be had by not attending every scheduled meeting. I know there are many organizations where meetings are the cultural way of doing things. If possible attend meetings virtually, learn to multitask and for sure learn how to use the mute feature on your phones. This can enable the saving of another block of time per day. Multitasking is a *"must learn"* skill for working effectively today. It is threatening to those running the meetings but it can work, and they will learn to get things done in that environment. I even know many men who have learned to multitask successfully.

There are two other critical skills that will contribute to a productive virtual work environment. The need for self discipline and the value of being organized are always important, but will be even more so when working from home. Plan your day, make sure you have access to what assets and people you need, or know the best way to get them. Clearly schedule people's time and get commitments that they will be available, learn to be effective and efficient in your communication and become an expert in using your technology tools. The technology is there to enhance your capabilities, not hinder them. These few suggestions will add at least two hours to your available work time each day. With this time and a greater amount of flexibility afforded by working from home, you can achieve a better work/life balance.

So the value to the virtual home worker can be:

- More flexibility in managing your time.
- A new level of convenience in your life.
- Improved availability for your family and colleagues.
- Elimination of the commute effort, frustrations and costs.
- The opportunity to achieve a better work/life balance.
- The satisfaction that comes from being more productive and delivering better quality work will reduce burn-out.
- A feeling of independence.
- Reduction of out of pocket costs.
- More freedom in where you live and how you dress—big potential savings.
- Dramatic elimination of office generated colds, stress and politics.
- Better opportunity for those with disabilities.

Each of these items identified will have a different weighting or significance for each individual. Some may even consider a few of them to be a negative to the case for the work-from-home individual. It is always the same; some see a glass as half full and some half empty. I believe the above list represents the potential for a substantial amount of personal value. If anyone is interested in realizing these benefits in their life, then look into the possibility of working remote. If your organization does not offer this work flexibility then it just may be time to investigate other employers that are more forward thinking and considerate of their employees.

My experience is that although organizations would like to realize the benefits from having employees work remote it is actually the employees that are taking the initial steps to work from home. Unfortunately organizations may see the cost saving and not the true value to the bottom line. That does not mean that all management will agree or be proactive with virtual initiatives. It will take well-informed executives that are comfortable with major organizational change and willing to be part of a much larger change involving globalization, knowledge, collaboration, technology and of course changing human behavior.

The first step is equipping the information workers with the tools to efficiently work in a Stage Two mobile environment if you have not already done so. Next, they must become experienced with the concept of leveraging capabilities from around the global (the first step may be outsourcing). They need to assess their organization's readiness to move to a virtual model and the value of individuals working from home. They need to change their thinking; recognizing that not only can they establish international supply chains and sell their products and services in other countries; they can hire the cleverest people in the world without making them immigrate. Once these changes have percolated and become common, the benefits will be accepted, and then the move to a virtual world of work is possible.

Let's look at the value that an organization can realize:

- The substantial reduction of facility costs.
- An increase in productive hours.
- More scheduling flexibility and longer workdays.
- Achieve around the clock global performance.
- Fewer workdays lost.
- More responsive and available workforce.
- Less turnover, reduced hiring and training costs.
- Greater retention of retirement aged employees.
- Superior resourcing and retention of the best workforce.
- Happier workforce and more motivated workers.
- Fewer office problems.
- Improved productivity and quality.
- Digitally connected resources working from literally anywhere.
- More timely decisions.
- More attractive culture for attracting the next generation of workers.
- New capabilities to achieve competitive advantage.

The benefits are all available to be harvested. I will cover in a later chapter several case studies that demonstrating actual savings and improvements to the business.

The best way to approach an organizational movement to the virtual world of work is to have a shared vision of where you are going. This vision needs to be balanced, representing equally the individual and organizational perspectives. A vision must contain the following 4 Ps and be launched with a comprehensive communication program:

- **PICTURE**—A vivid picture and description of how things will work and how they will look once the end state is achieved. A picture communicates at least a thousand words and is the visual image that people will remember.
- **PURPOSE**—The purpose must be well articulated so it is clear to everyone why the organization has selected the particular path and what the targeted outcomes are. It needs statistics that validated the

decision and references that confirm that other respected organizations are taking similar action. This is an internal sales job and you had better close the sale.

- **PLAN**—There must be a well thought out plan that goes step by step describing what the road map, schedule, program management structure, and objectives are. Explicit in the plan will be how the program will be tracked and measured. Major decision gate points need to be identified and the communication portion of the plan well done.

- **PEOPLE**—The vision must be personal enough to explain what this change will mean to everyone involved. Every person must be able to see what the impact will be for them and how it will impact the other people. Everyone is reluctant to change if they do not understand what will happen and how they, their friends and colleagues will be affected. Expectation setting is a critical component to a smooth change and a smooth change is dependent on its acceptance. People need to understand their options and to whom they escalate concerns. Who the change team is, who is in charge, and who do they interface with.

Communicate, listen, analyze, and communicate again and again. These are very simple words, laid out in a start forward sequence that is very helpful when trying to successfully transition organizational change. On average people need to hear a message eight times before they accept it. Like any standard change, the adoption curve will show a dip in personal performance during the early part of the change. You must manage the depth and the width of any reduction in performance. Remember we have two ears and one mouth, and a good habit is to use them in that ratio.

Implementing organizational change always introduces some risk. The risks in committing to a mobile work strategy as described in Stage Two are relatively low. That should not be a surprise because every organization is already involved with mobile activities. There is a risk that moving through Stage Two may not be viewed as part of an organizational change that will lead to a much larger social change, Stage Three. If your organization is viewing the change as simply riding a technology wave, then you have a major risk of buying your future problems now. Making a successful transition from Stage Two to Stage Three will require a master plan and a program office to make the right commitments, at the right time to both manage risks and maximize value.

The real risk is of *not doing anything* or *reacting too slow*. Attempting a transformational change without the proper assessments or planning can turn your organization into an unattractive employer, supplier or partner in the expanding global business world. This is the major risk.

You are not Captain Picard on the Enterprise, you can't just say, "Make it so Number One." There is a strong probability that the attitudes, habits and mental models of some of the people involved may not be ready for the virtual world of work. You very well may need to conduct some assessments, education and training before people buy-in. If you have a unionized labor force you will probably have a problem on some humanitarian position that the change will not be good for its members. You will need to discuss this with the union leadership and negotiate a resolution.

You may have too many personality types that are not self-starters or independent enough to be trusted to motivate themselves to work in a physically isolated environment. Many may need to come to the office every day to attach to the office umbilical cord. Others may just not be able to work from home for valid personal reasons. An assessment of the workers and their capabilities will help in planning for the transformation. It is possible to change and be prepared for a virtual work life; remember the first time I tried working from home it did not work for me.

Many organizations may not have the capability or capacity to plan and manage the required organizational change program. The worst thing you can do is start a change that gets so badly screwed up that it needs to be stopped. This would lead to frustration and arm the nay-sayers, making the program more difficult to restart. The nature of a program level change like this is that it will take a considerable amount of time. There is always the risk that a take-over, acquisition, merger or a reorganization could take place introducing new players with new ideas. Last but not least, you will need to deal with the different levels of government that have influence over your business. They will constantly be behind where aggressive, agile organizations need them to be. Remember, persistence is the most powerful trait in accomplishing difficult tasks.

Competitive advantage is more often based on your information workers than your products and services; they are the ones that understand your customers, innovate and design your products and services, create and execute your strategies, decide who to partner with, buy the infrastructure tools, and make the decisions that will power your organization. The information flow doesn't just happen up and down the hierarchy. The information should be available to all that need it, and the role of the hierarchy is much more to set strategy, and provide leadership than simply to be a conduit for information.

Jack Welch's book, *Winning*, is a great book that has lots of ideas about how organizations can work better and discusses the new business imperatives that tie with a virtual world of work. Tom Friedman's book, *The World is Flat*, points out that globally there were about 800 million people in the global economy. Today, between technology reach and what's happened in a lot of countries, particularly Russia, China and India, you've got a potential of more like 4 billion people integrating and participating. It does not matter whether that is your market for talent, manufacturing, or selling products or services, that scale really changes things. Friedman's book was very good at saying that it is not just what's happened politically, or what's happened technically, it is the way those things come together that will make the difference. When you introduce the other forces, like demographics, social change, attitudes, collaboration, security, globalization and knowledge, they all influencing our move to a new world of work, the possibilities are truly infinite.

Chapter Summary

- If an organization could create an environment where employees worked longer, performance better, produce greater quality, all at less costs—you would think it sounds too good to be true.
- Work creep is affecting people in all walks of life—the majority regularly work more than 40 hours a week and nearly half have passed up part of their vacation from last year.
- We have to understand that there are limits to how much time we have and how much we can misuse it. Time is the most perishable commodity we have.
- The same technology that is enabling the work creep can be deployed to contribute to a solution but it will take personal discipline.
- Statistics show that approximately half of the time savings from reduced commuting is retained by the employee, the other half is invested in work.
- Multitasking is a "must learn" skill for working effectively today.
- The value to the virtual home worker can be considerable and are summarized in the text.
- Organizations must become experienced with the concept of leveraging capabilities from around the global.
- Organizations need to assess their readiness to move to a virtual model and the value of having positive dealing with individuals working from home.
- The value that an organization can realize is substantial and is summarized in the text.
- The best way to implement an organizational movement to the virtual world of work is to have a shared vision of where you are going.
- The vision should include, a vivid picture or visual image that people will relate to, a purpose that must clearly answer why, an explicit step by step plan and articulate an understanding of what will happen to each individual and what will be the effect on their friends and colleagues.
- Communicate, listen, analyze, and communicate again and again.

- Implementing organizational change always introduces some risk but I believe the real risk is in not doing anything or reacting too slow.
- There is a strong probability that the attitudes, habits and mental models of some of the people involved may not be ready for the virtual world of work.
- The worst thing you can do is start a change program that gets so badly screwed up that it needs to be stopped.
- Competitive advantage is more often based on your information workers than your products and services; they are the ones that understand your customers, innovate and design your products and services, create and execute your strategies, decide who to partner with, buy the infrastructure tools and make the decisions that will power your organization.
- It does not matter whether the global economy is your market for talent, manufacturing, or selling products and services, the global scale involving billions of people really changes things.

CHAPTER 18

GLOBALIZATION

Globalization is a modern term used to describe a process or movement that has existed since our earliest ancestors left Africa 75,000 years ago to inhabit the world. It is an expanding exchange that has the potential to encompass the entire globe. It is the result of greed, profit, curiosity and survival that have driven mankind to dramatically increase international exchanges at different points in history. It is trading goods and services, or cultural and political exchanges beyond the borders of a single country or territory with other parts of the globe. There is, and will be, resistance as we work across national boundaries, religious strongholds and cultures, because globalization involves great change.

Only two *nations* need to be involved to make something international, but many must be involved before it becomes global. Logic would require all nations to be involved to make globalization truly global, but this is just not likely, thus for this purpose, having the majority of the peoples of the world involved is sufficient to be considered global.

The creation of trade routes, empires and colonization are all early flavors of past attempts to create a global presence. The British Empire once boosted that the sun never set on its territory. Some think of globalization as the creation of a global village. Basically, globalization is closer contact between the dispersed people of the world to extend the possibility of personal exchanges, understanding and friendship that leads us to global commerce. A few believe it could ultimately bring about the establishment of a global citizenship. It will certainly take a global effort or a global village to expand our meaning of globalization to someday include other planets or worlds.

The Virtual World of Work, pages 149–159
Copyright © 2008 by Information Age Publishing
All rights of reproduction in any form reserved.

I am not thinking quite so grand for this book. In the context of the virtual world of work I am referring to, at least initially, a selective economic globalization. Selective globalization includes those parts of the world that are actively integrating their national economies and the intellect of its people into a global economy. I believe selective globalization is the required first step in attempting to create a total global citizenship. For this to be successful the participants must agree on economic rules and security rules to promote, preserve and protect its participants. This is particularly true for the U.S. since the September 11 terrorist attacks and the declared global war on terrorism.

Many leaders in the past have tried to unity the world through religion, government, business, language, ideals or military might, and they have all eventually failed. The movement to a more global economy has prospered and been set back many times. World War I and II caused such political and economic upheavals; it dramatically reducing the volume and importance of international trade flows. All of the gains created from the1870s to 1914 were wiped out during this period of self-destructive nationalism. In the post war environment, international economic institutions and rebuilding programs once again caused a rebirth of international trade, but it was somewhat tempered by the Cold War. This period was the first time in history that the human race could have been annihilated by the use of its weapons. The Cold War reached its most dangerous moment in 1962, with the Cuban missile crisis; the danger was so great that the two super powers were held in check by the realization of the nuclear consequences. Most people agree weapons of mass destruction pose an unacceptable risk to humanity and their proliferation must be controlled and eliminated if possible. It took until the first Strategic Arms Limitation Talks (SALT), in 1972, to formally start to end this nuclear arms standoff. With the end to the Cold War, the effects of the dramatic increase in trade became increasingly visible, both in terms of the benefits and the disruptive effects.

A little more history will help to set the stage of how we got to where we are today. During the 1970s through the 1990s the world evolved very rapidly. China moved from Mao's isolationist society to Deng Xiaoping's emerging markets, a joint effort in India thrust them into the outsourcing business making them a player on an international level, and there were advances in Latin America plus other parts of Asia. The Middle East moved to prominence through the formation of OPEC. Oil became a powerful weapon that can disrupt economic stability. Without the Soviet's support many terrorist groups around the world reinvented themselves into religiously motivated terror movements, which later became "*transnational terrorism.*" This subject is well covered in Daniel Benjamin and Steven Simon's book, *The Age of Sacred Terror.* The impact of terror is incredible, between

1987 and 1994 there were 9,575 global casualties of terrorism and that has skyrocketed to 27,608 in the period from 1995 to 2003.

Thomas Barnett in his book, *The Pentagon's New Map*, describes globalization through a vision of those connected and those disconnected from the global economy. He labels them the functioning *Core* and the lawless *Gap*. His view is that the radical Muslim terrorist groups use fear, death and hatred to accomplish their dream of controlling a vast part of the planet. Their goal is to take it off-line and create an alternative global society where our rules do not apply, where our money cannot be used to buy anything and where our power has no reach. In recent times, the Soviet led Communist movement attempted the creation of such an alternate world and for a time encompassed more than 1/3 of the world's population.

Most writers today describe economic globalization as having four distinct components of cross border flows: goods and services, people, capital and technology. In today's digital global world I strongly believe we must also include the exchange of information, knowledge, ideas, intellectual property and intellect. Even sports today are totally impacted by an expanding global influence. Canada no longer wins the World Hockey Championships; in 2006 America did not make it past the first round of the World Baseball Classic, the MVP of the NBA for the last three seasons is not from the U.S., the top professional tennis players are from Belgium, Russia and Switzerland, the best distance runners are from Africa, and even the top Sumo wrestler in Japan is from America. Everything it seems is becoming more and more global.

I thought it wise to check out how some of the most well known international agencies describe globalization. The International Monitory Fund (IMF) defines globalization as,

> The process through which an increasingly free flow of ideas, people, goods, services, and capital leads to the integration of economies and societies. Major factors in the spread of globalization have been increased trade liberalization and advances in communication technology.

The World Bank refers to economic globalization as,

> The most common or core sense of globalization. In recent years a quickly rising share of economic activity in the world seems to be taking place between people who live in different countries (rather than in the same country). This growth in cross-border economic activities takes various forms: international trade, foreign direct investment and capital market flows.

Another common definition of globalization is the freedom and ability of individuals and firms to initiate voluntary economic transactions with residents or organizations of other countries.

Unfortunately there are many in business who think of globalization as a sales and marketing term that refers to the access of international markets to sell their consumer goods, usually without an in-depth understanding of the local needs and desires. They try and sell the same products and services that were designed for the seller's domestic market, with the same ad campaigns, often with unfavorable results. Some then try to cover their lack of success with allegations based on unfair trade practices. A better term used is internationalization, which describes the same process with tailoring to account for local language, cultural and market differences.

Other even more negative views can be heard from those who believe globalization involves the use of legal trickery and shady financial means to take advantage of cheap labor, causing an erosion of national boundaries and patriotism. Globalism can be thought of as the opposite of localism and contrasted with economic nationalism or protectionism, sometimes even portrayed as the elimination of nation states. I am not using such a radical meaning and do not think we will see the day when country borders are eliminated. I think globalism actually causes an increase in national patriotism. This is good as long as it does not get confused or replaced by a more aggressive form referred to as national protectionism.

The emergence of an economic and intellectual global movement is indisputable, as demonstrated by the inclusion of the world's largest countries, Russia, India and China into the global economy. We have had a working mini global economy for the last part of the 20th century that included primarily, North America, Japan, Western Europe, and a sprinkling of other countries like Australia, Korea and Israel to name some. Today, with the latest inclusions our global economy includes more than 2/3 of the world's population or approximately four billion people. The total size of the global market will dictate the potential capital growth that can be generated by that market. So, the larger the better in my view.

The future of the virtual world of work will be influenced heavily by what happens in China. How the Chinese government and its people feel about connectivity and the digital world will determine how freely they will integrate into the global economy. Trust will need to be earned through actions and not political rhetoric. I recently heard that over a quarter of the world's construction cranes are in China and that the Chinese are passionate about having their factories certified as ISO 9001. These are encouraging signs of vibrant investment. To be successful in the global economy, China and its corporations will need to develop their own unique competitive positioning.

This is something that India has done. It pulled together the necessary infrastructure and is rapidly investing in the human capital to go way beyond its initial success. Russia and the other former countries of the Soviet Union are progressing but not as quickly. They have a well-educated population and given a chance, they probably will figure it out and that's what we all need for them to do.

Globalization is our best chance to increase our world economy and improve the lives of its participants. Organic growth from within each nation cannot match the potential created by a global market. Growth creates opportunity and opportunity taken means a better future. The virtual world of work is a key factor in making globalization a reality. It is our strategy, our plan, our future!

Globalization has become identified with a number of trends or events:

- Increase in international trade of goods and services.
- Connectivity to most of the world's population.
- Reduction or elimination of tariffs; establishment of free trade zones.
- Increase in international flow of capital including private investments.
- International agreements have created; WTO, OPEC, EU and NAFTA.
- Development of global financial systems to efficiently handle exchanges and settlements.
- Multinational corporations have increased their share of the global economy.
- Increase of economic outsourcing practices like "*off-shoring.*"
- Greater international cultural exchange, multiculturalism and cultural diversity.
- Much greater variety in what we grow, eat and know.
- Greater international travel and tourism.
- Greater immigration, including illegal immigration.
- Development of a satellite telecommunications infrastructures.
- Airplanes that can connect any two cities in a single flight.
- Greater trans-border data flow and information access through the Internet.
- Increase in the number of global standards and guidelines.
- Creation of International Criminal Court and International Court of Justice.
- Terrorism unfortunately has also developed global reach.
- Improved global environmental protection of our world.

Globalization can be one of our greatest gifts to the future of mankind; how do we make certain it will succeed? This is undoubtedly one of the most important questions we must answer in the advancement of the virtual world of work. So, how do we make globalization a reality? First, their needs to be a set of comprehensive rules or laws that can be used to monitor, guide and manage the global economy. These rule sets need to be understood, accepted, fair, and enforceable. We need an enforcement capability that has the power to do its job. Disputes inside the global economy need to be settled with armies of lawyers not soldiers.

If the rules are clear and equitable then most participants will abide by them with little need for enforcement, but when the rules are not clear, agreed to, or not well aligned, then they will break down. For globalization to work, we need both political and business leaders to compromise so that national interests do not outweigh global interests.

Unfortunately we will need tougher security rule sets to protect those in the global economy from those outside who oppose it. The security protection will need to be strong enough to absorb and withstand attacks. Shared intelligence will need to be sufficient to anticipate disruptive blows whether they are economic, network or terror based. To enforce the security we must have a deterrent ability capability of swift and lethal response. Uneven globalization means we are living in a world divided. Freidman in his book, *The World is Flat* describes the situation as the *Lexus world and the olive tree world.* Samuel Huntington controversial book, *Clash of Civilizations* predicts there will be major conflict where the Core and the Gap meet, a kind of *Fault line wars,* that we see today.

In *The Pentagon's New Map,* Barnett poses two critical questions with regard to globalization:

1. *"What constitutes the rules for who is in and who is not?"*—The size of the Gap will be a major factor in determining the nature of war in the 21st century.
2. *"Will political and security rule sets catch up to connectivity fostered by the economic and technological advances?"*—It could be national self-interest versus global stability.

Globalization is the best logical strategy and vision for the future. The best outcome from my perspective is to not just grow the Core but to shrink the Gap. Most are thinking of national interests being served primarily by the extension of global economic markets for our goods and services. I believe the real gain will come from the creation, storage and access of community knowledge. Community thinking and connectivity will be how we get nearly everything done in the future. It will be an intellectual connectivity that will provide for our future.

It is really very simple—peace enables globalization to flourish and advance, which in turn will provide the stability to assure the existence of the new virtual world of work. Better rules allow faster growth, but require a fair play mentality in the adherence to a wider array of political, economic, technical and security rule sets. Global dependence will provide a control over power disputes or war among its members. The more a country and its people are integrated into the global economy, the less chance they will find the need for major conflict. To be disconnected in the intellectual globalized world would be an economic disaster.

The rogue nations and radical groups of the Gap were satisfied with isolation, but their fear of globalization is so great they now have a strategy of attacking and disrupting the Core at any cost. Al Qaeda has rejected the notion that Muslims should join this larger global community. The threat to globalization will not come from evil empires or evil nations directly, but by evil doers that have no hope of a better future and are disenfranchised and disconnected from the economic and intellectual advances made possible by globalization. A country's economic success will be directly linked and measured by their participation in the global economy. Make no mistake, we are at war with those that hate what we are achieving and we had better take it seriously or the future will materialize in a way we currently do not expect. Our economic future is at stake.

When did the threats begin and when did this war on terrorism start? Many would say September 11, 2001, but the attacks started much earlier. Actually, my recollection is that the major blatant attacks, by radical religious groups, against America, started in 1972 with the Iran Embassy hostages. In 1983 there were attacks in Beirut on the Embassy and the Marine barracks. The Lockerbie Pan-Am airplane was downed in 1988 which was followed by the first World Trade Center attack in 1993. In 1996 the Khobar U.S. military base in Saudi Arabia was bombed. Two more U.S. Embassies were attacked in 1998 in Kenya and Tanzania, as well as the USS Cole in Yemen. In fact, the period from 1981 to 2001 there were 7,581 terrorist attacks worldwide. All of these attacks were carried out by radical Muslims and most were actually against other Muslims to intimidate them. The Muslims make up 25 percent of the world's population so controlling them is key to the radical Muslim's goals. The terrorists are focusing their hatred on Israel and America, but will kill anyone in the way, Muslims or infidels. We are now well into what has been described as a 100-year Holy War.

For the benefits of globalization to be realized we must not lose the war on terror or be frightened into submission by terrorist threats. Spain has given into the terrorists. When a Spanish train was bombed and they were threatened by more attacks they did what the terrorist demanded and pulled their troops from Iraq. France is vulnerable and could be the next major target of the radical Muslims; with 20 percent of its population Muslim it will be difficult for the French to resist and win on their own.

If more countries fold, then the promise of a fantastic global economy may fade with them. There is a problem right now—America, the only remaining super power, is taking the lead on the war against terrorism and is assuming the role of global enforcer, without the backing of many of the participants in the global economy. The global economy and the virtual world of work are dependent on controlling the seriousness of the terrorist threats.

As reported in a circulated email by Dr. Vernon Chong, a retired medical Major General in the USAF,

> We are all to blame for blithely assuming we can maintain our political correctness and all of our civil rights during this conflict, and have a clean, lawful, honorable war. Some have gone so far in their criticism of the war and/ or the Administration that it almost seems they would literally like to see us lose. I hasten to add that this isn't because they are disloyal; it is because they just don't recognize what losing means. Nevertheless, that conduct gives the impression to the enemy that we are divided and weakening.

This does great damage to our cause of creating a new global virtual world of work. If we are united, there is no way that globalization will be stopped and our goal of shrinking the Gap will happen for the benefit of the citizens of the world.

On a more mundane note, globalization requires considerable effort to secure our networks, infrastructures, proprietary information, intellectual property, the movement of goods and services, as well as the control of currencies and capital. If the politicians can handle the rules and the militaries focus on the bad guys, then business, enabled by technology, will invest and progressively integrate the parts of the world that provide economic and intellectual benefits. The evolution of this global economy will determine how and where we conduct business in the future. Global organizations will inevitable become more and more virtual in their structures.

As individuals and business become more virtual, this will present a problem for countries to control their operations. Virtual organizations may very well become the most common structure for future global corporations, just like our societies will become more virtual as the individuals move rapidly in this direct. A good book on the advent of virtual organizations is by Abbe Mowshowitz, called appropriately the *Virtual Organization*, in which he discusses a theory of societal transformation stimulated by IT. Mowshowitz's work provides an excellent framework for approaching transformation and how to achieve a seamless organization. You can use this book to determine where you stand on a continuum between an organization that has a rigid structure and one that has a flexible virtual one.

In his book, Barnett defines globalization,

> It is a condition defined by mutual assured dependence. To globalize your economy and your society, you must accept that the world will reshape your future far more than you can possibly hope to influence the world in return. Moreover, if you globalize, you will import from that world outside far more than you can possibly offer in return.

Globalization will change countries, organizations and individuals. Our society is changing and the pace will only quicken.

Americans tend to forget how difficult the early compromises were in shaping our nation, because most of the very difficult compromises now seem far behind us. Today's problems are much more fluid and it is difficult to predict with any accuracy who will support what and who will not. The time to react is so short that by the time governments move, everything will have already changed. There will likely never be clear-cut situations and decisions that seem obvious. It is never as easy as in the old movies with the bad guys wearing black hats and the good guys white hats. All this said, things do not look bleak, in fact, I personally am very optimistic about the future and the positive role globalization will have in the formation of the vision for the virtual world of work and the improvement to our lives that will accompany these changes.

Chapter Summary
- Only two *nations* need to be involved to make something international, but many must be involved before it becomes global.
- Globalization is closer contact between the dispersed people of the world to extend the possibility of personal exchanges, understanding and friendships that leads us to global commerce.
- Selective globalization includes those parts of the world that are actively integrating their national economies and the intellect of its people into a global economy.
- The movement to a more global economy has prospered and then been set back many times during periods of self-destructive nationalism.
- History has set the stage of how we got to where we are today—China moved from Mao's isolationist society to Deng Xiaoping's emerging markets, India thrust itself into the international outsourcing business, the Middle East moved to prominence through the formation of OPEC and the Soviet Union split apart ending Communism in those countries.
- Thomas Barnett in his book, *The Pentagon's New Map*, describes globalization through a vision of those connected and those disconnected from the global economy—the Core and the Gap.
- The emergence of an economic and intellectual global movement is indisputable, as demonstrated by the inclusion of the world's largest countries, Russia, India and China into the global economy.
- Globalization is our best chance to increase our world economy and improve the lives of its participants.
- The virtual world of work is a key factor in making globalization a reality—it is our strategy, our plan, our future.

- Globalization can be one of our greatest gifts to the future of mankind.
- Unfortunately we will need security rule sets to protect those in the global economy from those outside, who oppose it. The force will need to be strong enough to absorb and withstand attacks.
- Uneven globalization means we are living in a world divided and there will be major conflict where the Core and the Gap meet, a kind of fault line wars, that we see today.
- In *The Pentagon's New Map*, Barnett poses two critical questions with regard to globalization:
  1. "What constitutes the rules for who is in and who is not?"
  2. "Will political and security rule sets catch up to connectivity fostered by the economic and technological advances?"
- Community thinking and connectivity will be how we get nearly everything done in the future—intellectual connectivity will provide for our future.
- The more a country and its people are integrated into our global economy, the less chance they will find the need for major conflict—to be disconnected in the intellectual globalized world would be an economic disaster.
- I believed that these rogue nations and radical groups of the Gap were satisfied with isolation, but their fear of globalization is so great they now have a strategy of attacking and disrupting the Core at any cost.
- The threat to globalization will not come from evil empires or evil nations, but by evil doers from those disenfranchised and disconnected from the economic and intellectual advances made possible by globalization.
- A country's economic success will be directly linked and measured by their participation in globalization.
- Make no mistake, we are at war with those that hate what we are achieving and we had better take it seriously or the future will materialize in a way we currently do not expect.
- For the benefits of globalization to be realized we must not lose the war on terror or be frightened into submission by terrorist threats.
- If the politicians can handle the rules and the militaries focus on the bad guys, then business, enabled by technology, will invest and progressively integrate the parts of the world that provide economic and intellectual benefits.
- To globalize your economy and your society, you must accept that the world will reshape your future far more than you can possibly hope to influence the world in return.

- I personally am very optimistic about the future and the positive role globalization will have in the formation of the vision I have for the virtual world of work.

CHAPTER 19

DEMOGRAPHICS

The term *demographics* is the study of human population, its structure and change, also referred to as population geography. Demographics is a word often used erroneously for demography which is a descriptive and predictive science, demographics is an applied art and science. In both cases however, the objects of study are the characteristics of human populations. In the case of demography, the characteristics being studied tend to emphasize biological processes such as population dynamics, whereas demographics is concerned with a wide range of economic, social, and cultural characteristics. Demographics is interested in any population characteristic that might be useful in understanding what people think, what they are willing to buy, and how many fit in a particular profile. Recent demographic trends studied include the rise of the two income family, the single parent family, the nuclear family, retirement, health care, and Social Security implications.

Researchers typically have two objectives in this regard: first to determine what segments or subgroups exist in the overall population; and secondly to create a clear and complete picture of the characteristics of a typical member of each of these segments. Authors, Ken Dychtwald and Joe Flower in their book *The Age Wave*, convincingly argue that the changing age distribution of the American population is "the most important trend in our time."

Most references to demographics are to support marketing opportunities, buying patterns and preferences. The term is used in our context to examine the age segmentation of the workforce, for example the information can be used to predict the impacts caused by the retirement of the boomers. With this information we can analyze the possible impacts the

The Virtual World of Work, pages 161–166
Copyright © 2008 by Information Age Publishing
All rights of reproduction in any form reserved.

Gen-X and Gen-Y will forge on the virtual world of work. A concept introduced many years ago, called cohorts, has lead to our current use of segmentations like baby boomers, echo-boomers and Net-gens. Strauss and Howe, Tapscott, Schuman and Scott have all conducted interesting studies and written books that introduce us to many fascinating conclusions about the segmentation groups.

A *generational cohort* has been defined in Wikipedia as "the aggregation of individuals, within a population definition, who experience the same events within the same time interval." It is critical to understand the various cohorts or segmentations of the population. This allows the ability to more accurately predict how each cohort is different and how they may interact with each proceeding and following groups. If we can analyze how each cohort thinks then we can better understand their actions. Cohort studies often display the most repeated memorable events and attitudes experienced in each grouping. One of the problems with cohort studies are there is no commonly accepted names or timeframes for each cohort. Without a single event to tie the cohort to, such as the end of WW11 for the start of the Baby Boomers, the dates are tied to specific research studies. Here are examples of segmentations, sub groupings and events, representing cohort of those still living to demonstrate the point. These specific cohorts are from a demographics study by Schuman and Scott, done in 1989, of some U.S. generational cohorts that are reported in Wikipedia.

Depression cohort (born from 1912 to 1921):
- Memorable events: the Great Depression, high levels of unemployment, poverty, lack of creature comforts, financial uncertainty.
- Key characteristics: strive for financial security, risk adverse, waste not want not attitude, strive for comfort.

WW11 cohort (born from 1922 to 1927):
- Memorable events: men leaving to go to war and many not returning, the personal experience of the war, women working in factories, focus on defeating a common enemy.
- Key characteristics: the nobility of sacrifice for the common good, patriotism, team player.

Post-war cohort (born 1928 to 1945):
- Memorable events: sustained economic growth, social tranquility, The Cold War, McCarthyism.
- Key characteristics: conformity, conservatism, traditional family values.

Baby Boomer cohort #1 (born 1946 to 1954):
- Memorable events: assassination of JFK, Robert Kennedy, and Martin Luther King, political unrest, walk on the moon, Vietnam War, anti-war protests, social experimentation, sexual freedom, civil rights

movement, environmental movement, women's movement, protests and riots, experimentation with various intoxicating recreational substances.

- Key characteristics: experimental, individualism, free spirited, social cause orientation.

Baby Boomer cohort #2 (born 1955 to 1964):
- Memorable events: Watergate, Nixon resigns, the cold war ends, the oil embargo, raging inflation, gasoline shortages, introduction of computers, trips to the moon.
- Key characteristics: less optimistic, distrust of government, general cynicism.

Generation X cohort (born 1965 to 1982):
- Memorable events: *Challenger* explosion, Iran-Contra, social malaise, Reaganomics, AIDS, safe sex, fall of Berlin Wall, single parent families, general use of computers.
- Key characteristics: quest for emotional security, independent, informality, entrepreneurial.

N Generation cohort also called Generation Y (born 1983 to 2003):
- Memorable events: rise of the Internet, 9–11 terrorist attack, cultural diversity, two wars in Iraq, life with technology, exploration of the universe.
- Key characteristics: quest for physical security and safety, patriotism, heightened fears, acceptance of change.

Demographic profiling is essentially an exercise in making generalizations about groups of people. As with all such generalizations we must be aware that many individuals within these groups may not conform to the profile. Demographic techniques are simplifications of reality and should not blind us to the richness of individual complexity. Most important, we must not prejudice our view of specific situations by creating expectations about individuals based on generalizations about groups to which they belong. Demographic information is aggregate and probabilistic information about groups, not about specific individuals, but as such it is still very useful for planning. For specifics about an individual we have other techniques like assessments.

One thing about the generations is certain—the causes and events in one generation will dramatically impact the following generation. What one causes the other will live with. I believe that one such observation is: due to the dramatic decrease in the size of families and the increased sharing of parenting duties, young parents today are much more protective of their children, particularly if they only have one. I think it is their way of protecting their precious investment. There are other social influences but

I still think parents in small families tend to want much great structure involving their children and scheduling their activities. Culturally we have created an atmosphere in which parents are focused on children, with protection and development carried to the point that parents are intensely intertwined in scheduling and controlling their child's life. This protection extends even into their college years.

Another summary technique is called the *life table.* For a cohort of persons born in the same year, it traces and projects their life experiences from birth to death. For a given cohort, the proportion expected to survive each year, or decade, can be shown in an *abridged life table.* This is presented in tabular or graphical form for study. Many valuable analyses show us important aspects of our society, allowing us to better understand what is going on and how to predict the future impacts of change. Since 1900, the average life expectancy has increased from 47 years to 77 years. This represents a huge demographic shift and the largest increase ever achieved in human history.

There is a lot of economic and demographic data from the Census Board and over the Internet, relevant to the workforce. In America today about half of all employed men work in professional, managerial or other white-collar jobs, while less than 1 in 6 works in manufacturing. Our best-known cohort, Baby Boomers, contains 76 million Americans born between 1946 and 1964. Combining multiple analyses can show other critical data, as in how the increase in life expectancy can amplify the Boomer effect.

Since 1980, the number of U.S. workers over the age of 40 has increased significantly. By 2010, more than 51 percent of the workforce is expected to be 40 or older, a 33 percent increase since 1980, while the portion of the workforce aged 25 to 39 will decline 5.7 percent. At the same time, the median age of U.S. workers has continued to rise and is expected to increase by six years, from 34.6 to 40.6, by 2010. The number of workers aged 55 and older will grow from 13 percent of the labor force in 2000 to 20 percent in 2020.

Information Workers make up 56 percent of the work force, or 81.8 million workers. There is no doubt that we have transitioned from a manufacturing economy to a service economy, and are now moving rapidly to an information economy. Making it all possible are the advances in technology. In the last 10 years IT and its related services spending has risen to $65.7 billion, a doubling in one decade. The Bureau of Labor Statistics projects a 2010 labor force of 157.7 million people. But, the Bureau also pegs the total number of jobs in 2010 at 167.8 million. Some of that 10 million or so gap between jobs and workers is due to the fact that some jobs are part-time. But today that gap is only 4.7 million workers. A difference this big between the size of the labor force and the number of jobs most certainly means a return to labor shortages greater than was experienced in the late 1990s.

Another analysis I have done is to consider what the rate of retirement will be in organizations that I am familiar with. I only looked at governments and large corporations but the estimates are scary. If an organization has an average age of mid to late 40—then they will be retiring 4–5 percent of their employees each year over the next 10–15 years. This means a department of 1,000 employees will retire approximately 40 to 50 per year and in just 10 years more than half will leave, not counting normal unplanned attrition. How will you operate without these resources and what are you doing to alleviate this lose?

What is certain is that understanding global demographics are critical to understanding the future world of work. To accurately predict the future workforce needs we need to know globally by job type and competency levels the following information:

- The age of the various workforces in place.
- What the productivity of the workforces are currently.
- What the productivity could be.
- What investments this performance improvement will require.
- How many will leave the workforces through retirement and resignations.
- When will these retirements happen.
- What birth rates exist that will produce the future workforces.
- What portion of future needs will be supplied by immigration.
- How many are available to enter the workforces through graduation from the preferred programs.
- Where are the necessary workforces located and do they need to be moved.
- How best to attract and retain the necessary workforces and how best to train them.
- What will be the costs for these future workforces.
- How will each cohort react to the virtual world of work.

This level of knowledge requires considerable work, but until robotics gets a lot more advanced, we will still require competent, motivated workers to keep the global economy turning in the right direction. An analysis of the most appropriate demographic facts will encourage us to prepare for the transformation to the virtual world of world.

Chapter Summary
- Demographics is an applied art and science study of the economic, social, and cultural characteristics of human populations.

- Researchers typically have two objectives in regard to demographics: first to determine what segments or subgroups exist in the overall population; and secondly to create a clear and complete picture of the characteristics of a typical member of each of these segments.
- Some experts argue that the changing age distribution of the American population is the most important trend in our time.
- We need to analyze the possible impacts the gen-X and gen-Y will forge on the virtual world of work as the Baby Boomers exit the workforce.
- A concept called cohorts, has lead to our current use of segmentations defined as the aggregation of individuals, within a population definition, who experience the same events within the same time interval so we can do a better job of understanding each cohort, how they think and predict their actions.
- Demographic profiling is essentially an exercise in making generalizations about groups of people and as such are simplifications of reality and should not blind us to the richness of individual complexity.
- Demographic information is aggregate and probabilistic information about groups and as such it is very useful for planning.
- One thing about the generations is certain, what one causes the next will live with.
- Since 1900, the average life expectancy has increased from 47 years to 77 years, this represents a huge demographic shift.
- In America today about half of all employed men work in professional, managerial or other white-collar jobs (information workers), while less than 1 in 6 works in manufacturing.
- Our best-known cohort, Baby Boomers, contains 76 million Americans born between 1946 and 1964.
- By 2010, more than 51 percent of the workforce is expected to be 40 or older, a 33 percent increase since 1980.
- The Bureau of Labor Statistics projects a 2010 labor force of 157.7 million people and a total number of jobs at 167.8 million, the 10 million or so gap between jobs and workers mean a rapidly approaching labor shortage.
- If an organization has an average age of mid to late 40 – then they will be retiring 4–5 percent of their employees each year over the next 10–15 years not counting unplanned attrition.
- What is certain is that understanding global demographics are critical to understanding the future world of work.

CHAPTER 20

KNOWLEDGE

The more turbulent the times, the more complex the world, the more knowledge will be required. Knowledge is our link to the past and our path to the future. Drucker noted that, "to remain competitive—maybe even to survive—businesses will have to convert themselves into organizations of knowledge specialists." Although Drucker died on November 11, 2005, we are fortunate that he was such a prolific writer and never lacked for something important to share. He was like Mr. Warren Buffett, he could talk for hours and we would all listen intently. At one session Drucker was reported to say, "As long as I keep talking, they can't ask any more questions."

In business our knowledge gurus used to quote Carla O'Dell, "If only we knew what we know." If this was possible then we would do a much superior job in whatever our tasks are. Globally there is a tremendous store of information, knowledge and expertise, what we lack are the tools, desire and access to efficiently and effectively leverage much of this knowledge.

To realize our vision of the virtual world of work, we need the technology and software tools to make it happen. Whoever supplies the best work management software (WMS) will be in the cat-bird seat for the future. The vision is for software to manage each task performed better than the best personal assistant could. The software would need to be used by all team members so that all tasks could be coordinated and integrated to achieve the desired outcomes. Knowledge is the true enabler of performance. Those with it will prosper and those without it will not.

I have always been fascinated by the idea of knowledge, so to better understand what knowledge is, I have endeavored to trace the history of human knowledge and how it has enabled our evolution. Every living thing on earth has a vast store of knowledge contained in each cell that is

The Virtual World of Work, pages 167–173
Copyright © 2008 by Information Age Publishing
All rights of reproduction in any form reserved.

referred to as their *gene memory*. We all share the ability to store and copy, using the language of chemistry, our inherited memory in our DNA. In each cell we have the instructions for all basic functions. The same bio-chemical structure exists in all DNA, whether the living creature is a single celled organism or a complex multi cellular mammal. We do not control this knowledge; it is our legacy from hundreds of millions of years of evolution. This knowledge is our link to the past.

The DNA knows! Humans have some 5 billion bits of information stored in 100 trillion cells, the equivalent of a library of thousands and thousands of books. For example, we possess the knowledge to control important metabolic processes, giving us the ability to absorb oxygen through the lungs and into the blood, turn sugar into energy, and many other amazing functions. Imagine if we had to learn these things before we could do them. In fact, everything we need to know, to create life, is stored in this amazing *gene library*.

But, when the gene library was not sufficient to manage our way in an increasingly complex environment, the brain started to emerge. The brain evolved from the inside out through a long evolutionary process. In simple terms, we developed a brain stem, next came several layers of old brain functions during our dinosaur and early mammal past, and most recently the new brain or cerebral cortex. The cerebral cortex makes up 2/3 of our total brain. The *cerebral cortex library* stores information in billions of neurons. The number of neurons we have is approximately, 10 to the 11th power (10 followed by 11 zeros). In addition there are trillions of connections linking all neurons to each other. This gives the brain the ability to store 10,000 times as much information as the gene library. This is the equivalent of millions of library books, on-line and instantly accessible.

The brain became our tool for survival and has propelled us to the top species on this planet. We use the brain for our conscious life. It is where we synthesis and analyze our thoughts, it is our thinking memory library and throughout our entire life we are constantly adding to it. Unlike the gene library we can control and are responsible for much of the content that goes into this knowledge store. This gives us an amazing ability to actually be able to change ourselves. It allows us to have feelings, emotions, ideas and thoughts. It provides us the capability to exist and thrive in an increasingly complex world. The brain is the source of our memory and our knowledge all nicely stored within our cerebral cortex library.

Memory is critical to us, it is a very powerful tool and we are totally dependent on it, yet it is also mysterious, erratic and frustrating. Memory is divided into implicit and explicit. Explicit memory is further segmented into short term and long term memory. Short term is where we store information for a short period of time. A good example is how a waitress functions; she takes order, passes them to the kitchen and then forgets about them forever. Long term memory is very important to us—it is what shapes us into whom we are and gives us our personality. By holding onto new information we can adapt to new situations and build our personal store of knowledge.

The brain does not work like a computer, nor does it store information like a camera, video, or disk drive. Memory is not stored in one place in the brain; it is stored in small bits in different regions of the brain. Memory recall is our ability to reference all the bits in combination to retrieve what we need. There is no such thing as perfect memory, but we do tend to remember the things that are important to us. A problem with memory is that it is fragile and can be lost in a dramatic event or injury. A person's life can be erased in a single incident.

Implicit memory is where we store very familiar information we regularly use. Earlier we referred to this information as habits. We are still learning how the brain works, how we store information in short term memory and transfer it to long term, and how we retrieve the right information from our stored memory are all still puzzling to researchers. Much of our knowledge about memory is learned from studying damaged brains or memory disorders that can stop our memory from working or provide individuals with extraordinary memory.

In the next incredible step we used our brains to develop a third fantastic knowledge store; this library is the exclusive domain of the human race. With the advent of language and writing, the greatest of human achievements, we extended our capability to record, store and distribute knowledge independent of time or location. At first we used rock drawings, clay tablets, papyrus paper, wood, and silk to record our words. The Chinese invented printing, using carved wooden blocks; this made it practical to have multiple copies that could be shared across many libraries, thus allowing greater access to the printed information. It also made it practical to back up the information to preserve it forever.

This made it possible to capture someone's knowledge, and allowing others to use it without the need for the original person to be present. This meant that we could leverage an individual's knowledge in multiple places at the same time. Today we have electronic environments that allow us to have *digital libraries* of a goggle size. These repositories of knowledge can be distributed via extremely high speed lines, satellites and wireless connectivity to humans anywhere. Again we have greatly extended and supplemented our human knowledge capabilities.

Now we have the capacity to connect every human to our global digital knowledge stored in our third library. As we learn and use the knowledge generated by the people on this planet, we will surely develop a new *fourth library* capable of dealing with the knowledge gained from contacts out in the cosmos. I believe this fourth knowledge capability will be very different from the third. We may not have time to evolve a new ability, so it very well may come from biotechnology improvements that we learn from other species in the universe. I think it will probably involve the direct exchange of thoughts between us and alien species. *If only we knew what they know!*

I went to one of my favorite sites to see what Wikipedia has to say about knowledge. There I found the term Epistemology which is the branch of philosophy which studies the origin, nature, and scope of knowledge. The word epistemology originated from the Greek words *episteme*—knowledge and *logos*—word/speech. There are different approaches to the theory of knowledge. Thus, philosophers have developed a range of epistemological theories to accompany their general philosophical positions. More recent studies have rewritten centuries-old assumptions, and so, the field of epistemology continues to be vibrant and dynamic.

Searching further on Wikipedia I came across the term DIKW; which stands for data, information, knowledge, wisdom: an information hierarchy where each layer adds certain attributes over and above the previous one. *Data* is the most basic level; *Information* adds context; *Knowledge* adds *how* to use it; and *Wisdom* adds *when* to use it. As such, DIKW is a model that is useful to understanding the analysis, importance and limits of conceptual works. Data has commonly been seen as simple facts that can be structured to become information. Information, in turn, becomes knowledge when it is interpreted, put into context, or when meaning is added to it. The idea of the levels is a widely adopted theme. Despite the increasing wealth of information readily available, it is not clear that we're more in control of our lives, or more able to make better decisions. We probably have too much information, and what we really need is the knowledge to know what information we need.

The common idea is that data is something less than information, and information is less than knowledge. Moreover, it is assumed that we first need to have data before information can be created, and only when we have information, knowledge can emerge. Data are assumed to be simple isolated facts. When such facts are put into a context, and combined within a structure, information emerges. When information is given meaning by interpreting it, information becomes knowledge. At this point, facts exist within a mental structure that consciousness can process, for example, to predict future consequences, or to make inferences. As the human mind uses this knowledge to choose between alternatives, behavior becomes intelligent. Finally, when values and commitment guide intelligent behavior, behavior may be said to be based on wisdom.

There are many terms floating around associated with knowledge management. For example, the term *knowledge technologies* refer to a set of tools including languages and software enabling better representation, organization and exchange of information and knowledge. Think of it as an added layer of intelligence to information, to filter appropriate information, and deliver it when it is needed. When we have the complete work management software, we will be able to access and tailor it for each worker, just-in-time, just-enough and just-in-place, exactly what we need to do our jobs in the new virtual world of work.

It is time to see what the experts are saying about knowledge and how it can affect us. The manner in which companies acquire knowledge from data can vary. Ikujiro Nonaka in, *The Knowledge Creating Company*, suggests that creating new knowledge requires, in addition to the processing of objective information, tapping into the intuitions, insights and hunches of individual employees and then making it available for use in the whole organization. Within this framework is an understanding of two types of knowledge: tacit and explicit. Both of these have to exist in an organization and exchange between and within each type is needed for creation of new knowledge. Another point in Nonaka's work is that the creation of new knowledge is not limited to one department or group, but can occur at any level. It requires a system that encourages frequent dialogue and communication within the organization and outside the organization.

Similar but more defined ideas are presented in David Garvin's, *Building a Learning Organization*. Garvin's approach focuses on the importance of having an organization that learns. He defines a learning organization as one that is "skilled at creating, acquiring, and transferring knowledge, and at modifying its behavior to reflect new knowledge and insights." He describes five activities/skills that are the foundation for learning organizations. These are, systematic problem solving, experimentation, review of past experiences, learning from others, and transferring knowledge.

Teaching Smart People How to Learn by Chris Argyris, deals with the way individuals within an organization can block the acquisition of new knowledge because of the way they reason about their behavior. In order to foster learning behavior in all employees, an organization must encourage productive reasoning. One caution is that use of productive reasoning can be threatening and actually hampers the process of learning if not implemented throughout the whole organization.

Leonard and Straus in *Putting Your Company's Whole Brain to Work*, address another way in which knowledge can be acquired. They identify two broad categories: left brained and right brained individuals, with different approaches to the same concept based on cognitive differences. Within these categories, there is great potential for conflict, which can stifle the creative process. However, these different perspectives are important for full development of a new concept. Innovative organizations should keep a balance of these different personality types to avoid stagnation and to encourage development of new ideas. In today's global race for innovation, it is not as much about leveraging what's inside the factories and distribution centers, as it is what's inside the employees' heads.

My colleague, Chris Riemer, uses this definition:

> Knowledge is a matter of layering context. Consider data to be raw facts. Data becomes information when facts are associated in meaningful ways. Information becomes knowledge when it's linked in some way to other information. Wisdom is knowledge that is associated with other knowledge over time, or with knowledge from other domains. Knowledge is information that leads to action. People have knowledge when they know what to do, and this is very useful when working as a virtual worker.

Today we are at a critic point in our move to the virtual world of work. We have the technology to capture, store and distribute knowledge, we have access to the majority of the world's human capital through digital networks; with our changing attitudes and global behaviors we have the appetite as learning humans to make a virtual world a reality. We can collect knowledge from everyone who has some to share. We can digitize it and make it available to anyone selected in the world to have access. It is obvious; to have the best and most complete knowledge will improve all work and all decisions. Soon we should have the comprehensive work management tools that will automatically select and guide us in the use of the knowledge. So, software suppliers, please let's just do it!

Chapter Summary
- The more turbulent the times, the more complex the world, the more knowledge will be required.
- If only we knew what we know.
- Drucker noted that, "to remain competitive—maybe even to survive—businesses will have to convert themselves into organizations of knowledge specialists."
- Globally there is a tremendous store of information, knowledge and expertise, what we lack are the tools, desire and access to efficiently and effectively leverage this knowledge.
- Knowledge is the true enabler of performance—those with it will prosper and those without it will not.
- Knowledge is our link to the past and our path to the future.
- I have always been fascinated by the idea of knowledge, so to better understand what knowledge is, I have endeavored to trace the history of human knowledge. I have identified the major stores of knowledge leveraged by mankind:
  - Gene library
  - Brain library
  - Digital library
  - Future library

- If only we knew what they know.
- DIKW; which stands for data, information, knowledge, wisdom: an information hierarchy where each layer adds certain attributes over and above the previous.
- We probably have too much information, and what we really need is the knowledge to know what information we need.
- We will be able to access and tailor knowledge for each worker, just-in-time, just-enough and just-in-place, exactly what we need to do our jobs in the new virtual world of work.
- Creating new knowledge requires, in addition to the processing of objective information, tapping into the intuitions, insights and hunches of individual employees and then making it available for use in the whole organization—thus requiring both tacit and explicit knowledge.
- A learning organization is one that is skilled at creating, acquiring, and transferring knowledge, and at modifying its behavior to reflect new knowledge and insights.
- Left brained and right brained individuals, have different approaches to the same concept based on cognitive differences, these different perspectives are important for full development of a new concept.
- In today's global race for innovation, it is not as much about leveraging what's inside the factories and distribution centers, as it is what's inside the employees' heads.
- People have knowledge when they know what to do, and this is very useful when working as a virtual worker.
- People have the capability to collect knowledge from everyone who has some to share, we can digitize it and make it available to anyone selected in the world to have access.

CHAPTER 21

CASE STUDIES

Let's explore the results some of the leading companies are achieving as they progress into the virtual world of work. It is only fitting that we first examine the experiences of those who are actually providing us the technological innovations that are enabling this work changing world.

Intel Corporation

Intel, the world leader in chip and circuit innovation initiated an internal study in November of 2003. They selected 100 employees to understand the business value to the corporation of going wireless, and they were very interested in the personal benefits experienced by the employees. The conclusion was very dramatic—"wireless mobility changes the way employees work."

Intel did a thorough study by surveying the employees before and after the study period. To make the study as accurate as possible they conducted extensive interviews, collected self assessments and reports, kept detailed systems logs and actually performed lab-based user performance testing. Here is a brief summary of their results; the study can be reviewed on the Intel Web site at intel.com/ebusiness/wp033101_sum.htm:

- **Qualitative benefits**—employees perceived a benefit through—time shifting, location flexibility, time slicing, and greater availability. They reported that the wireless notebook became like a cell phone, watch or wallet—always with them (don't leave home without it).
- **Quantitative benefits**—impact on productivity—the study showed two hours and eight minute per week or 100 hours per employee per year improvement—across 25 K employees this is like adding 1,250

The Virtual World of Work, pages 175–185
Copyright © 2008 by Information Age Publishing
All rights of reproduction in any form reserved.

experienced employees or approximately $5K per employee in savings that covers the additional costs. The big surprise was that the improvements started in days of the beginning of the study.

Nissan

Some organizations have made the investment and are well ahead of the curve when it comes to the use of mobile technologies. "We were one company operating as different companies," says John Schaefer, Technology Strategist, Nissan North America (NNA). "There was no common, global directory, calendars and shared resources—such as conference rooms—visible to people across domains. Meetings took four times as long to arrange as they should have," says Larry Berger, Manager, Computer Services, NNA. "Because of the delays, sometimes the meetings didn't happen at all."

Nissan executives, like most who travel frequently depend on dial-up connections and were at the mercy of unreliable hotel Internet connections when they wanted to retrieve email or access the corporate intranet. At Nissan's locations, they had no way of gaining network access in the offices they were visiting, because network access and authentication systems varied from region to region. Many simply didn't take their portable computers at all, further impeding their ability to respond quickly to changing events.

As early as 1999, CEO, Carlos Ghosn began to address the company's IT issues with moves calculated to reduce costs, streamline company operations, and improve worker productivity. The WIN project—for *Workforce Integration @ Nissan*—was born. The key to WIN was the goal of boosting employee productivity with better collaboration and knowledge sharing. Also, key to the project was the provision of universal connectivity for Nissan employees (including full mobile access) and the creation of a common employee portal.

Steve Mejia, Senior Manager, Information Systems, NNA said,

Moving to Windows Server Systems was crucial—it gave us the ability to provide anywhere, anytime access to our mobile workforce in a way that was almost identical to being in the office.

Steve continues:

The software allows all Nissan employees to check their e-mail or access the corporate intranet from their portable computers, home computers, kiosks, or any Internet-connected devices. The solution is proving to be increasingly popular with Nissan employees. Soon after it became available, it was accessed 41,000 times in July 2004; within five months that monthly access number had doubled to more than 83,000.

"At Nissan, we expect to save at least $135 million over the next few years thanks to the efficiencies that Windows Server 2003 and Exchange Server 2003 are helping us to achieve," says Toshihiko Suda, Senior Manager, Nissan Motor Company, Ltd. "That savings comes from increased productivity of our staff at the same time that we are able to spend less on technology, maintenance, travel, printing, telephone, and outsourcing. It makes executives more productive and even contributes to better customer service." Further detail can be accessed through Nissan or Microsoft Web sites.

The Boeing Company

The following information is from an article written by Jennifer German from Boeing.

"The Boeing 787 program benefits from collaboration methods, said Frank Statkus, vice president of Tools, Technology and Processes for the program. Statkus calls this "the partnership of the future," redefining development activities to include an international team of engineers working around the world literally 24 hours a day to support the program's schedule. In addition, this partnership includes other parts of Boeing such as Operations, Tooling and Quality.

Partnership at this level requires much more than redefining roles and responsibilities. To successfully reap the rewards of this structure, the 787 team, in conjunction with Dassault Systemes, developed a suite of software solutions to design, build and test the airplane digitally prior to production. The software suite includes CATIA, the computer-aided design tool; DELMIA, the manufacturing software; and ENOVIA, the engineering interface. Together they offer what is known as a Product Lifecycle Management (PLM) solution.

The team built specially equipped conference rooms, called Global Collaboration Centers, to use in conjunction with the software toolset. This arrangement creates a "virtual workspace" for engineers on the 787 program at Boeing and partner locations worldwide to make design changes to the airplane in real time.

Through the global collaboration environment, the combination of the conference rooms and the advanced software permit visualization and analysis of specific components of the airplane during design reviews. As a result, the team is seeing a high level of interaction that allows engineers to review technical design issues—meeting face-to-face but not in person—from a common database being developed as the entire airplane is defined.

As an example, in the past parts would be designed in an engineering language or format. Manufacturing engineers would translate the data to a language compatible with manufacturing software. Incompatibilities between the software tools resulted in errors during the translations. These errors needed to be resolved through numerous iterations in the design, analysis, tooling and manufacturing cycle before proceeding to part fabrication. Because the suite of new tools developed by Boeing and Dassault do not require translations, this time-consuming process is no longer required.

In addition, the tools enable relational design, where the software analyzes design changes and automatically adjusts adjacent geometry to accommodate the new or modified configuration. All automatic changes are reviewed and approved or modified by the person responsible for the initial design. This allows you to see the benefits or issues of the change immediately—a huge benefit of real-time interfaces, said Statkus.

To underscore the point, Statkus recounted all of the design effort required using previous tools and processes to move a passenger door by two inch*es*.

It would literally take a team of engineers weeks to figure out all of the components that the move would affect, to redesign those components and to work through any new issues. Now, that process is greatly simplified with the use of these tools through relational design.

The new suite of software will span the total development of the 787—from conceptual design to detailed engineering and analysis, from manufacturing and final assembly to in-service support. In this environment, the program can maintain the configuration of the 787 throughout its life cycle.

Right now more than 11,000 Boeing employees have work agreements with their managers to work away from the traditional office—from hotelling centers, the offices of business partners or customers, or from their own homes. These telecommuting and "virtual" work agreements create clarity about employee and business expectations, goals, and objectives, and about how communications with business partners and customers will be maintained. A recent Boeing Employee Survey showed those with these virtual work agreements feel as connected and engaged with their work groups as those who work in a traditional office setting.

Chevron

This is an extract from a presentation by Alan Nunns, who is General Manager of Global Technology and Strategy at Chevron, during Microsoft's 2005 CEO Summit.

The real business of Chevron is making business decisions using digital information, that really is, in a sense, our core business. We make all of those decisions, basically, with people working together, generally collaborating using digital information. All of the people, the 60,000 people we have working in 186 countries exchange about a million e-mails per day. So, we're doing teamwork across geographies, where people in Angola are working with people in Houston, are working with people in the Bay Area to make capital and real-time decisions.

Our commercial transactional systems are processing about four million commercial transactions per day. So, we've got this really data rich environment. We've got this two petabytes of data, about half of that is what you would call structured data in big databases, big files. The other half are documents, e-mails, PowerPoints, Excels, all sorts of other documents. And there are probably about 100 million of those. 2001–2002 we were actually merging Chevron and Texaco when we rolled out XP across the enterprise. We also significantly improved our network infrastructure, and improved our security infrastructure, a globalization of work processes, and a focus on people actually in more or less real-time across geographies. So, we made a lot of use of NetMeeting, a lot of use of instant messaging, and so on. So, we really created a global community at that point.

Sun Microsystems

Sun Microsystems was one of the early adopters of employee flexibility based on a forecast that they will save $71 million annually on real estate costs by allowing 17,000 employees to work part of the time from home, thus reducing the need for office space. According to Crawford Beveridge, Chief Human Resources Officer and Executive Vice President in charge of people and places for Sun Microsystems, Inc.:

> The iWork program has already helped Sun reduce real-estate holdings and lower operating costs by $50 million in the first year, and $63.8 million the second. We believe it has the potential, through cost savings and cost avoidance, to have a bottom-line impact of $140 million a year when fully implemented. Today's office is anywhere your employees happen to be . . . and that could be anywhere. Through mobile technology, employees can connect to the office at anytime, from anywhere, using any device.
>
> This choice of work environments goes beyond telecommuting and includes the mobility to be closer to colleagues, partners and the global marketplace. These new levels of workplace flexibility create a compelling opportunity for organizations to rethink how they manage their real estate portfolios.
>
> The Sun Open Work Practice leverages the mobile employee revolution to help develop a 21st century workplace. This improved access to office resources not only means that employees can choose how and where they work; through the Sun Open Work Practice, enterprises have an alternative to centralized, monolithic office buildings or huge, sprawling office parks. It means that major real estate events, such as mergers and lease terminations, no longer need to lead to excess capacity. And, it means that employee and process disruption can be minimized when moving to outsourced or off-shoring models.

Based on a "Network of Places," the Sun Open Work practice employs a mixture of workplace types and locations that match the needs and habits of your mobile and distributed workforce with your corporate strategy and vision. It allows the company to optimize near-term and long-term real estate portfolio goals against key people, workplaces and technology elements. This network can include central campuses, regional hubs, drop-in centers, flexible field offices, work cafes and home offices. It also includes access to browsers through non-company locations like airports, hotels and coffee shops.

Of course the cornerstone of the liberated work environment is flexibility. Depending upon their category, employees are given the option to work in a variety of physical settings. Flexible Campus-based Offices provide open and enclosed workspaces for employees who work primarily on campus or at centrally-located buildings. Flexible Zones are blocks of flexible seats in predominantly assigned buildings. These seats are available by advance reservation through SunReserve, a central workspace reservation system.

Drop-In Centers provide workspaces and resources so any employee can use them on a drop-in basis. No advanced reservations are permitted. Work from Home employees make a mutual agreement with their managers to work from home from 1–5 days a week. Again, assuming they have suitable space and a conducive home environment, employees are outfitted with all the technology and tools they need to remain connected securely to the network 24/7.

The Sun Open Work Practice has revolutionized what it means to be virtual and connected to the office. Average fixed office vacancies sometimes approach 50–70 percent. Sun's successful transition from a centralized campus-based environment to a Network of Places resulted in cost avoidances of more than $300 million since the program's inception, with substantially lower IT and support costs and improved employee job satisfaction scores.

Implementing the Sun Open Work Practice can directly contribute to a more physically and economically agile organization. Flexible offices and mobile workstation sessions mean that you can incur zero-cost moves during reorganizations and real estate events. Greater access to office resources via Internet and networked communications means employees can be deployed where they are most productive. The Sun Open Work Practice provides an alternative portfolio options to expensive, centralized office buildings and monolithic office parks. The key is something we call iWork—a system of workplaces, work practices, and technologies designed to support an increasingly mobile workforce.

It's also proving to be a real benefit to our workers. On average, users of our drop-in centers save 6.6 hours of driving time a month (and give 4 hours of additional work time to Sun). Work-from-home participants save 12.4 hours a month (and give 8 of them to Sun). One of the side benefits of iWork is that it enhances our ability to attract and retain the best talent available. In fact, we estimate that, so far, the work-from-home aspect of the program has enabled us to keep 680 employees who otherwise would have left the company.

We have started to think of our main campuses as town halls or community centers—places where groups can gather to foster team spirit and tackle specific tasks. In the cafeteria of our Menlo Park, Calif. campus, we even opened a prototype iWork Cafe, with networked lunch booths, countertop Sun Ray stations, and other casual, open work settings for individuals and small groups. As always, we'll monitor usage and collect feedback to determine whether we want to extend the cafe option to other campuses.

Best Buy

Best Buy is the nation's leading electronics retailer and it is in the process of transforming itself to an ultra flexible organization. Michelle Conlin describes Best Buys radical reshaping in the December 11, 2006 edition of *Business Week*. She states that,

> Best Buy had a culture known for killer hours and hard driving bosses. Through a grass roots led movement they are trying to break an age-old dogma that equated physical presence with productivity. In fact, the goal is to judge performance based on output instead of hours.

> In a dramatic move Best Buy head office employees are free to work wherever, whenever they want—as long as the work gets done. Critics worry that they will lose some of the interoffice magic when they don't gather together all day, every day. They are concerned that the value of riffing on one another's ideas, teamwork and camaraderie will be lost. The company's findings show that absolutely some of that is lost, but what they get back far outweighs anything they have lost.

> Best Buy was afflicted by stress, burnout and high turnover. The hope was that the new program ROWE (Results-Only Work Environment) would free employees to make their own work-life decisions, boost morale and productivity. The risky program has proven successful with department voluntary turnover down dramatically (50 to 90 percent), productivity up an average of 35 percent and employee satisfaction way up. ROWE'ers are processing orders 13 to 18 percent more than the in office workers and the quality metrics are also better.

Erin Kelly and Phyllis Moen, of the University of Minnesota researches work-life issues says,

> Most companies are stuck when it comes to employees' and managers' relationship to time and work. Our whole notion of paid work was developed within an assembly line culture. Showing up was work. Best Buy is recognizing that sitting in a chair is no longer working.

Best Buy has several great tips for those organizations trying to create, what they call the post-geographic workplace:

- Managers and employees need to tailor schedules to their needs.
- Location-agnostic work is a hard concept to grasp—education is a must.
- Before unplugging workers, metrics are key to ensure that productivity, engagement and turnover improve.
- Inevitably untethered workers will slack off. Managers need to trust—then rely on data to assess performance.
- When workers are nomads, regular gatherings, in person or by videoconference, help retain a team dynamics.
- Management must "model the behavior."

Washington Ferry System

The information is from their Web site.

Washington State Ferries operates the largest ferry system in the U.S., serving 2 countries on 10 routes, with 20 terminals by 29 vessels. Every weekday more than 75,000 regional residents commute to work or school using the ferry system. It is the equivalent of a moving highway system. Recognizing that wireless consumer technologies are enabling commuters to work and be productive during travel times, the State's management wanted to provide this amenity to its customers.

The wireless system is now used by more than 27 million annual passengers, with a potential demand of 300–400 concurrent users per ferry per trip. The system needs to accommodate stationary terminals, parking lots and fast-moving ships. Making wireless work for moving platforms involves an advanced network, complex switching to allow passengers to stay connected while they work. One of the basic promises of mobile work is to increase productivity; therefore, the speed of the system is invaluable for driving usage.

Users of the Internet and corporate intranets using laptops, PDAs, 802.11 enabled phones and other hand held devices also demand better connectivity and security than available with mobile phones. In our virtual world of work you must be able to work no matter where you are, the method of transportation, or how fast you are traveling, connectivity must be assured. The ferry system wanted to make certain its users did not need specialized software and did not force them into connecting to one specific ISP. They needed complex usage tracking to be bulletproof, allowing the State of Washington a new source of revenue.

The Washington Ferries choose a WLAN system from Siemens to meet its mobility requirements. The HiPath Wireless Portfolio mobile solution was selected not to just provide easy connectivity to its employees for data only, convergence of voice and data over IP (internet protocol), as most companies do, but as new valued revenue services for their rider-ship. Each HiPath Wireless Controller is a full-functioning router that aggregates all access points—the HiPath Wireless Access Points as well as third-party access points—into what appears as individual, centrally managed IP subnets to the rest of the network. As a result, network management, which is centralized at the HiPath Wireless Controller, is greatly simplified, eliminating the need to physically visit the remote HiPath Access Points.

Whether it is simply reading, accessing information, sending emails or participating in collaborative work sessions, commuters now have the option to work remotely, regardless of speed, location, weather or time. The Washington State Ferry connectivity service has demonstrated it can scale and meet the mobility demands associated with remote travel.

Wireless applications are starting to make their way into some of the smallest and least high-tech businesses in the country, and even there, they are proving their value. Construction workers, electricians and repairmen are hardly known for their high-tech approaches to doing business. In these blue-collar industries, much of the business is handled with the same old-fashioned, hardcopy work orders that have been used for decades. Still for many, the days' job lists and work orders are handed out in the morning, before the worker goes out into the field to do their thing. Parts are carried in the truck or ordered over the phone, which requires more paperwork. At day's end, a stack of paperwork is dropped off on an administrative worker's desk. Experience shows that this manual process causes call-backs, errors and a tremendous amount of extra work.

Mobile applications are ideal for helping in these situations. The worker can use a wireless system to receive their work orders digitally, saving a trip to the workshop. They can be guided to the work site by a GPS system, eliminating confusion and time-consuming directions, with just an address. Once at the job site they log onto a time-tracking system which will eliminate error prone manual time reporting. The information can be integrated with inventory systems and accounting software to handle billing, receivables and financial reporting. Any questions, comments or problems can be entered directly into reporting systems for further action. This kind of mobile system can save both time and money by reducing the costs and problems associated with the old practices.

More sophisticated systems can be deployed on a tablet PC to accommodate on-line access to engineering drawings, product repair procedures, or product specification manuals for field workers to use. In some, very exacting work can be improved with the use of 3D visual displays used in the aerospace industry for quality control and fault detection in wiring applications. Mobile applications to continually monitor cement trucks, delivery vehicles and even packages are becoming common.

There are even examples, like in New Mexico, where they are deploying mobile systems in courthouses; the wireless connectivity allows perspective jurors, while waiting selection, to use their mobile devices to be productive by connecting to work. A mobile capability can also be used by the courts to allow dangerous criminals to attend court through secure video on-demand from a special room in the jail. This provides saving on security, transportation and reduces the risks associated with moving criminals. The new mobile systems will accommodate an increased effectiveness of judges, lawyers and staff through wireless connectivity.

Many large universities and small colleges through wireless initiatives across their campuses are attracting students, increasing productivity and enhancing their reputations as world-class institutions of higher education. As mentioned earlier even K–12 private schools are better preparing their pupils for the future by implementing and using WiFi technologies. I also heard that the City of New York is implementing WiFi in many of their parks for the growing number of people who work with mobile technologies. Some communities are implementing wireless capabilities in all public places. What are the schools, parks and communities in your area doing?

Chapter Summary
- **INTEL** initiated an internal study to understand the business value to the corporation of going wireless:
    - They concluded—wireless mobility changes the way employees work.
    - Employees perceived a benefit through—time shifting, location flexibility, time slicing, and greater availability.
    - The impact on productivity showed 2 hours and eight minute per week or approximately $5K per employee.
- **Nissan North America** initiated the WIN project (Workforce Integration @ Nissan) to boost employee productivity with better collaboration and knowledge sharing. The key to the project was the provisioning of universal mobile connectivity for Nissan employees. Nissan expects to save at least $135 million over the next few years thanks to increased productivity and reduced costs.
- **BOEING** has developed a global collaboration environment or virtual workspace for the 787 program redefining development activities to include an international team of engineers working around the world literally 24 hours a day to support the program's schedule. The advanced software permits the team to achieve a high level of interaction allowing engineers to review technical design issues—meet face-to-face but not in person—from a common database being developed as the entire airplane is defined. The new suite of software will span the total development of the 787—from conceptual design to detailed engineering and analysis, from manufacturing and final assembly to

in-service support, reducing development time and cost and providing the highest-quality and safest product to their customers.

- **CHEVRON** has created a global community through their technical environment allowing teamwork across 186 countries, where people in Angola are working with people in Houston, are working with people in the Bay Area to make capital and real-time decisions. The implementation of a standard platform has significantly improved their network infrastructure, and improved their security infrastructure, a globalization of work processes, and a focus on people actually in more or less real-time across geographies.
- **SUN** Microsystems was one of the early adopters of employee flexibility based on allowing 17,000 employees to work part of the time from home, thus reducing the need for office space. The Sun Open Work Practice leverages the mobile employee revolution to help develop a 21st century workplace that employs a mixture of workplace types and locations that match the needs and habits of their mobile and distributed workforce with their corporate strategy and vision. Sun's successful transition from a centralized campus-based environment to a Network of Places resulted in cost avoidances of more than $300 million since the program's inception.
- **BEST BUY** is in the process of transforming itself to an ultra flexible organization. Through grass roots led movement they are trying to break an age-old dogma that equated physical presence with productivity. The hope was that the new program ROWE (Results-Only Work Environment) would free employees to make their own work-life decisions, boost morale, and productivity. The risky program has proven successful with department voluntary turnover down dramatically (50 to 90 percent), productivity up an average of 35 percent and employee satisfaction way up.
- **WASHINGTON FERRY SYSTEM** operates the largest ferry system in the U.S., serving more than 75,000 daily commuters. Recognizing that wireless consumer technologies are enabling commuters to work and be productive during travel times, the State's management has provided this amenity to its customers. Whether it is simply reading, accessing information, sending emails or participating in collaborative work sessions, commuters now have the option to work remotely, regardless of speed, location, weather, or time.

Section Four

HOW WILL THE VIRTUAL WORLD WORK?

CHAPTER 22

SECTION INTRODUCTION

To make the virtual world of work effective and efficient requires leadership, collaboration and the latest technologies, but to gain momentum and acceptance we need credibility generated through lessons learned and case studies. Technology enables the virtual world of work through four distinct but integrated components, *connectivity, software, hardware,* and *security.* The virtual world of work enables turning information and people into actions that provide extra value for organizations and individuals.

The total connectivity chain must handle the movement of digital information, electronic money, people, products and services. Any breakdowns in any of these connectivity components will weaken our future virtual world of work and the global economy. In this book the focus for *connectivity* is of course the digital connectivity we enjoy today globally. We can move digital packets at very high speeds along wires, wirelessly through the air, or directed from distant orbiting satellites.

Connectivity is a derivative of the word, connect, which comes from the Latin *connectere,* to fasten together—*com* (together)—*nectere* (to bind, tie). It can be used today as a verb or a noun. As a transitive verb it is used to describe the act of joining any two or more things, or to join an electrical or telephone line between physical places. When used as a noun it describes the state of being tied together, the ability to make a connection between two or more points in a network. Connectivity is the route, wire or transmission that connects; it is the mode of transfer; while the content that travels the connection is closely related but separate from the connectivity. A simple example, the telephone wire is connectivity while the conversation is communication content; it is why the wire exists.

The Virtual World of Work, pages 189–198

We have seen this definition partially clarified in 1968 when the Federal Court mandated that telephone service be defined as the lines to the jack on the wall and does not include the telephone (this was the Carterphone decision). Until then, we could not plug in our own phones or other devices. The phone companies saw themselves as providing phone calls or communication rather than connectivity. The whole content market is relatively new and was not considered as relevant at the time of the Court decision, where today the voice, video, music, and data (pictures, files, documents, engineering drawings or other forms of digital information) that travel the connection is the critical component.

We now have home networks running at 100 megabits per second and soon, a billion bits per second will be common. We already have Internet backbones that support trillions of bits per second, per strand of fiber, used for the transport of voice, data, video and TV, basically anything that can be digitized. Digital connectivity is the unbiased transport of packets of data between at least two points on a network. This is also the definition of IP (Internet Protocol) popularized by the usage of the World Wide Web in the 1990s. Although there were individual networks earlier, this was the rise of global connectivity as we know and enjoy today.

Computer software or just *software* is defined in Wikipedia as "the programs, instructions and procedures required to enable the physical components of the computer hardware to perform specific tasks." The term *software* was first used in this sense in 1957 and has been generally attributed to John W. Tukey. The concept of reading different sequences of instructions into the memory of a device to control computations was invented by Charles Babbage in 1823 as part of his Difference Engine which led in 1833 to his work on the Analytical Engine. The theory that is the basis for most modern software was first proposed by Alan Turing in an essay where he described the Universal Machine in the 1930s.

Computer software is so called to contrast it from computer hardware, which encompasses the physical interconnections and devices required to store and execute, or run the software. At the lowest level, software consists of a machine language specific to an individual type of processor. A machine language consists of groups of numeric values; in my early days at IBM we used binary (0 or 1), octal (8) and hexadecimal (16) based numerals. Processor instructions were in object code which was used to run these ordered sequence of instructions to change the state of the computer hardware in a particular way to create a specific meaning through computation, storage or resequencing.

My career began by learning to program in machine language that made the hardware do exactly what you instructed it to do, even if it was not really what you wanted it to do. Next, the software was written using an assembler language, which was a mnemonic representation of the machine language using a natural language alphabet. Assembler language programs needed to be assembled into object code via a compiler before they could be run by the computers. Eventually programs were written in high-level programming languages that were easier and more efficient to use, being much closer to natural language than machine or assembler languages.

High-level languages are compiled or interpreted into machine language object code by other software so that programmers do not have to do this work or even understand the complex and tedious machine language. Today we have software that runs embedded systems like those found in the cockpit of our airplanes, analog computers used in industrial equipment, and sensors. Supercomputers are used for scientific studies, business applications that run our business processes, and personal software we use for everything from emails, games, or analyzing investment portfolios.

People who use modern, general purpose computers, experience three layers of software performing a wide variety of tasks.

- **Platform software or system software**
  Platform software includes the basic input-output system or firmware, device drivers, an operating system, and a graphical user interface. These allow a user to interact with the computer and its peripherals, which include such devices as storage units, printers, screens, keyboards, etc. Platform software comes bundled with the computer and generally is only understood by software engineers developing or maintaining this software.
- **Application software**
  Application software is what most people think of when they speak of software. Typical examples include business process applications like SAP, personal applications like PhotoShop or even video games. Application software is most often purchased separately from the computer hardware and provides the interface level between users and the platform software.
- **User-written software**
  User software tailors application software to meet the user specific needs. User software includes spreadsheet templates, word processor macros, scientific simulations, graphics and animation scripts to name only a few. Even email filters are a type of user software. This software is often integrated into or operates with purchased application packages. When the user-written software is supplied by your employer or a co-worker, you may not even know it is not part of the off-the-shelf application package.

The advances in hardware have come in the areas of speed, miniaturization, efficiency, price and integration. Software has advanced in the areas of incredible complexity, the enormous size and sophistication of the programs, and its integration with the data, other software and hardware. Two of the most sophisticated software packages ever written were tested and then used to manage the Deep Space 1 spacecraft which began its mission in 1998. The space mission tested 12 new revolutionary technologies including the new Ion engine. But, it was the following two advanced intelligent software systems that interested me the most.

- *"Remote Agent"* (**Autonomous Operations System**)
  This system is composed of an *"agent"* that can plan, make decisions, and operate by itself. Sophisticated software is programmed into the spacecraft's computer to allow it to think and act on its own, without human intervention or guidance. The agent knows when a failure has occurred, how to isolate and analyze what to do about it, and when to call Earth for human help. During a mission problem the agent analyzed the situation and chose an optimum corrective path that its handlers back on Earth did not anticipate. We all know computers can do things much faster than humans but this is the beginning of them doing things smarter than humans.
- **"Auto Nav"** (**Autonomous Optical Navigation System**)
  This intelligent software takes thousands of images of asteroids, comets, stars and galaxies; collected by the onboard camera system to plot and guide the selected missions. The onboard navigator system computes and corrects the spacecraft's course using its own observations. Earlier spacecraft navigation systems relied on human controllers back on Earth but with the great distances this is no longer practical.

There may very well be more sophisticated software today that runs intelligent robots, scientific experiments or medical devices. The point of these space mission examples is that we are truly in the time of intelligent software and its involvement in our virtual world of work is going to be unimaginably powerful.

Wikipedia defines, *hardware,* as

those objects that you can actually touch like: panels, disk drives, display screens, keyboards, printers, boards, and chips. In contrast, software is untouchable. Software exists as ideas, concepts, and symbols, but it has no physical substance. Books provide a useful analogy. The pages and the ink are the hardware, while the words, sentences, paragraphs, and the overall meaning are the software. A computer without software is like a book full of blank pages—you need software to make the computer useful just as you need words to make a book meaningful.

Early in my career I was part of a small group that traveled internationally to deliver software programs to be tested. The programs we carried were in the form of punched cards. As the customs agent tried to understand what we were transporting, things got a little silly. I told the agent that we had four programs in the two boxes but when he looked he was alarmed to estimate that we had hundreds of them; try explaining this to somebody that had never heard of software. Things got even crazier when he told us he was going to charge us a couple of bucks, based on the weight of the paper card stock, because they did not have any duty rates for software. We then had some more fun telling him that the paper cards actually were worthless because all we really needed were the holes. The paper only held the holes in the right position and it was the holes that were of value and they had no weight. Well, the short version of the story is that we paid the duty and thought we had been quite funny, yet nobody was laughing.

Computer hardware has become a commodity purchase and there are way too many types and kinds of hardware or devices to list here. What is critical about hardware is that you understand your present and future needs for these magnificent examples of advanced technology. The hardware must satisfy your requirements for speed, capacity, size, capability, integration, reliability, supportability, and cost, and be consistent with your technology architecture and future direction. No organization and most individuals are no longer starting with a "green field," and as such, most purchases are already biased by what decisions you made in the past. This is what make standards and compatibility, or as IT folks say interoperability, so critical.

The most important rule to use when selecting new hardware is to make certain, or at least as certain as possible, that you "do not buy your future problems today." Individuals can and do discard purchases easily but organizations have such large investments in hardware they cannot employ such a wasteful strategy. The larger and older your organization's technology environment, the more complex and difficult even straightforward decisions can become.

Purchase decisions should be made using portfolio management investment techniques and tools, and must involve the right people from the technology group as well as the appropriate business groups and levels of management. In the early years most computer-related acquisition decisions did not involve the chief executives because they felt they did not understand the ramifications, thus they took a position that allowed them the ability to blame someone else if it did not work properly. Today these decisions are much too important for such a ridiculous luxury. If your organization is visible, publicly traded or provides critical services, and if your systems fail or your security is breached, the consequences by the media and the market will be immediate and hash.

The term *computer system* is the one most commonly used because it is the synthesis of hardware, software and data. Many people use the simple term, *system*, because it is difficult to imagine an example that would not involve the integration of software, hardware and information. It can get tricky when people discuss things like the Internet, which does not exemplify a computer system per se, but rather a network of computer networks. The real power of the system comes with interconnectivity. Computer systems today can interconnect, that is, join to become a bigger system. Interconnecting computer systems can prove difficult due to vendor incompatibilities. Sometimes these difficulties occur between differing hardware and sometimes between differing software.

They are like the parts on different cars. The engineers of different computer systems do not necessarily aim to interconnect their creations with other systems. Technically knowledgeable people can often configure disparate computers to communicate using a set of rules and constraints known as *protocols*. Protocols attempt to precisely define the communication within and between computing endpoints. If two computer systems define the same protocols, they are capable of interconnecting and become a part of a larger system.

To demonstrate how powerful it can be to interconnect computer systems we just need to visit Virginia Tech University. In the summer of 2003 they assembled one of the world's fastest supercomputers, System X. It comprises 1,100 Apple PowerMac G5 computers. System X is currently running at 12.25 teraflops (a measure of computational speed), making it the second fastest supercomputer used by an academic institution, second only to the MareNostrum in Barcelona, Spain. System X was ranked #20 in the list of the world's most powerful supercomputers.

The supercomputer's name originates from the use of the Mac OSX operating system for each node, and because it was the first university computer to achieve 10 teraflops, it is known as "Big Mac." It is also touted as "the world's most powerful and cheapest homebuilt supercomputer." System X was constructed with a relatively low budget of $5.2 million, in the span of only three months; this was made possible in large part because it used off-the-shelf G5 computers. By comparison one of the largest super computer systems, the Earth Simulator, cost somewhere in the range of $400 million to build.

All this investment, capability and dependence require us to protect these critical assets. *Technical* or *cyber security* is becoming increasingly necessary as we move further toward a connected world. Operating globally means we are sharing more and more proprietary information across more and more dispersed people. Securing the extended enterprises that make up a major portion of the global economy is one of our greatest challenges.

Security planning and effective operations must start at the top of the enterprise and take its place at the table during executive strategic planning sessions. If we can't trust our ability to secure our connectivity then the virtual world of work will not be successful. I do not understand why our digital world is so under siege. Is it people lashing out against technology, is it pranksters, are they criminals looking to make money, is it the fact that they can supposedly attack systems with anonymity, or are they terrorists and should be treated like those we are fighting in our war on terrorism? The weakest link in information security is the people not technology. We need to embed security into the organization structure, culture and the daily behavior of our people to continue our battle with the risks that are just too real.

So what is being done to protect our future? In 1996, the National Research Council recognized that the rise of the Internet simultaneously increased societal reliance on computer systems while increasing the vulnerability of such systems to failure. They defined a "trustworthy system" or components as one "that will not fail." The Committee on Information System Trustworthiness was convened, producing the work, *Trust in Cyberspace*. This report reviews the benefits of trustworthy systems, the cost of untrustworthy systems and identifies actions required for improvement.

Microsoft launched its Trustworthy Computing initiative in 2002. This program was in direct response to Internet devastation caused by the Code Red and Nimbda worms in 2001. Bill Gates announced the initiative and redirected the company's software development activities to include a "by design" view of security. Microsoft in defining their framework for trustworthy computing identified four key pillars.

1. **Security**
   Microsoft's first pillar of Trustworthy Computing is security. Security has always been a part of computing, but now it must become a priority. According to Microsoft, security goes beyond the technology to include the social aspect as well.

2. **Privacy**
   For computing to become ubiquitous in connecting people and transmitting information over various networks and services it is critical that information is protected and kept private.

3. **Reliability**
   Microsoft uses a fairly broad definition to encompass all technical aspects related to availability, performance and disruption recovery. It is intended to be a measure not only of whether a system is working, but whether it will continue working in non-optimal situations.

4. **Business Integrity**
   Microsoft's fourth pillar of Trustworthy Computing is business integrity. Many view this as a reaction to software developer integrity and responsiveness.

While the computer industry is generally supportive of Microsoft's efforts to improve the reliability and security of its software, the initiative is not without controversy. The open-source community has expressed concern that a trustworthy computing implementation will require authenticating programs as well as content. Such an approach could be used to hinder the progress of non-Microsoft software and operating systems. Some observers view digital rights management as an attempt to not only protect, but also control the content on users' computers.

In doing my research for this section, I came across many organizations with reference to different aspects of security. The Cyber Security Policy and Research Institute, which is a center for George Washington University and the Washington area, promotes technical research and policy analysis of problems that have a significant computer security and information assurance component. The Institute bridges discipline barriers to bring together researchers from all of the Schools with interests in policy issues related to computer technology, the Internet and security of critical infrastructure. Outside of the University, it works with governments and private organizations to study the impact of rapid technological change on business, government, society and the infrastructure security problems caused by the convergence of data and organizations in a networked world. For more detailed information I would suggest contacting this organization or the Cyber Security Industry Alliance which is more oriented to congressional policy matters.

There are software packages, individuals and organizations that can conduct a wide variety of security services. They call their offerings computer security audits, information technology audits, penetration tests, security breach analysis, spyware or virus analysis, intruder detection, anti-virus management, vulnerability scans, threat evaluation, or just about any other clever word combination you can think of. There are simple, easy-to-use security software and updates that can and must be used. In today's connected world if you do not protect yourself then you are a potential threat to your friends and colleagues.

Leadership in the new world of work is rapidly changing and the role and definition of a leader are also changing. The old world practices of command-and-control will not be accepted by the net-gen workforce. If you are micro managing, then one of you will need to leave. The job of passing on communications, down to the troops, from the senior leaders and filtering the information that goes back up to those same leaders, will not exist in the new virtual workplace. Leaders will need to embrace the newest technologies that enable information to be instantly available within all levels of the information infrastructure.

Why would a leader wait for employee feedback or the workforce wait for information and decisions to be delayed by intermediates? Leadership will be cascading throughout the disbursed global organizations. Leadership will be more about multiple two-way conversations, enabled by technology, not by one-way quarterly mass broadcasts or unread emails. Leaders will need to establish new dialog channels like internal chat sights and blogs. Done properly, leaders and employees can leverage these technologies to be more informed and knowledgeable about important issues on-line and real-time.

For people to perform or contribute at a greater level, dictates that they will need to be more interested in what is happening, self-managed, and understand the context of how, what they are doing fits into the bigger picture. My experience is, when information workers get this type of information directly from the leaders, motivation will be higher, and the individuals will collaborate more and contribute more. They will begin to not only deliver more but be smarter about what they contribute. If they can visualize how their work products or efforts provide value, then you will have hit the jackpot, there is a much greater chance they will take pride in what they do and feel good about themselves. Leadership will be about making bold decisions about direction, choosing the right vision, selling that vision and mission to all, selecting the right people, motivating them and getting out of the way.

Leaders that see their jobs as instructing people what their individual tasks are and enforcing the bureaucracy are obsolete and will soon be irrelevant. They instead need to set expectations, define the deliverables and outcomes, and remove the bureaucracy. This will require not only the organization to change but also the individuals. Leadership styles and behaviors will have to adjust to the virtual world. People will be working in teams that are more diverse and dispersed. Leaders will need to deal with work groups that comprise individuals from anywhere on the supply chain and anywhere they can be productive regardless of geography or time. It will be difficult and some will not make the transition, this is sad, but evolution and change are hard and sometimes not fair.

Knowledge is food for those anxious to learn and collaboration is the best way to share and leverage this knowledge. Sharing knowledge is the most efficient way to learn. To use that knowledge is also the most effective way to work. We have the technology, which is rapidly improving, and we have the necessary changing behavior and attitudes to leverage our global knowledge using the power enabled by collaborative practices. Soon we will have the tools to work in the most efficient and effective collaborative ways. The issue will be, do we have the learned behavior and practices to capitalize on this powerful collaborative approach? The virtual world of work is supported by these amazing forces, it will continue to become accepted and be the future way we do our jobs and live our lives.

Section Introduction Summary

- The virtual world of work is about turning information and people resources into actions that will provide extra value for organizations and individual workers—how it works is through connectivity, software, hardware, security, leadership and collaboration.
- Digital connectivity is the unbiased transport of packets of data between at least two points on the network. This was popularized by the usage of the World Wide Web in the 1990s and has given rise to global connectivity as we know and enjoy today.
- Software is the programs, instructions and procedures required to change the state of the computer hardware in a particular way to create a specific meaning through computation, storage or resequencing.
- Hardware are the objects that you can actually touch like: panels, disk drives, display screens, keyboards, printers, boards, and chips.
- Computer system is the term most commonly used because it is the synthesis of hardware, software, and data.
- Computer systems today can interconnect, that is, join together through networks to become a bigger system.
- Technical or cyber security is becoming increasingly necessary as we move further toward a connected world.
- Leadership in the new world of work is rapidly changing and the role and definition of a leader are also changing.
- Collaboration is the best way to share and leverage knowledge in the virtual world of work.

CHAPTER 23

CONNECTIVITY

Communicating over vast distances is one of mankind's greatest innovations. This has contributed to the reality for us humans that the world is getting smaller and smaller. We have collapsed distance and time through connectivity. The Soviets launching Sputnik in 1957, today there are more than 2,000 satellites in orbit allowing people to be connected worldwide. Our global economy, its individuals and societies are linked by both mobility and bandwidth. We have transformed from the novelty of flying to some three million people daily boarding more than 42,000 flights on jetliners to almost every country in the world. These technologies are changing our attitudes toward communicating, traveling and working while remote from the traditional office.

How many times have you heard people say, I was out of town so I did not get your message, or we better not talk long because this is a long distance call? For many mobile plans there are no cost differences between local and long distance. As the price of communicating has come down, because of advances in connectivity, we are gradually getting comfortable staying in touch without regard to where we are communicating from. A consequence of this satellite coverage is that we increasingly get bombarded with editorials, videos and pictures disguised as breaking news, especially if it is bad, from every corner of the planet. People are traveling more, seeing more and learning about people and places we never heard about before. The world is becoming more familiar.

Boeing's new 777 LR and the 787 can connect any two cities in the world with nonstop flights. We are no longer surprised that flowers can arrive from across the globe the same day they are cut and fish are transported fresh daily to markets anywhere people will pay for them. Here in some

The Virtual World of Work, pages 199–210
Copyright © 2008 by Information Age Publishing
All rights of reproduction in any form reserved.

cites each year there are even contests to see who can be first to drink the newest Beaujolais Nouveaux wines from France.

Connectivity is the *how*, communication is *what* we can now do around the world and around the clock. Collaboration is the *way* we will work when we leverage global knowledge. Connectivity is no longer the overriding barrier to humans having long distance conversations. It is now primarily our behavior and attitudes that are the true obstacles. Many societies are controlled by their culture when it comes to open communications. In Japan and other countries you may even need to be introduced to a person before you can engage in a conversation.

With so many Internet conversations and the possibility of meeting bad people, introductions may not be as bad an idea as I first thought. If you are young and innocent there are just too many predators trying to befriend you or your children, trying to con somebody. Be careful how you or your children use bulletin or message boards. There are evil people constantly looking for victims and they regularly check their trap-lines electronically.

The Internet and cell phones are truly the prominent symbols and enablers to connecting the world. We are connected and increasingly depend on each other, very similar to what you would find in a small town or village through human networks. We have reached the point where email and instant messaging can be sent and received much easier than phone messages. Fiber optics capacity is tripling every year. The third generation fiber optics can push ten billion bits per second down a single strand enabling nearly unlimited communications.

Did you ever wonder how the email addresses work? This was something that puzzled me. Unlike regular mail they do not have street addresses, city, country zip or postal codes. Unlike the telephone they do not have area and country codes. They work by incorporating a "@" symbol in the email address to separate "the who" from "the where." Who decided that convention?

Well, I am glad you asked. The @ sign came into use sometime in the 18th century in England as a symbol used in commerce to indicate price per unit, as in "2 chickens @ 10 pence." Later the symbol became a standard key on typewriter keyboards in the 1880s and a standard on QWERTY keyboards (the ones used today) in the 1940s. But, it was not until 1972, that Ray Tomlinson sent the first electronic message, now known as email, using the @ symbol to indicate the location or institution of the email recipient. Tomlinson, using a Model 33 Teletype device, understood that he needed to use a symbol that would not appear in anyone's name so that there was no confusion. The logical choice for Tomlinson was the "at sign" both because it was unlikely to appear in anyone's name or address, and also because it represented the word "at," as in a particular user is sitting @ this specific computer. Now, aren't you glad you know this bit of trivia?

Modern long distant communication started with the telegram. The word, telegraph, is from the Greek words *tele* meaning—*far* and *graphein* meaning—*write*. It is the long distance transmission of the equivalent of a written message over a wire. Messages sent by telegraph operators using Morse code were known as telegrams or cablegrams, often shortened to a cable or wire message. Later, telegrams were sent by a switched network of teleprinters similar to the telephone network, known as telex messages. Before long distance telephone services were readily available or afford-able, telegram services were very popular.

The telex network is the connectivity while the Morse code is the method for communicating information, using standardized sequences of short and long marks or pulses—commonly known as dots and dashes—for the letters, numerals and special characters of a message. The code was cre-ated for Samuel Morse's electric telegraph in the mid-1830s; it was also extensively used for early radio communication beginning in the 1890s.

I have two cute stories to share about the use of telegrams. I was born at a remote air force base during WW11. Because you paid by the letter for sending telegrams, people became very ingenious with their messages. The message sent by my Father to my grandparents announcing my arrival sim-ply read, "Mother's features, father's fixtures, everyone fine." The second story is from when we had rotary phones; my wife knew Morse code and could actually dial the phone by clicking the receiver button to enter the dots and dashes into the phone. Today we have extremely sophisticated telecommunication networks that could not be imagined in Morse's time.

Connectivity really started to take off with the invention of the tele-phone. I have drawn from Tom Farley's telephone history series. For a lot more detail check out his series at *www.privateline.com/TelephoneHistory/ History1.htm*. People have always wanted to communicate over long dis-tances and used smoke signals, mirrors, jungle drums, carrier pigeons and flags to get a message from one person to another. But, until the electrical age began, a real telephone could not be invented. The electrical princi-ples needed to build a telephone were known in the early 1830s, but it wasn't until 1854 that Bourseul suggested transmitting speech electrically.

On March 10, 1876, in Boston, Alexander Graham Bell invented the telephone. His partner Thomas Watson fashioned the device enabling the first telephone call between them—"Mr. Watson, come here, I want you!" Bell filed his patent application in a controversial move just hours before his competitor, Elisha Gray. What's more, though neither man had actually built a working telephone; Bell made his telephone operate three weeks later using some of the ideas outlined in Gray's Notice of Invention.

At this time in history inventors focused on telegraph improvements since these had a waiting market and a chance to make a lot of money. Developing a telephone, on the other hand, had no immediate market, if one at all. Elisha Gray, Alexander Graham Bell, as well as many others, were trying to develop a multiplexing telegraph, a device to send several messages over one wire at the same time. Such an innovation would greatly increase traffic without the powerful Western Union telegraph company having to build more lines. As it turned out, for both men, the desire to invent one thing turned into a race to invent something altogether different. This is truly the reality of most inventions.

Bell's entire education and upbringing were quite different from the other inventors, as it revolved around the mechanics of speech and sound vibration, not electronics. Bell experimented to make an ear like membrane work in a telephony application by using the membrane to vary an electric current in intensity with the spoken word. Such a current could then replicate speech with another membrane. Bell had discovered the principle of the telephone, the theory of variable resistance. Bell feverishly pursued his real interest, the telephone, and not the harmonic telegraph which his financial backers wanted. Bell told Watson, "If I can get a mechanism which will make a current of electricity vary in its intensity as the air varies in density when a sound is passing through it, I can transmit any sound, even the sound of speech." With Bell's patent, U.S. Number 174,465, the telephone had been invented. This patent has been called the most valuable ever issued.

On July 9, 1877 with investors, Sanders and Hubbard, Bell formed the first Bell telephone company. Against tough criticism, Hubbard decided to lease telephones instead of selling them and license franchises. In an effort to compete, Western Union decided to buy patents from others and start their own telephone company. They were not alone, at least 1,730 telephone companies organized and operated in the 17 years Bell was supposed to have a monopoly on his patent.

On January 28, 1878, the first commercial switchboard began operating in New Haven, Connecticut. It served 21 telephones on 8 lines creating the first party line. The switch board meant callers were no longer limited to talk to people on the same wire; folks could now talk to others on different lines. The public switched telephone network was born. On February 21, 1878, the world's first telephone directory came out, a single page with only fifty names. In the same year President Rutherford B. Hayes' administration installed the first telephone in the White House and the first outgoing call went to Alexander Graham Bell himself, a distance of thirteen miles. Hayes' first words instructed Bell to speak more slowly. The first phone did not reach the president's desk until the Hoover administration at the start of the Great Depression.

Bell himself became more optimistic about the telephone's future, prophetically writing, "I believe that in the future, wires will unite the head offices of the Bell Telephone Company in different cities, and that a man in one part of the country may communicate by word of mouth with another in a distant place." The Bell Telephone Company reorganized in June 1878, forming a new Bell Telephone Company as well as the New England Telephone Company, a forerunner of the strong regional Bell companies to come. Growth was steady, and with 10,755 Bell phones installed the first telephone numbers were issued.

In 1879 Bell won its patent infringement suit against Western Union and in the resulting settlement, Western Union gave up its telephone patents and the 56,000 phones it managed, in return for 20 percent of Bell rentals for the life of Bell's patents. Theodore Vail became chairman and began creating the Bell System, composed of regional companies offering local service, a long distance company providing toll service, and a manufacturing arm providing equipment. Vail's restructuring was so successful it lasted until modern times. In 1976, on the hundredth anniversary of the Bell System, AT&T stood as the wealthiest company on earth.

In January 1927, commercial long distance radiotelephone service was introduced between the United States and Great Britain by AT&T and the British Postal Office. Nearly thirty years would pass before the first telephone cable was laid under the Atlantic, greatly expanding calling capacity. The United States Congress created the Federal Communications Commission in 1934 to regulate telephones, radio, and television. It was part of President Roosevelt's New Deal plan to bring America out of the Great Depression. In 1937 Alec Reeves of Britain invented modern digital transmission when he developed Pulse Code Modulation and became known as the father of modern telecommunications.

On July 1, 1948, the Bell System unveiled the transistor, a joint invention of Bell Laboratories scientists William Shockley, John Bardeen, and Walter Brattain. It would revolutionize every aspect of the telephone industry and all of communications. The invention of the transistor, which incorporated a flowing stream of electrons, along with the special characteristics of silicon, made possible the development of hearing aids, satellites, computers and most other technologies. Siemens, in Germany, was the first to introduce the dial tone into the public switched telephone network. In 1963 the first modern touch-tone phone was introduced and in 1965 the first commercial communications satellite was launched using the first central office computerized switch.

In 1969 Microwave Communications International (MCI) began transmitting business calls over their own private network bypassing Bell System lines, at cheaper prices. This brought about unprecedented jumps in usage and this demand caused service deterioration in several large cities causing huge public outcries. The experience showed for the first time how vital telephones had become to modern life. In 1971 General Telephone and Electronics (GTE Sylvania) introduced a data system called Digicom that let police dispatchers communicate directly with patrol cars to run license plate checks. On August 24, 1982, after seven years of wrangling, the Bell System was split apart, succumbing to government pressure. Most modern countries have surpassed the U.S. in providing better telephone connectivity from that point to today.

The use of wire line connectivity has now been surpassed by the use of wireless connectivity. Let's take a few moments and see how this technology evolved. Ham radio gear installed in cars, taxicab radios, and two way radios in police cruisers was the predecessor of mobile phones. The first real mobile phone, in the sense that it was connected to the telephone network, was tested by the Swedish police in 1946 for use in police cruisers but only a half dozen calls could be made before the battery died. The first truly successful public commercial mobile phone network was in Finland, launched in 1971. This connectivity technology is sometimes viewed as a zero generation (0G) network, being slightly above previous proprietary and limited coverage networks. Modern mobile telephony is often considered to have started on April 3, 1973, when Motorola employee Martin Cooper placed a call to rival AT&T's Bell Labs while walking the streets of New York City talking on a Motorola DynaTAC.

Let's look at Wikipedia to see what is meant by the different generations of mobile connectivity:

- **First generation (1G)**
  Mobile phones began to proliferate through the 1980s with the introduction of *cellular* phones based on cellular networks with multiple base stations located relatively close to each other, and protocols for the automated *handover* between two cells when a phone moved from one cell to the other. At this time analog transmission was in use in all 1G systems. Mobile phones were somewhat larger than current ones, and at first, all were designed for permanent installation in cars (hence the term *car phone*).

- **Second Generation (2G)**
  In the 1990s, 2G mobile phone systems such as GSM, IS-136 (TDMA), iDEN and IS-95 (CDMA) began to be introduced. The first digital cellular phone call was made in the United States in 1990 and in 1991 the first GSM network opened in Europe. 2G phone systems were characterized by digital circuit switched transmission and the introduction of advanced and fast phone to network signaling. Coinciding with the introduction of 2G systems were trends which meant that the larger handsets (*bricks*) disappeared and much smaller 100–200g hand-held devices became the norm.

- **Third Generation (3G)**
  During the development of 3G systems, 2.5G systems such as CDMA2000 1x and GPRS were developed as extensions to existing 2G networks. These provide some of the features of 3G without fulfilling the promised high data rates or full range of multimedia services. At the beginning of the 21st century, 3G mobile phone systems such as UMTS and CDMA2000 1xEV-DO became publicly available. The final success of these systems is still to be determined.

Now, let's look into the Internet and how it has changed everything with regard to connectivity and much more. The Internet is a worldwide broadcasting capability, a mechanism for information dissemination, and a medium for collaboration and interaction between individuals and their computers without regard for geographic location. The Internet today is a widespread global information infrastructure, and connectivity is now usually referred to as the network or network infrastructure.

The first recorded description of the social interactions that would eventually become the Internet came from a group at MIT. Leonard Kleinrock published the first paper on packet switching theory in July 1961 and the first book on the subject in 1964. In a series of memos by J.C.R. Licklider of MIT in August 1962, he discusses his "Galactic Network" concept and convinces others of the importance of this networking concept.

Kleinrock of UCLA convinced Lawrence Roberts at MIT of the theoretical feasibility of communications using packets rather than circuits, which was a major step along the path toward computer networking. They then connected their computer over a dial-up line. Roberts developed the computer network concept and quickly put together his plan for the ARPANET (Advanced Research Projects Agency Network), publishing it in 1967.

Donald Davies and Roger Scantlebury in the UK and Paul Baran and others at the RAND Group in Europe had proceeded in parallel without any of the researchers knowing about the other work. Kleinrock's Network Measurement Center at UCLA was selected to be the first node. One month later, when Stanford Research Institute (SRI) was connected, the first host-to-host message was sent. Two more nodes were quickly added at UC Santa Barbara and University of Utah.

Thus, by the end of 1969, four host computers were connected together into the initial ARPANET, and the budding Internet was off the ground. Crocker finished the initial Host-to-Host protocol, called the Network Control Protocol (NCP). As the sites completed implementing NCP, the network users finally could begin to develop applications. Ray Tomlinson wrote the basic email message "send and read" software, motivated by the need of the developers for an easy coordination mechanism.

Roberts expanded its utility by writing the first email utility program to "list, selectively read, file, forward, and respond" to messages. The original ARPANET grew into the Internet.

The Internet was based on the idea that there would be multiple independent networks and soon included packet satellite networks, ground-based packet radio networks, and other networks. Kahn decided to develop a new version of the protocol which could meet the needs of an open-architecture network environment. This protocol would eventually be called the Transmission Control Protocol/Internet Protocol (TCP/IP).

While NCP tended to act like a device driver, the new protocol would be more like a communications protocol. So armed with Kahn's architectural approach to the communications side and with Vint Cerf's NCP experience at Stanford, they teamed up to spell out the details of what became TCP/IP. Email was the first hot application and provided a new model of how people could communicate with each other, and changed the nature of collaboration for much of society.

David Clark and his research group at MIT set out to show that a compact and simple implementation of TCP/IP was possible. This meant that workstations, as well as large timesharing systems, could be a part of the Internet. The shift to a large number of independently managed networks (e.g., LANs) meant that a single table of hosts was no longer feasible, and the Domain Name System (DNS) was invented by Paul Mockapetris of USC/ISI.

At the same time that the Internet technology was being experimentally validated and widely used amongst a subset of computer science researchers, other networks and networking technologies were being pursued. The backbone had made the transition from a network built from routers out of the research community to commercial equipment. The Internet has grown to more than 50,000 networks on all seven continents and outer space, with approximately 29,000 networks in the United States. The U.S. government provided $200 million from 1986 to 1995 to get the Internet on its way to becoming the backbone service for the Global Information Infrastructure.

The Internet is as much a collection of communities as a collection of technologies, and its success is largely attributable to both satisfying basic community needs as well as utilizing the community in an effective way to push the infrastructure forward. The Internet has changed much in the two decades; it started as the creation of a small band of dedicated researchers, and has grown to be the enabler of the global economy. Without the Internet specifically and connectivity in general the virtual world of work could not exist.

The key architectural advance for the industry is taking the low level connectivity that the Internet has given us and turning that into high level connectivity, where industry standard formats and organizational standard data dictionaries allow information to move between systems without loss of semantics.

The way this is done is through a service-oriented architecture and the standards that are called Web Services, organizations have embraced writing software that can talk to software on any other machine, independent of what language it is written in or what operating system it is on, simply by using the rich data standards that grew out of XML and is now part of Web Services. This has simplifying connectivity for everyone.

We still have unevenness in connectivity, businesses are very connected, and individuals are only somewhat connected to broadband networks. In the United States, there are only 31 percent of households that have implemented a high speed connection. This is an increase over a year ago but it still greatly lags behind other countries. Korea, for example, is more than 70 percent. That's the model that we need to aspire to as quickly as possible.

Wireless networks are becoming much more important to the mobile and virtual workers. The wireless network I am referring to is called Wi-Fi and the growth in this technology has doubled in the last year. Every portable machine sold now have the Wi-Fi capability, and corporations now take it as common sense that they're going to need a wireless network. Wi-Fi is the standard in hot spots around the world, in homes, in businesses, and is well entrenched with anyone having a mobile device.

According to M. Scott Peck in the book, *The Different Drum: Community-Making and Peace,*

> It is clearly no longer enough to be simply social animals, babbling together at cocktail parties and brawling with each other in business and over boundaries. It is our task—our essential, central, crucial task—to transform ourselves from mere social creatures into community creatures. It is the only way that human evolution will be able to proceed.

A virtual community is a group whose members are connected by means of information technologies, typically the Internet. Similar terms include online community and mediated community. The term *virtual community* is attributed to the book of the same title by Howard Rheingold in 1993. The book discussed a range of computer-mediated communication and social groups. In our movement to a global community, organizations involved in the virtual world of work are creating *Virtual Teams*—also known as geographically dispersed teams. A virtual team is a group of individuals who work across time, space, and organizational boundaries with links strengthened by webs of communication technology. The team members have complementary skills and are committed to a common purpose, have interdependent performance goals, and share an approach to work for which they hold themselves mutually accountable.

Geographically dispersed teams allow organizations to hire and retain the best people regardless of location. A virtual team does not always need to mean work from home members. Virtual team members are defined as individuals who work from wherever they are situated at the time. Most virtual teams in today's organizations consist of employees both working at home and in the offices that are in different geographic locations. The future virtual world of work is dependent on the formation of virtual teams and virtual individuals willing and capable of connecting and working from anywhere at any time to improve productivity and overall performance.

Connectivity in the future will be very different and I believe will be based on what we think of now as the holographic theory. Space and time are all part of the holography theory that involves physical and nonphysical components. We will increasingly use holograms for connectivity whether they represent an abstract work of art or a "holo-view" connecting individuals to each other or individuals to computers. The holographic theory explains the ability to travel from one point to another without having to transverse the space or time between the two. This premise may prove to be one of the most significant theories of this 21st century enabling the future virtual world of work.

Applying holographic principles to the arts, sciences and humanities may connect us to our brains in ways not possible in a two-dimensional media. The concept of thinking in a spatial, rather than linear, manner is at the very heart of holographic principles. While the clock and calendar seem to remind us that things move forward in a linear manner, holography theories teach us that thoughts exist simultaneously. According to Ken Wilber in his book, *The Holographic Paradigm and Other Paradoxes,* the brain functions using neurotransmitting peptides and frequencies to connect us to the underlying thoughts. The brains own holographic functioning when used with holographic images may just be how communication takes place in the future virtual world of work.

The world leading telecom companies are building very high bandwidth Internet networks that can deliver TV over the Internet. Video on the Internet is exploding, and the ability to access news and sports clips is now a reality. The Greek Olympics was a good example; you could narrow your choice by sport, and then pick the highlights you are most interested in. These types of connectivity are making for a very compelling experience over the Internet.

Chapter Summary
- We have collapsed distance and time through connectivity.

- People are traveling more, seeing more and learning about people and places we never heard about before.
- Connectivity is the how, communication is what we can now do around the world and around the clock, and collaboration is the way we will work when we leverage global knowledge.
- Modern long distant communication started with the telegram which transmitted the equivalent of a written message over a wire.
- The telex network is the connectivity while the Morse code is the method for communicating information.
- Bell told Watson, "If I can get a mechanism which will make a current of electricity vary in its intensity as the air varies in density when a sound is passing through it, I can transmit any sound, even the sound of speech."
- On July 9, 1877, Bell formed the first Bell telephone company.
- Bell wrote, "I believe that in the future, wires will unite the head offices of the Bell Telephone Company in different cities, and that a man in one part of the country may communicate by word of mouth with another in a distant place."
- In 1937 Alec Reeves of Britain invented modern digital transmission when he developed Pulse Code Modulation and became known as the father of modern telecommunications.
- In 1965 the first commercial communications satellite was launched using the first central office computerized switch.
- In 1982 the Bell System was split apart by the government and since then most modern countries have surpassed the U.S. in providing superior telephone connectivity.
- Modern mobile telephony is often considered to have started on April 3, 1973, when Motorola employee Martin Cooper placed a call to rival AT&T's Bell Labs while walking the streets of New York City.
- By the end of 1969, four host computers were connected together into the initial ARPANET, and the budding Internet was off the ground.
- Email was the first hot application and provided a new model of how people could communicate with each other, and changed the nature of collaboration for much of society.
- The U.S. government provided $200 million from 1986 to 1995 to get the Internet on its way to becoming the backbone service for the Global Information Infrastructure.
- The Internet has changed much in the two decades; it started as the creation of a small band of dedicated researchers, and has grown to be the enabler of the global economy.

- A virtual team is a group of individuals who work across time, space, and organizational boundaries with links strengthened by webs of communication technology.
- Connectivity in the future will be very different and I believe will be based on what we think of now as the holographic theory.

CHAPTER 24

SOFTWARE

Software is the artificial intelligence that makes technology work the way it was intended. The objective for software is to enable workers to use information effectively and to work efficiently. It provides the instructions, structure and rules to be able to connect talented resources anywhere in the world and enable them to work collaboratively. Whether the information workers are inside or outside your company, on different technologies, situated in a structured form, or scattered in an ad hoc fashion, software enables them all to work together. The value realized from software is the execution of consistent rule-sets; the value from people is innovation.

Most organizations start with a people-centric view of work, but software is the component that can facilitate and enable workers to "be more than they can be," to use a quote from the military. Yet most application software is actually very rigid and does not draw out people's capabilities, makes it cumbersome to use, and causes workers to not use their creativity. Good software on the other hand provides humans with the greatest opportunity to continuously improve work processes and make the world a more productive, secure and a fun place to be.

Software has historically been considered an intermediary between electronic hardware and the data which is created, manipulated and stored. The hardware processes data according to the sequence of instructions defined by the software. As the complexity of the processes increases, the distinction between software and data becomes less precise. Data originally was considered either the output or input of executed software. Remember the old clique, "garbage in garbage out." Today the output of a particular piece of executed software is more than likely integrated with other executed pieces of software. Therefore, software may be considered an inter-

The Virtual World of Work, pages 211–220
Copyright © 2008 by Information Age Publishing
All rights of reproduction in any form reserved.

face between hardware, data, and/or other software. Hardware provides the *how* to do something and is the more familiar and visible part of technology. Software dictates *what* it is you will do when data is transformed into action, and information is *why* we utilize technology.

In the introduction to this section, we discussed the layers or types of software. So now we will cover the things software is used for and how these are related to the virtual world of work. The basic software delivered with the computer is what controls and manages the internal hardware. It comprises an operating system, device drivers, diagnostic tools, utilities, communication protocols, error messaging, libraries, storage management, as well as many other more specific software functions. Also included with the system can be programming languages and their text editors, compilers, interpreters, linkers and my favorite, debuggers. Portfolio, program and project management software and the associated methodologies, techniques and tools are normally purchased separate from the hardware, as are the service management tools used to monitor and optimize the systems.

When one thinks of software, the vast majority of what is envisioned is the application layer. These are the programs that contain our business process rules and associated data stores. The largest cost for these "apps," as they are usually called, is for maintaining them over their life. Legacy applications run the current business but they represent a major obstacle in migrating or transitioning to newer and more capable and flexible software. The fact they work, people are familiar with them, and the large investments in the legacy software all mean they are hard to get rid of. My experience is that implementing new software packages seldom replace 100 percent of the old software that has evolved to handle exceptions unique to each business.

Early in my career all application software was specifically written for the client and referred to as *custom software*. The demand for software was immature without a large enough target market to justify package development, or COTS (Commercial off the Shelf) software. When packages first emerged they were utilities, programs like sort programs, these were followed later by spread sheet and word processing packages. I do not remember commercial business applications being available until mini computers became plentiful enough to create sufficient demand. There was no open concept at that time, each computer required proprietary software, so software from one type of system would not run on another manufacture's computer.

Once the small to medium sized businesses bought desktop computers in large numbers, the commercial market for packaged software became viable. The prime driver was that these companies needed software but could not justify the costs or time for custom software. In the early 1970s software services companies were emerging and by the early 1980s they were faced with directional decisions. Some companies wanted to focus on the large companies that had larger budgets and more specific requirements, still justifying custom work. Others wanted to write packages that could address this small to medium sized emerging market and be distributed across America. Still others thought the best path was to sell and implement the early packages from across America within geographic locations. At this time I heard the term, *killer apps* for the first time. These were the spread sheet and word processing packages that made the desktop computer a success just like the email software made the Internet a success. One thing was sure the application software business was changing fast and forever.

One of our good friends worked for a record manufacturing and distribution business in the Bay Area, his task was researching new ways to expand the business. He soon convinced the owner to try securing licenses with the emerging software companies and then distributing the software packaged floppies through their record store distribution network. As unbelievable as it sounds today the issue was; would there ever be a consumer retail market for software? After a short period of time the owner decided this was not going to work. But, in putting this opportunity together our friend became convinced it could work. In his travels he met two young techies in Albuquerque NM that were going to move their small software business to Redmond WA. Well he joined them and as they say the rest is history.

Today software and the software industry have changed more than it seems possible. The Internet has enabled interoperability from around the global. In 2006, more than 250 million PCs and more than 47 million laptops were sold, that's more than a 10 percent increase from 2005. The increases are from across the board: business, education, medical, government and personal buyers. They all need software and a lot of it to do what is now expected from computer systems. There are many software success stories but two that I find most incredible are Microsoft and Goggle. It is amazing to me that they each envisioned one of the main pillars of the future virtual world of work. Microsoft's original vision was "a computer on every desk, and in every home." I think Bill Gates and Paul Allen have succeeded on their first part of their vision but with more than 6 billion people on this planet it is still a stretch to meet the second part of the vision.

Google's mission is to "organize the world's information and make it universally accessible and useful." To fulfilling that mission, Google's founders, Larry Page and Sergey Brin, developed a new approach to online search in a Stanford University dorm room and it has quickly spread to information seekers around the globe. Google is now widely recognized as the world's largest search engine, providing an easy-to-use free service that usually returns relevant results in a fraction of a second even though there are billions of information sources on the Internet.

It is harder and harder to isolate the contributions of the software from that of the hardware. As the technology moves to the 64 bit chip, multi-core, miniaturization, and more broadband, the opportunities for software to become more are being realized. As the economy continues to digitize and the world globalizes, the reach of software is dominating our lives. Although software has come a long way, it can do much more than it is today. It will enable greater levels of personal productivity and organizational performance as it is improved.

I think the most important trend in systems is the mobilization of people, allowing them flexibility to connect to wireless networks across the world. This requires new performance improvements with the wireless WiFi, Bluetooth and the ultra-wide band technologies. The mobile form factor is allowing people to carry or wear technology that provides them with a quantum improvement in capabilities and it is software that is making it happen. Both the software and the hardware can run multiple threads in parallel enabling organizations to realize greater benefits with this capability.

The first objective for computers was to automate manual processes and tasks by putting them under software control. This expanded to the computerization of new and more sophisticated tasks that could not be accomplished with manual processes. With the advent of mobile computing, endeavoring to do new tasks, we can now see new opportunities to a greater extent than any time in the past. Software is enabling totally new businesses, products and services that were simply not possible earlier.

The way we think about systems and interact with them is rapidly changing. I assume all interfaces with technology will soon become interactive, allowing us to deal with computers more like we deal with people. The trend will not be to just make software easier to use, but to make it more useful for humans. We have evolved a range of senses in our four-dimension world (including time) and future systems will need to more completely engage all of our senses for us to perform at our potential. We do not live in a two-dimension world, so software must enable us not to work that way.

Software should at least install and configure itself in a new environment, by learning from the existing software installed. There is a lot of interest with software virtualization and the capability to create virtual machines. Microsoft's SharePoint and IBM's WebSphere platforms are becoming the focus for collaborative virtual work; maybe one or both of them will soon get us the necessary software to enable our vision of the virtual world of work.

In this kind of environment blogs, wikis and other emerging approaches will be commonplace in improving how we work together. We are seeing the use of video communication evolving very quickly and expect it will surpass voice in the near future. If a picture is still worth a thousand words then this will dramatically change how we think about communication and how we will perform our collaborative tasks and interface with technology, all within the new secure virtual world of work.

Software can do a lot more than it's doing today, but to realize this dream we need software companies to aggressively drive forward and for organizations to enable new applications that will innovate how organizations do their business. Going forward expect software to simplify the act of working together, improve communications, emancipate knowledge, and allow the visualization of co-workers and computers. We desperately need it to be easy to find anything that is digitized and available, even if you are not sure where to look.

We need sophisticated software that enables better ways to manage content, provide rights protection and access the huge store of global knowledge that exists in the digital world. We need software tools to implement compliance processes and standards that allow traceability and transparency to those that need that visibility. With people traveling more, we need the capability to safely and efficiently duplicate our own personal workplace on other computers without running into insurmountable technical road blocks. Above all else we need computer software that can recognize and understand a familiar user and help, just like a personal assistant would help that person achieve their potential. Software will provide us the tools to work collaboratively, leveraging global resources and knowledge to perform at a higher level. Software companies please hurry!

To be assured your organization is ready for the future of software you need an architectural view of where you are and where you intend to go. The architecture must include business process, hardware, software, data, workforce and cultural views, as well as the integration of each. Remember that good architecture should provide a simple picture of something complex and not the reverse. Business users often see things differently than the technical IT staff, so if your models resemble wiring diagrams then the onus is on you to incorporate more animation objects to communicate the purpose, meaning and value of the work.

Our vision is that software will help virtual workers around the world get connected and stay connected to people, information, other software and technology. Our goal is to have software that makes working or playing seamless regardless of how people work, where they work, or when they want to work. The future software will enable virtual workers to function in their own language and culture without any degradation in team performance.

The game and entertainment segments of the technology industry are playing a significant role, introducing new software techniques that are being used by the virtual world of work to make things more real, compelling and interesting. We need software to be more agile and intuitive, while providing more transparency in what it is doing. Like what we have with the Internet applications, we need better monitoring of software and how individual users work with the systems. This will help in making software more sensitive to why people do certain things so the software can personalize itself to be more familiar to the user. The future virtual world of work will see the existence of interactive relationships between people and technology.

Not long ago email was the greatest breakthrough for communicating, sharing information and collaborating. It has already advanced to the point of now being one of the obstacles to higher levels of collaboration. When you have lots of people collaborating and many large attachments are going back and forth, the systems bogs down. We now have new tools emerging so that whenever you want to work with somebody, you just create a website that everybody authorized can go to and see what's going on.

This will save us from sending huge documents, but we will need management tools to organize and track, through an affinity code or a very sophisticated RSS (an acronym with several meanings—the one I prefer is *Really Simple Syndication*)—it will monitor and connect you to a specified number of websites that you need among the hundreds or thousands of sites that will appear in organizations. Things like wikis and blogs are allowing users to be more creative, faster. With the RSS you will be notified if someone has changed something that is important to you so you can respond quickly. I have a personal plea, although responsiveness is good we also need to be more reflective in what people respond with.

We will know when this is working because people will build communities and work teams around group websites. Look at the incredible success of the world's largest encyclopedia, an example of a wiki, named for the technique it uses, Wikipedia. In writing this book, it has been of tremendous value. Every organization should have on their corporate website chat facilities for their customers, their suppliers, individuals, to interact using these new techniques. This will allow their employees to see the dialogue taking place and to talk to those people to help them and build relationships.

People have been talking about videoconferencing for years. Personally when I have been involved in video conferences they have either been derailed by technical problems only an expert can solve or been less than impressive. This is not acceptable; we desperately need simple, cheap and easy to use visual conferencing. As we move more and more to a virtual world of work we need more face-to-face meetings without physical attendance. We have the very inexpensive cameras; we now need the software and reliable connectivity to add value in the meeting environment without the need for a technician. In the virtual world of work, no matter how isolated your workplace you need never be alone.

A fundamental technology called Web Services and the tools have gotten a lot better partially because the standards are now in place. This has come about because Microsoft and IBM have put their best people on developing the standards and assuring that it will not be proprietary to anyone. IBM understands long-running transactions, mainframe data access and the world of corporate application portfolios arguably better than anyone, while Microsoft understands the desktop, XML and information worker software requirements better than anyone else. Many other companies have helped but to get something really important done we still need the two gorillas.

We have a major technology hurdle and it will take the gorillas, the specialty players, in fact, most of the IT industry will be required to put the pieces together to solve what I perceive as "the software challenge." The challenge is for software that enables virtual workers to function in collaborative teams, from anywhere, at a highly effective level. Even during handoffs, having real time access to the right information and knowledge, no matter where it resides, enables all of our human abilities. Much of the world's information is stored in people's heads, in private organizational applications, databases, spreadsheets and documents. Information is both structured and non-structured and we very often know it exists but not where it is or how to locate it. On the Internet there have been amazing breakthroughs with search engines invaluable in finding public information, but we are not so fortunate in easily accessing organizational information, and there is no automated way to get at the information in human brains.

We are progressing, we can see the possibilities and taste the promise of what software could be, but there is still a lot of work ahead to meet the information/knowledge challenge and achieve the results that will propel us through the present and prepare us for the future. The organizational, geographical and technological boundaries still remain current barriers to real progress. Making the information workers, mobile workers and virtual workers efforts more enjoyable, easier and productive is the job of Jeff Raikes, Ray Ozzie and their Information Worker teams at Microsoft. Since Microsoft already owns the software tools that most information workers use worldwide, they are the ones we expect to solve this momentous challenge. There are other individuals and organizations (SAP and Oracle) that may emerge with new innovations but they will need to provide an integrated, seamless, complete platform for us to reach our goal.

The factors influencing and enabling the virtual world of work has changed so quickly it would be unimaginable for anyone suddenly placed in the 21st century from the beginning of last century. They would not believe what they would see today, so imagine what we will see by the end of this century. The nature of work is, has, and will continue to fundamentally change. New mobility and connectivity technologies, made usable by software, are emerging on a daily basis. Given what we know about the sociological profile of net-gens, many of these workers will probably find surprising applications for the new technology, resulting in exciting changes that we couldn't possibly predict today.

Increasingly, the virtual workplace is defined as wherever you and your technology happen to be, whether in a customer's conference room, airplane, car, hotel room, coffee shop, park bench or a home office. More often than not, the collaborative work teams now comprise partners, customers, contractors and others who don't share a common network or IT infrastructure. Software needs to evolve even faster so all the components can come together to fulfill the needs of the Virtual Worker Stage.

Web Services are now allowing software to be run outside your company; you simply connect up to it over the Internet. Virtual Earth is a great example; it provides you with a 2D and 3D digital representation of the real world. This software is too costly to purchase and maintain by individual organizations. In the future there will be a smorgasbord of Web Services for us to choose from.

The future of software is directly connected to having all of the related speech or language handling capabilities so the workplace of the future can operate in multiple languages and cultures. Software will integrate all of the phone services with the computing services to provide ease of use. It will let us conduct live real-time holographic meetings and simplifying working with technology by making the interfaces interactive. Software will continue to make technology more intuitive and sensitive by becoming more familiar with user needs. Business applications will become more agile and adaptive without months of programming effort to meet each new request. Software is perhaps the most critical component to making the future world of work a reality.

Chapter Summary
- The objective for software is to enable workers to use information effectively and to work efficiently.
- Software has historically been considered an intermediary between electronic hardware and the data which is created, manipulated and stored.

- Hardware provides the how to do something, software dictates what it is you will do when data is transformed into action and information is why we utilize technology.
- The vast majority of what is envisioned when one thinks of software is the application level software, the programs that contain our business process rules and associated data stores.
- Early in my career all application software was specifically written for the client and referred to as "custom software."
- Once the small to medium sized businesses bought desktop computers in large numbers, the commercial market for software packages became viable.
- Microsoft and Goggle each envisioned one of the main pillars of the future virtual world of work—Microsoft's mission was a computer on every desk, and in every home—Google's mission is to organize the world's information and make it universally accessible and useful.
- As the technology moves to the 64 bit chip, multi-core, miniaturization and more broadband, the opportunities for software to become more are being realized.
- I think the most important trend in systems is the mobilization, allowing people to carry or wear technology that provides them with a quantum improvement in capabilities and it is software that is making it happen.
- Software is enabling totally new businesses, products and services that were simply not possible in the past.
- With the advent of mobile computing software we are now enabling totally new businesses, products and services that were simply not possible in the past.
- I assume all interfaces with technology will soon become interactive allowing us to deal with computers more like we deal with people.
- Going forward I expect software to simplify the act of working together, improve communications, emancipate knowledge, and allow the visualization of co-workers and computers.
- We need computer software that can recognize and understand a familiar user and help, just like a great personal assistant would help that person achieve their potential.
- Future software will enable virtual workers to function in their own language and culture without any degradation in team performance.
- We desperately need simple, cheap and easy to use visual conferencing so in the virtual world of work we can have more face-to-face meetings without physical attendance.
- IBM understands long-running transactions, mainframe data access and the world of corporate application software arguably better than

anyone, while Microsoft understands the desktop, XML and information worker software requirements better than anyone else.

- The challenge is for software that enables virtual workers to function in collaborative teams, from anywhere, at a highly effective level even during handoffs, having access to the right information and knowledge no matter where it resides, in real time, enabling all of our human abilities.
- Software will continue to make technology more intuitive and sensitive by becoming more familiar with user needs.

CHAPTER 25

HARDWARE

In the earlier chapter, *The Pace of Change,* we talk about Moore's Law and the idea of exponential improvement. The computer chip speed has doubled every two years for decades, but amazingly the optic fiber speed for communication has increased faster than that, and the disk storage industry has actually even done much better. For example, IBM introduced the hard disk drive 50 years ago and today the density of data storage has increased by an unbelievable 65 million times—much of that increase coming in the past decade.

Seagate and Hitachi are the big disk drive makers and are already shipping hard drives with a new architecture known as *perpendicular recording* that is replacing the current *longitudinal recording.* The perpendicular drives start at 130 gigabits per square inch, while the older longitudinal drives have maxed out at a density of 100 gigabits per square inch. The perpendicular technology is projected to get us to 500 to 700 gigabits before a newer technology will be required. This will allow us a 10-fold improvement; this means that video iPods will be able to store 1,500 hours of video instead of 150 as reported by Mark Fischetti in a disk storage article, "Working Knowledge: Going Vertical" in *Scientific American.*

These incredible developments allow us the ability to have a different way of thinking about storage capacity, a different way of thinking about what we can do. This makes it possible to digitally record every meeting, have all training information online, access the information anywhere, and the actual cost of doing that storage is almost a rounding error in an IT budget. Only a decade ago it would have been completely impractical, way too expensive in terms of not only storage costs, but network bandwidth

The Virtual World of Work, pages 221–227

and network access costs. This is the mindset change that is possible in the new digital age of amazing hardware.

The breakthroughs that are required to keep on Moore's incredible improvement curve are coming very rapidly. Some of the changes are brought about by new ways of thinking, like why have one large expensive computer when we can have many smaller and cheaper computers, operating as one as effectively for a lot less money. Parallel processing and other techniques that allow us to run software across many machines are becoming increasingly prevalent. What I discussed earlier in the field called supercomputing is now actually becoming part of the mainstream computing, it's no longer a niche. Those supercomputing techniques are being used to provide the necessary power to run and manage the virtual world of work.

The devices are getting lighter and more capable, greatly encouraging mobility. This is evident in the use of tablet technology, which lets you not only use the keyboard but also the pen for taking notes, doing annotations, and having it in a meeting environment connected to a high speed wireless network for accessing the world. People are moving from their PC, to their phone, to their Blackberry, so what they really want is their information to instantly be available on any device. They want it to be user-centric so what they have been working on just appears automatically the way they want it.

In the few months it took me to research the technology releases across the main types of hardware, there was a plethora of new releases. Even to narrow the new developments down to a single class or industry is difficult. Thus, I will attempt to report on only a selection of new technologies in this chapter that I think are interesting and will have a significant impact on our ability to conduct business and enjoy ourselves virtually. I realize that as soon as this book is published this chapter will be dated.

I have a positive technology teaching experience to share that is being used to help prepare our young students for a work life integrated with technology. This is critical because of our desperate need to improve our education system and its ability to prepare our future workforces. The North Shore Country Day School in the northern suburbs of Chicago supports a K–12 private education program. The school implemented a complete wireless infrastructure in 2003, ahead of most businesses and universities. The school supplies all teachers with laptops as well as 1 laptop for every 4–5 students in the lower school and 1 for every 3–4 in the upper school. Students check out laptops for use at the school depending on the classes they are attending. This has reduced the need for expensive computer labs.

The school is also using a SmartBoard technology. It is a dry-eraser touch board that is 4' by 6' with a 4-color stylus. The students or teacher can hook their laptop to a projector that displays on the board so all students can easily participate in a lesson. You can edit, circle, underline or move anything displayed on the board with the stylus. One popular lesson the grade 4 students enjoy is the "*silly sentence*" exercise, where they make grammar and spelling corrections on the SmartBoard with the stylus.

Other lessons involve the students learning to access and display sites like NASA and the Smithsonian to support learning. The whole technical environment—cords, projector, stereo, VCR, DVD, is on a SmartCart which can easily be moved between classrooms. I found another private school that includes a personal tablet for each student as part of their tuition. It is critical for all students to learn computer skills as early as possible to prepare them for their future in a digital, global world.

There is a technology called RFID (Radio Frequency Identification). You may have already heard about it. It was the focus of a very clever IBM technology solution TV ad a while back. Like all new technologies, it got hyped up a few years ago and has become successful overnight. There is likely an RFID tag in your corporate ID, conference or visitor badges. It can enable incredible new services when embedded in any physical item.

The chip is so small that it can become integrated into any sized item that can be transported, carried, stored or worn. It connects the item to a computer so it can be tracked on-line to determine location, direction, usage, identification, temperature or any number of other useful data. In the global economy we are moving more and more items further and further, so knowing exactly where things are is essential. I can only try to imagine the number of security and military applications that may be enabled by this type of technology.

Oakley has eyewear, the O ROKR, which combines their patented optical technology with Motorola's leadership in the global wireless communication market. The eyewear enables hand-free mobile communications for compatible Bluetooth enabled handsets and takes mobile music to a whole new enriched level. The O ROKR is changing how people think and experience personal wearable technology by incorporating functionality with fashion. With the touch of a button you can play your favorite tunes or answer an incoming call, from your sunglasses, while jogging in the park. This very much helps prepare us for the future occasion when we will be wearing much of the technology we will need to be an effective virtual worker.

There are many good examples of regional technology innovations that have led to global solutions. Motorola is a great example of a corporation that encourages this style of global innovative thinking at the regional level. Motorola Labs Shanghai developed the technology to "*finger write*" in their natural style, Xing Shu, over a traditional handset key pad. You simply write the characters on the handset surface. The keys are not elevated but flat with the surface of the handset. The whole surface of the keypad is used to record the finger writing.

The regional challenge was the complexity of the Chinese written language making it impossible to add simple text messaging to a mobile phone. Existing text-input systems rely on mapping key presses to letters or characters superimposed on the numbers of the key pad. With more than 19 thousand traditional or 6.7 thousand simplified characters, the mathematical permutations could potentially be in the billions, making mapping totally impractical for the Chinese language (we can't quite get our 26 letters on the numeric keyboard). The finger writing technology has been recognized as a tremendous breakthrough in the communities across Asia. This solution to a local problem is now well on its way to being included into technological products around the global. Innovations that enhance global connectivity and communications are what will spur the virtual world of work forward.

North American sales of mobile hand devices, basic phones, smart phones and PDAs, rose nearly 25 percent in 2004 according to industry research, to more than 135 million units. The handsets sold will more than double by the end of this decade. There are many hot technologies that will dominate sales at the close of this decade: CDMA EV-DO, HSPA and EDGE are the most likely, and probably in this order. In this same time frame the costs for the handsets will be cut by approximately two-thirds. In the first half of this decade sales were driven by new users, churn and replacement units. The North American market has been largely penetrated, the sales in the second half of this decade will be lead by replacement units as the price tumbles and features continue to be enriched. The current race is to include all types of entertainment features, and the handsets will become an all-in-one device with many more mobile capabilities. People in other major portions of the globe are becoming mobile.

Motorola delivered *Q* the world's thinnest, lightest QWERTY phone last year. The Q delivers a fully-loaded package of email, voice, and entertainment in one rich but thin device. The name must be a play on the technology inventor, Q, from the James Bond movies. The Moto Q includes flexible mobile email featuring Microsoft's 5.0 Windows Mobile software, advanced cellular phone technology, rich multimedia capabilities, and an easy-to-use one-handed navigation thumbwheel. An all-in-one hand set is designed to deliver true seamless connectivity, helping mobile professionals improve productivity through the power of seamless mobility. The global competition is fierce and the devices get better and cheaper allowing more and more to be productive while mobile. The so-called smart phones are truly making those using them, more responsive while also looking smarter.

There are so many cool technologies being released like the ultra-mobile Tablet PC that lets you use the edges to navigate. The beautifully designed devices even have features like the new ultra-intuitive interface that are easily customizable to match your style when listening to music or viewing videos and pictures. The Samsung thin-film-transistor liquid crystal display (TFT-LCD) is bringing moving images to life on portable PCs. The devices have 2–5 gig flash drives that allow synching between the devices through the Internet or peer-to-peer connections.

The device capabilities are being pushed by applications offering new functionality. Non-volatile memory allows us to improve performance dramatically. All hand held devices are offering secure connectivity over Bluetooth and/or WiFi. New flexibility and greater capability are enabled as we move to the unified extensible firmware interface and away from the older BIOS technology. Again, all these innovations are making the mobile worker more and more capable of working anywhere and at anytime.

We see other things going on in the industry that just did not happen in the past. Apple was confident enough to supersede its best-selling product, the iPod mini, to introduce their replacement. With 74 percent of the digital-music-player market all the competitors were targeting the iPod when Apple announced the replacement for its highest-volume product. It exemplifies the pace of change in the industry and the philosophy of its founder, Steve Jobs, to "eat his own lunch" before anyone else can. They have just entered the competitive communication market with the new iPhone that pushes us to more usable technology solutions. Going forward I suspect if an organization with a dominant product position is not willing or confident enough to compete with its own products, they simply will not be the leader for long.

The mobile phones are, of course, been delivered with great color screens, capabilities and keyboards. They will have hard disks, will run Windows XP and Microsoft Office. All of this and full fidelity and richness, and will actually fit conveniently into a pocket or small purse. Once the data networks become more pervasive, you'll see a lot more mobile use of these devices in the virtual world of work.

To work effectively from anywhere we need a lot more than instant messaging, we need all possible communication channels to be integrated so one tool will let people manage all of the different types of communications. Some people do not like the impersonal nature of instant messaging so they will want to invoke video conferencing on the same system they are using for communicating.

Very inexpensive cameras can add value when in a meeting environment. We need software so at the same time collaborate teams can share computers, applications, data on each other's screens without needing to go to separate systems. We need it to be easy to add members to a work team from around the world, without the need for outside administrators, so they can access all documents and deliverables once authenticated and authorized.

The virtual private network (VPN) is one of the easiest ways to control access. With the VPN token you can work from your mobile and/or home computer and have full access to the corporate network. You can have the full functionality of your email client and be able to access public networks and internal intranet sites. Using a VPN connection is one of the most secure ways to connect to an organization's virtual work teams. A VPN creates an encrypted digital "*tunnel*" between your computer and your organization or work team members.

Mobile communication is the most visible aspect of the changing virtual world. When surveyed many more people in third world nations want mobile phones before they want mobile laptops. We see some major consolidations in this mobile sector in the last decade. In the wireless industry Cingular acquired AT&T Wireless, Sprint has gobbled up Nextel, the big three carriers all are adding subscribers and increasing sales. Verizon and the others have sold more than 1.6 billion cell phones worldwide over the past few years; cell phone companies need new services to keep growth going, like entertainment oriented add-ons that would have been unfathomable just a year or two ago. Phones are quickly evolving into mini-PCs. Cingular says its 50 million subscribers sent 4.4 billion text messages in the first quarter of 2005. Image the numbers today. The next generation phones will need to be managed in the same way that we do business PCs, making sure things are up to date and secure.

As a last note for now, under the hardware chapter, I would like to describe something I learned about that is in the research labs right now. There are new developments being investigated every day that may never reach the public as a commercial product. But if this one does, and I hope it does, we will be in for a treat. Imagine two devices the size of fountain pens. When placed in a small flat holder they stand upright and communicate with each other through a Blue Tooth connection. The one device displays a screen on any flat surface, like a wall, and the other displays a keyboard on a flat surface, like a desk. You have a working computer with flash memory, Wi-Fi connectivity, and the software necessary to work in the virtual world of work. How cool will this be?

Chapter Summary
- The computer chip speeds are doubling every two years, but amazingly the optic fiber for communication is increasing faster than that, and the density of data storage has increased by an unbelievable 65 million times in the last 50 years.

- The devices are getting lighter and more capable, greatly encouraging mobility.
- People are moving from their PC, to their phone, to their Blackberry, so what they really want is their information to instantly be available on any device.
- There are some positive technology teaching experiences used to help prepare our young students for a work life integrated with technology, but we need more.
- A new technology called RFID (Radio Frequency Identification) is a communicating chip so small that it can become integrated into any sized item that can be transported, carried, stored or worn.
- Oakley and Motorola are changing how people think and experience personal wearable technology by incorporating functionality with fashion.
- We will be wearing much of the technology we will need to be an effective mobile virtual worker.
- There are many good examples of regional technology innovations that have led to global solutions.
- There are many hot technologies that will dominate sales at the close of this decade: CDMA EV-DO, HSPA and EDGE are the most likely and probably in this order.
- Global competition is fierce and the devices get better and cheaper allowing those using them to be more responsive while also looking smarter.
- New flexibility and greater capability are enabled as we move to the unified extensible firmware interface and away from the older BIOS technology.
- To work effectively from anywhere we need a lot more than instant messaging, we need all possible communication channels to be integrated so one tool will let people manage all of the different types of communications.
- A VPN creates an encrypted digital "tunnel" between your computer and your organization or work team members.
- Mobile communication is the most visible aspect of the changing virtual world.
- There are new developments being investigated every day that may never reach the public as a commercial product.

CHAPTER 26

SECURITY

Computer or system security is an essential component of our future. Without a secure working environment our future will not evolve the way we desire it. Global connectivity, the global economy, and the virtual world of work will not be possible if virtual workers and their information cannot be secured. System security is the science concerned with the management of risks related to computer usage, networks and the protection of information. Digital security needs to be part of an overall comprehensive threat management strategy to truly protect an organization. There are four major components that make up a secure virtual work environment.

- **Outside Access**
  Protecting all systems and networks from unauthorized entry is the objective. Protection is primarily enabled through firewall protections and positive identification of your specific rights to access the systems and that you are who you say you are. This is the equivalent to perimeter protection in the physical world, denying access to the grounds and buildings or the people and products during transport.
- **Inside Access**
  Managing the specific rights that an authorized user has to specific resources, places and information is the objective. Authorization is more complex because users will be allowed access to specific systems and information but not other resources. Or they will be allowed access to view information but not to add, modify, copy, send, or destroy information. They may also be limited to specific versions of the information. In the physical world this would represent what an employee can do, where they can go, and what they can see.

The Virtual World of Work, pages 229–237
Copyright © 2008 by Information Age Publishing
All rights of reproduction in any form reserved.

- **Physical Protection**
  The objective is simple, to protect all physical components from being shut down, damaged, removed, used, copied, stolen or compromised in any way. This includes all the resources; the people, central computers, power, servers, desktops, laptops, mobile phones, PDAs, Blackberries, networks, devices, vehicles, lines, dishes, satellites, media storage, printed documents, drawings, notes, etc. This task is becoming increasingly difficult as more and more vulnerable components become very mobile, out of site and dispersed.
- **Audit Trails**
  All activity, movement or access, whether physical or electronic, must be captured and maintained by cameras, readers, sensors and/or digital logs. The objective is to present a formidable deterrent and the ability to immediately detect breaches or attempts against any secure resource. This information is invaluable for prosecution and analysis of possible vulnerabilities leading to better risk management.

What makes the security challenge difficult is to do all of the above without interfering with the efficient use of all resources by any authorized user worldwide. The challenge is to establish the right balance between locking everything down tight and making systems easier to use in a connected collaborative work world.

Security prevention investments have to be appropriate for the risks that exist toward your organization and the consequences of those risks. If your organization is a likely candidate for certain threats then you must invest in the necessary protection. If the consequences are catastrophic, a larger investment is appropriate. To protect life is different from protecting property, or confidential competitive information requires a greater degree of protection than preventing possible inconveniences. In today's connected world of work threats can change daily or even hourly from both inside or outside your organization.

As more and more of the world is connected and a much greater part of the global economy is dependent on digital information transmitted electronically, the vulnerabilities have become considerably greater. Security is one of the fastest growing segments of the overall IT industry. It is also a very active area for research; both private and public organizations are investing heavily in standards and solutions. The Trusted Computer Group and the Next-Generation Secure Computing Base are indicative of this focus on standards.

In the past security has tended to be built onto systems and not into them. Into the hardware, software, and application systems, we will need to design much more sophisticated protections from an increasing array of threats. Fire-drills are not sufficient, just because you have not been hit does not mean you will not be hit. Closing the door after the horse has escaped is a worthless strategy.

Security strategies have focused on numerous security engineering approaches. Let's review a few of the obvious and most useful.

Cryptography

Cryptography is a discipline of mathematics and computer science concerned with information security using encryption and authentication techniques. *Encryption* is the process of obscuring information to make it unreadable without special algorithms for encryption and decryption. Encryption can be used to ensure secrecy of the information, but other techniques are still needed to make communications secure, particularly to verify the integrity and authenticity of a message. Encryption or software code obfuscation is also used in software copy protection against reverse engineering the software.

A *cipher* is an algorithm for performing encryption or decryption. The original information is known as plaintext, and the encrypted form as ciphertext. You may see the word "code" used for cipher but they are not the same. A code works at the level of meaning—that is, words or phrases are converted into something else. Ciphers, on the other hand, work at a lower level—the level of individual letters, small groups of letters, or, in modern schemes, individual bits. The operation of a cipher depends on a piece of auxiliary information, called a key. As the key size increases, so does the complexity, to the point where it becomes infeasible to crack the encryption key directly.

Cryptography has a long and colorful history. Generally, the earliest forms of "secret writing," as it was known, required little more than pen and paper. The main classical cipher technique was transposition ciphers, which rearrange the order of letters in a message (e.g., "Help me" becomes "ehpl em"), and substitution ciphers, which systematically replace letters or groups of letters with other letters or groups of letters (e.g., "Fly at once" becomes "gmz bu podf"). An early example, and one of the simplest substitution ciphers, was the Caesar cipher, used by Julius Caesar during his military campaigns.

Early in the 20th century, several mechanical encryption/decryption devices were invented, and patented, including rotor machines. The most famous was the Enigma machine used by Germany in World War II. Extensive open academic research into cryptography is relatively recent beginning as recently as the mid-1970s with the public specification of Data Encryption Standard.

Authentication

Authentication is the act of establishing or confirming something or some-one as authentic. We sometimes interchangeably use words with different meanings to be equal. In this case the precise IT security usage describes authentication as the process of verifying a person's identity, while authoriza-tion is the process of verifying that a known person has the authority to per-form a certain operation. Authentication, therefore, must precede authorization. The process is to apply one or more tests which, if passed, have been previously declared to be sufficient for the person to proceed with entering a facility, an application or a network. The problem is to determine which tests are sufficient based on the risk and the need for security.

The methods by which a human can authenticate themselves are gener-ally classified into three cases:

- Something the user *is* (e.g., *fingerprint* or *retinal* pattern, *DNA* sequence, voice pattern, signature recognition, unique bio-electric signals produced by the living body, or other *biometric* identifier).
- Something the user *has* (e.g., ID card, *security token, software token* or *cell phone*).
- Something the user *knows* (e.g., a *password,* a *pass phrase* or a *personal identification number* or PIN) is also used.

Sometimes a combination of methods is used, such as a bank card and a PIN, in which case the term *two-factor authentication* is used. In IT, biometric authentications refer to technologies that measure and analyze human physical and behavioral characteristics for identification purposes. Physical characteristics include fingerprints, eye retinas and irises, facial patterns and hand measurements, while examples of mostly behavioral characteris-tics include signature, gait and typing patterns. Voice is considered a mix of both physical and behavioral characteristics.

In a typical IT biometric system, a person registers or enrolls, which means that the digital template of the biometrics is captured. This informa-tion is then processed by a numerical algorithm, and entered into a secu-rity database. The algorithm creates a digital representation of the obtained biometric. Each subsequent attempt to use the system, or authen-ticate, requires the biometric of the user to be captured again, and pro-cessed into a digital template. That template is then compared to those existing in the security database to determine a match. The comparison process involves the use of a Hamming distance. This is a percentage mea-surement of how similar two the bit strings are. Computer systems must also ensure communication end points are who they say they are.

Chain of Trust

Chain of Trust is used to ensure that all software loaded has been certified as authentic, and this includes all maintenance releases, patches and fixes. This approach provides controls that are needed both for security and operations. Only a select few can put any new software into production after it has been tested and approved for production. Publicly known flaws in commercial software is the most common entry point for *"worms"* to break into a system and then spread to other integrated systems. The security of your systems is only as good as the weakest link. People trying to penetrate your security are very sophisticated in scanning your environment for points of entry.

Computer Media Back-up

Computer Media Back-up is the physical copying, transporting and storing of versions of all software and data files on a recurring cycle. Depending on the transaction volumes and criticality of the systems to the organization, backups must be taken on monthly, weekly, daily, hourly or continuous. Some critical systems duplicate all data on a shadow back-up file as part of processing. These backups are critical when there is a need to rebuild the systems if a failure is detected or when audits are performed.

The back-up is typically stored on transferable media such as tape or disk. All organizations should employ the services of a professional company to ensure that backups are not compromised. The copies must be made on a regular cycle and transferred back and forth to a secure facility far enough away to be subject to a different set of risks. As organizations move to the new virtual world of work, it is even more critical that security issues including backups are part of the overall security or threat management procedures and processes.

Anti-Virus Software

Anti-Virus Software consists of computer programs that attempt to identify, thwart and eliminate computer viruses and other malicious software normally called malware for short. Anti-virus software typically uses two different techniques to accomplish this:

- Scanning files to look for known viruses matching definitions in a virus dictionary.
- Identifying suspicious behavior from any computer program which might indicate infection.

Most commercial anti-virus software uses both of these approaches, with an emphasis on the virus dictionary approach. In the virus dictionary approach, the anti-virus software examines a file and refers it to a dictionary of known viruses that the authors of the anti-virus software have identified. If a piece of code in the file matches any virus identified in the dictionary, then the software can take one of the following actions:

- Attempt to repair the file by removing the virus from the file.
- Quarantine the file so that the file remains inaccessible to other programs and its virus can no longer spread or do damage.
- Delete the infected file.

To achieve consistent success in the medium and long term, the virus dictionary approach requires periodic online downloads of updated virus dictionary entries. It is critical for all home users particularly in the virtual work world to continually have the virus software updated and also to send any viruses found to the company that supplies the anti-virus so they can update everyone's software. The creators of the viruses try to stay one step ahead of the anti-virus software and have currently resorted to software that encrypts itself to avoid detection.

The suspicious behavior approach, by contrast, does not attempt to identify known viruses, but instead monitors the behavior of all programs. If one program tries to write data to an executable program, for example, the anti-virus software can flag this suspicious behavior, alert a user and ask what to do. Unlike the dictionary approach, the suspicious behavior approach therefore provides protection against brand-new viruses that do not yet exist in any virus dictionaries. The modern anti-virus software uses this technique less and less because it causes a lot of false alarms.

Some anti-virus software uses other types of heuristic analysis to emulate the beginning of the code of each new executable that the system invokes before transferring control to that executable. A sandbox approach emulates the operating system and runs the executable in this simulation. After the program has terminated, software analyzes the sandbox for any changes which might indicate a virus. While the simplest approach is to look for file types that are suspicious. No approach is full proof so it is very important for users to use good computing practices and not download or open emails or files that you do not know or are not expecting.

Firewall

A *firewall* protects computers, networks and data from attacks and intrusions by restricting traffic based on a set of defined rules controlled by the systems administrator. A computing firewall can be hardware and/or software based which functions in a networked environment to prevent communications forbidden by the security policy. The original idea was formed in response to a number of major Internet security breaches, which occurred in the late 1980s, against the unprotected early Internet. The Internet community made it a top priority to combat any future attacks from happening and began to collaborate on new ideas, systems and software to make the Internet safer.

In 1988, Jeff Mogul from Digital Equipment Corp. (DEC) developed a filter systems know as packet filter firewalls that became the 1st generation firewall. The 2nd generation of firewall was known as circuit level firewall while the 3rd generation firewall known as application layer firewall. The first commercial product was released by DEC who named it the SEAL product. The 4th level packet filter firewall system was produced at USC and operated on both Microsoft Windows and Apple Mac/OS.

The software was commercialized in 1994 by Check Point and became readily available in the market. The 5th generation of firewall was based on Kernel Proxy technology. This design is constantly evolving but its basic features and codes are currently in widespread use in both commercial and domestic computer systems. Cisco, one of the largest Internet security companies in the world, released the product to the public in 1997 and it remains one of the top sellers of Internet firewall technology on the market.

There are basically three types of firewalls:

- The personal firewall that filters traffic entering or leaving a single computer.
- The network firewall that operates at a low level of the TCP/IP protocol stack as IP-packet filters, not allowing packets to pass through the firewall unless they match multiple packet attributes.
- The application level of the TCP/IP stack intercepts all packets traveling to or from an application.

Access Authorization

Access Authorization is the method of identifying users based on a rights management process and access control lists as a fundamental way of enforcing privilege separation. There are many techniques using passwords, ID codes, smart cards, biometrics, VPN tokens and many more that identify the user but do not authenticate the users. The authorization process is used to decide if the person, program or device is allowed to have access to data, applications or services. Most modern, multi-user operating systems must include an authorization process. When a user tries to access a resource, the authorization process checks that the consumer has been granted permission to use that resource. Authorization systems should only grant permissions that are needed for users to do their jobs.

Most websites encourage users to access them through the use of clever graphical presentations and provide permissions to do normal activities, like ordering products, searching information, copying information or asking questions. These users are referred to as anonymous consumers or guests and are not required to authenticate.

A trusted consumer is one that has been authenticated and is allowed access to specific resources. There are two philosophies, to allow permission to anything that has not been restricted or only to those specific things that have been granted and nothing else.

You will be tracked when you access or visit websites. Cookies and tracers are used by most organizations. A cookie is a small data file placed on your hard drive by the website server when you visit a site. They make it possible to track traffic patterns, see what visitors are doing and understand how they navigate. Tracers are tracking scripts that recognize a unique identification from a cookie and can be used to determine what sites or site areas you have visited. They know where you have been and may even capture personal information.

Cyber criminals are adjusting and getting more sophisticated in their methods. The new breed of "web criminals" are succeeding in finding novel new ways to convince users to open documents or click links that download data-stealing software. Instead of directly asking the user to enter personal data into a fake website, cyber criminals are embedding code into fake news articles or business-oriented "requests for proposals" (RFPs) which, when opened, install a backdoor into the computer. Security firms estimate the use of data-stealing code designed specifically to steal financial information, known as Trojans, is rising dramatically.

It appears fewer recipients are responding with personal or financial information compared to earlier, but fraud losses connected to the theft of such information off the web have risen substantially, with estimates now well more than a billion dollars per year. The criminals will do anything to make you trust them as their way of getting to larger and larger thefts.

The advances of opening the Internet to more and more people around the world has brought great benefits but has a side effect that is not good. The predators have a new and very large group to prey on. Be smart, learn the rules to protecting yourself and be vigilant in protecting those you know and love who may need your help. The new virtual world of work is opening fantastic new opportunities for us and unfortunately some of the bad guys.

Chapter Summary
- Global connectivity, the global economy and the virtual world of work will not be possible if virtual workers and their information cannot be secured.
- There are 4 major components that make up a secure virtual work environment: Outside Access, Inside Access, Physical Protection and Audit Trails.

- The challenge is to establish the right balance between locking everything down tight and making systems easier to use in a connected collaborative work world.
- In today's connected world of work threats can change daily or even hourly from both inside or outside your organization.
- Security strategies have focused on numerous security engineering approaches like: cryptography, encryption, cipher, authentication, chain of trust, media back-up, anti-virus software, firewall and access authorization.
- There are two philosophies: to allow permission to anything that has not been restricted or only to those specific things that have been granted and nothing else.
- When you access or visit websites, you must assume you will be tracked by cookies and tracers.
- The new breed of "web criminals" are succeeding in finding novel new ways to convince users to open documents or click links that download data-stealing software.
- The use of data-stealing code designed specifically to steal financial information, known as Trojans, is up tremendously.
- Fraud losses connected to the theft of personal information off the web rose from $690 million in 2004 to $1.5 billion in 2005.
- The new virtual world of work is opening fantastic new opportunities for us and unfortunately some of the bad guys.

CHAPTER 27

LEADERSHIP

For organizational change, often referred to as transformational change, to be successful several conditions have to be created or nourished through exceptional leadership. This involves the communication of a meaningful purpose, picture, plan and personal impact of change that are clear to people up and down all the levels of an organization. One fact is consistent; with great leadership much can be accomplished. We can easily see the results of powerful leadership throughout the history of the human race, some good and unfortunately some very bad. Transformational leadership needs to first communicate a believable reason for the upcoming change. The reason may be compelling or frightening enough for people to buy-in and precipitate an increased willingness to change.

Projecting a better outcome can cause change but there doesn't seem to be anything like a pending disaster to get people to co-operate and work hard to achieve a common objective. When the time is right, a leader can be tremendously effective if they have a plan that is clear, comprehensive and understandable. Leadership does not have to be as portrayed by Hollywood; in fact, I believe that broad, cascading leadership is the critical factor needed in business today. Under these circumstances individuals can jump in and assume a role of enabling change. This does not have to be the sole responsibility of the organizational chain of command. In fact, many significant changes grow out of ground up movements where individuals band together to bring about change based on the buy-in of the majority, sometimes even without managements full participation. This happens best when people understand what the change will mean to them.

There can be a dramatic difference between the words *leader* and *leadership*. Leaders fill a position, a formal or informal recognition of a person,

The Virtual World of Work, pages 239–250
Copyright © 2008 by Information Age Publishing
All rights of reproduction in any form reserved.

like the President or the expert, while leadership indicates behavior, actions or relationships which can be exercised by the leader or anyone else on more of an informal base, like in friendships or work groups.

This power may be the result of a personality trait that makes it possible for one to take the initiative to lead or assume the leadership by having the knowledge or expertise that is recognized by others who want or need someone to lead. To provide leadership requires others who are willing to follow the influence, advice, direction or guidance provided. Leadership implies a relationship of power, the power and responsibility to guide others.

There are many examples of leaders who have gained their influence or power using very different methods and techniques. Many leaders are put into place by formal processes, for example, election, selection, competition, seniority, birthrights, etc.; while others gain their position through actions, character, ambition, experience, relationships, etc. Looking specifically at organizations we may see a combination of the above factors, even pure chance or circumstances may lead to an individual becoming a leader. Some lead by providing wonderful visionary leadership qualities. Many high tech companies are lead by visionary leaders. Others may appear to gain a leadership role through more of a survival of the fittest, the toughest or most intimidating, and still others because they have the relationships with clients or investors. Some may be elevated to the role by being great managers or administrators of the complexities of a project, program or business. A few may just have been in the right place at the right time or conversely in the wrong place at the wrong time depending on your view.

It is one thing to become a leader yet a very different thing to provide great leadership. Our education systems do not teach leadership. Other than the military schools, we do not have any training for being a leader, providing good leadership or being a good follower. Too often it is a skill that one just has to somehow learn. This is very troubling because great leadership can make the difference between success and failure for most endeavors.

Work groups or teams without good leadership struggle and do not reach their potential. Many of today's good leaders have learned through mentoring from former good leaders. There is not a proven formula for making a leader, or for exactly how to provide great leadership, yet clearly some people do provide that elusive leadership that consistently makes the difference. Most business failures can be traced back to a series of bad leadership decisions. Individuals with the leadership responsibility may not see trends and patterns, nor pay attention to the situations that should have clearly predicted an alternate path or direction.

Let's look at a technology leader who takes his responsibility seriously, and is prolific at sharing and clearly articulating his technological vision of the future. Bill Gates is such a visionary leader for the whole world; here are some of his ideas about the new world of work he shared at the 2005 Microsoft CEO Summit:

> Technology innovation doesn't take place in a vacuum. The agile business deploys technology in response to changing conditions in the market, the workforce, the economy and society at large. While some aspects of the future will always remain uncertain until they happen, other trends clearly point toward the broader conditions and challenges that will define the business landscape in the coming five to 10 years.
>
> For those just barely catching up with the tools and practices of information work today, the value of some of these developments may seem elusive. But for the workers who will be delivering the innovations and productivity growth of tomorrow, this technology not only won't come as a surprise, it will be a positive expectation.
>
> The "net generation" that's coming of age today has lived its entire life in the digital age. They are rapid adopters of new information technology and are not only comfortable, but expect to work collaboratively with others. They multitask in ways that seem unfathomable to many. Email, the Internet, vivid real-time interactive games, instant messaging and mobile devices are as natural to kids today as the telephone, television and ballpoint pens were to the previous generation.
>
> In a business setting, information workers will have all their task-based data—project notifications, meetings, line-of-business applications, contacts and schedule—accessible within a single view, whether they're at their desk, down the corridor, on the road or working from home.

Gates provides us with the insights and knowledge of where technology in going. If you listen and learn from him and other visionary leaders in similar positions you will have a good idea of where you, your organizations and society are going.

So the question for this chapter is; how do organizations ensure the leadership and knowledge required to guide them in the transformational change to the new virtual world of work? To know or understand if our leaders have been successful, we need to agree on how we will measure success and against what goals, objectives or visions. James M. Burns introduced the idea of several different types of leaders. "An effective leader will unite followers in a shared vision that will improve an organization and/or society at large." Burns calls leadership that, "delivers true value, integrity, and trust *transformational leadership.*"

He also describes the *functional leadership* model which conceives leadership as a set of behaviors that help a group perform a task and reach their goal. In this model, effective leaders encourage functional behaviors and discourage dysfunctional behaviors. He also introduced the *transactional leadership* model that focuses on doing all the correct things to seemingly get check marks on their report card. In business all of these models exist but the first two models have to be active at many levels for a major change program to be effective.

Some leadership experts believe that a leader can be described by the sum of their traits or characteristics that they exhibit. This is popular because we can all agree on some of the common descriptors associated with a leader. But, some feel this is too simple and their research indicates that not so much as a set of traits, but a pattern of motives can define a leader. These motives include a high need for power, a low need for affiliation, and a high level of self-control.

According to the *situational leadership* theory no single optimal psychographic profile of a leader exists. This theory proceeds from the assumption that different situations call for different characteristics and that the leadership style must match the appropriate level of characteristics exhibited by the followers. In this model, leadership behavior becomes a function not only of the characteristics of the leader, but of the characteristics of followers as well. This would suggest a good feedback loop would be needed.

I personally have experienced both good leadership and ineffective leadership based on the leader's ability to accept feedback or criticism. The good ones would listen but not easily change their mind based on the last person they talked to. After all you really only want them to change when you think they are wrong and you are right. Right!

Leaders are usually caught in a continuing game of balance between their concern for people and their concern for goal achievement. I knew there was an imbalance when I heard, "the project was a success but there is blood everywhere." To me this indicates not a good leader but a strong authoritative person with too much power. It is not always easy to predict ahead of time how people will react if given the power to lead. We continue to expect people to move from the rank and file, take over a new management role and somehow know how to provide leadership. There is a huge difference in doing the business of a company, managing and administrating the business, and leading the business. I have seen excellent consultants become poor managers and none existent leaders with a promotion.

I am not aware of any single proven method for developing a continual supply of leaders in an organization other than mentoring, on-the-job training, or through selective recruiting. Mentoring and on-the-job training is a consistent theme with most job or career development plans. Although training classes and on-line learning events were a big part of the change services we offered when I was working, our studies showed that approximately 80% of what was needed to perform a task or role was learned on-the-job. I was also unable to find theoretical or empirical work that has been done to explore the complexity of the relationships that are required by exceptional leaders. This is particularly true in the case of developing transformational leadership.

In today's highly competitive business environment, long term organizational success depends on the development of transformational leaders who can motivate and inspire their organizations to innovate and change in a continually evolving environment. The best of these leaders can make their vision a group objective to be achieved by all. GE is viewed as one of the best corporations to consistently turn out good managers with leadership capabilities.

In the past many organizations prided themselves in generically growing their future leaders but in today's increasingly global environment corporations like IBM, Boeing, and many others have acquired senior executive officers from the outside. This practice will continue because working in a single organization may not gain an individual the variety of experience required to lead in unpredictable times, through unchartered global waters.

I was fortunate to learn the techniques and power of influence as a young child from my Mother. I was raised in a home where I never witnessed my parents arguing or significantly raising their voices in anger against each other, perhaps sometimes against me and my sisters but not each other. My Mother usually got what she wanted by using a more gentle approach. The ability to influence and compromise until I got my way was very helpful, but this particular home-grown mental model did little to prepare me for being able to confront, argue, yell, and fight to get what I wanted or needed.

Today more than ever in the past, transformational leaders need to set an expectation by the role model they display. Words are cheap but over time a good role models actions and behavior will set the stage for trust and great leadership influence. As I have heard clever people say, "It is easy to be tough but hard to be smart." It would be fantastic if the leaders also had the ability to inspire and motivate their followers. It is my experience that many business leaders need to hire others that have these interpersonal skills to do most of the job of motivating the troops. As long as the leader is seen to be directly involved, setting the future direction, and being optimistic about the future, this can be effective.

Truly motivated people can accomplish amazing tasks if they are encouraged to be innovative, take risks and be responsible for their efforts, and results they impact. A great leader makes every individual feel they are important to the outcome and that the leader understands, and is interest in their role. The leader is responsible for creating the overall environment people work in and for the direction the individuals and the business are going. Feedback must be encouraged through meaningful two-way dialogs that support collaborative work practices. These practices must be enabled by the leadership, and supported through an active mentoring and coaching culture.

In 1994, House and Podsakoff attempted to summarize the behaviors and approaches of outstanding leaders. These leadership behaviors and approaches do not constitute specific styles, but cumulatively they characterize the most effective attributes of a leader that make a difference. I have modified their summaries slightly to specifically mesh with our focus on the business context of leadership by eliminating some political and military content:

- **Vision**—outstanding leaders must have a vision that can be vividly articulated and consistent with the deeply-held values of the organization and its employees, and paint a picture of a better future for the participants.
- **Passion**—they must have a strong enough conviction of their vision or mission that they will make self-sacrifices in the interest of being successful.
- **Persistence**—the leaders must display a high degree of confidence in themselves and be determined in the attainment of the vision because their mission usually challenges the status quo, and therefore may offend those who have a stake in preserving the established order.
- **Image**—they must be concerned about their own image and recognize that they must be perceived by the employees as competent, credible, professional and trustworthy.
- **Role-model**—the leader's image must represent an effective role-model because employees will identify with the values of the role-model and perpetuate these values and behaviors.
- **Spokesperson**—they should be the internal and external image for their respective organizations and symbolically represent their changing organization.
- **Confidence**—the leader must communicate high expectations and strong confidence in their employee's ability to meet such expectations.
- **Motivate**—they must selectively arouse and motivate the participants of the necessity and relevance to successfully accomplishment the transition to the future state.
- **Change agent**—the leader must persuade followers to accept and implement *change*, and that they can lead them to the better future.
- **Inspirational communication**—outstanding leaders often, but not always, communicate their message in an inspirational manner using vivid *stories, slogans, symbols,* and *ceremonies.*

In my experience the most powerful of these traits is persistence, the ability to go on when things seem bleak, and the pressure is on to make compromises to the plan. Many organizational people are just like the media, they get very good at poking at things, picking things apart, and creating negative ideas, just to be recognition as a contributor and somebody that must be smart. This works too often for these purveyors of gloom and negative energy, but do not expect alternative visions, plans or suggestion of what to do from them. This never seems to be their jobs and whatever you do, don't give them the responsibility for a new direction. They are parrots, only selectively repeating what they hear and they will occupy everyone's time—you will surely regret you ever ask them to help.

A transformational leader's job is to create and communicate a vivid vision so that a sufficient number will accept the vision as their own and be the force that enables a successful journey that brings the remaining employees along. This action will encourage cascading leadership, buy-in and reduce the dependency on a single leader. The transformational leader's actions will get the change program started, and from that point their job is to support and eliminate obstacles when necessary. In the past leaders enforced the bureaucracy; now they need to eliminate it.

I always enjoyed relating organizational change to what an orthodontist does. They study the current problem or situation, establish a vivid picture of the future state, analyze the pressures that created the present state, and determine what pressure must be applied to achieve future success. They do this by designing a program with continuous monitoring and adjustments to cause change that is at a pace that is sufficient, but not so great that the pressure is removed and the change program stopped. Oh yeah, one more critical step, they pinpoint and extract any obstacle to the change that will impede success. The orthodontic approach is more reliable than doing nothing and less painful than using a hammer.

I do not subscribe to the belief that management and leadership are synonymous. Leaders are more generally concerned with direction, change and people, while managers are concerned more specifically with tasks, forecasts and performance. I certainly do not think the existing management should always be expected to draw double duty and lead a transformational program. The job of operating the existing business and managing the transformation is normally too great for one individual. Both are full-time jobs and you cannot afford to do both in a half-ass way.

Very often existing management are chosen, because of their knowledge of the business and buy-in to the change, and temporarily removed from the operations position to head the transformational team as a special assignment. These assignments can be a normal and useful part of a career development program. This is beneficial for succession planning. The special assignment will test the selected individual for further responsibilities and promotion. If the individual needs help with the transformation team duties, hire an expert to assist them. This could be a recently retired executive from your organization or an outside person with specific experience with such tasks and knowledge of your business.

Sometimes you do not get what seems obvious in a leader. I can recall situations where one leader portrayed an image of being very concerned with people and another who seemed much more concerned with performance. As I worked with these individuals their true nature in fact was just the opposite, but this was not apparent to most. I have worked with corporations that believed in group leadership or even a counter balancing of leadership. I have also seen organizations that encouraged leaders to take opposing teams and directions so that the act of competition determines the winners.

This is similar to, but not as visible and exhausting as our drawn-out process for selecting political candidates for the Presidency of the U.S. I find it interesting that some leaders try to become one with their constituencies and others take positions of the benevolent leader. This is usually much more evident in some nation states and religions than in business, but, given sufficient power and time some leaders become *"larger than life."* This may be very useful after they have retired in creating corporate stories that can be retold, but I do think this attitude can be problematic while they are still actively leading an organization.

Let's look at what two leaders, who managed a large global corporation, have to say about leadership. I observed them during an assignment I was privileged to lead in their company. Phil Condit was the CEO of Boeing and often spoke very eloquently about the importance of people and leadership. Here Laurette Koellner, Chief People and Administration Officer quotes Condit: "We work very hard and are very successful at delivering leading edge technology. We can work for years at a particular technology and be the first to market, but a competitor can come along and duplicate that technology immediately. However, they can't duplicate people. People are our competitive advantage. We can never lose sight of the fact that leaders need to focus on people every minute of every day."

Another line Condit uses and is often quoted by Koellner: "Great leadership and involvement by all = good business." She continues, "It's really that simple. It's not one at the expense of the other. It's not either/or, it's both. And, it's so simple. Yet, it is hard because many of us grew up in a 'command and control environment.'" That is, we did not invite—in all cases—employees to be engaged. And, we were rewarded and promoted for these actions.

Koellner in a great speech about leadership states:

Today's leaders must take courageous action. Business today is about action, bold action. Part of this action is...to "let go" of controlling everything. Leaders must support people in the risk-taking that is essential...not only for people's personal growth, but also for the successful growth of the company.

Now I'm not speaking of risk involving the safety or integrity of the product or the brand. I'm speaking of encouraging personal risk, career risk. I am talking about fostering the innovation that will take us successfully into the next century.

Leadership is not for the fainthearted. It takes courage, integrity, dedication and business savvy. Peter Drucker summed it up: "Whenever you see a successful business, someone once made a courageous decision."

We work in a fast-changing and evolving world. And we work in fast-changing and evolving organizations. Today's leaders, and the leaders of the future, must manage that change to keep competitive. We must do so in a world in which the nature of leadership itself is changing. I believe this is our challenge...and I also believe this is our opportunity.

What is it that's happening in our workplace that is causing the need for us to take a new look at leadership styles, and even a new look at the very role of leadership?

I believe one primary driver shaping leadership includes how work is being performed. Work is being performed more and more by small collaborative teams. Whether we are speaking of the smallest of businesses or massive global companies, or even of world powers...it is teams that are completing the work and accomplishing our goals. The ability to collaborate has become the key to the success of an enterprise. Today's employee recognizes that the power of ideas can multiply many-fold through collaboration. Today's employee is not a "soldier" who will stand for that command-and-control environment that has been mentioned earlier. Labor is starting to flow freely around the world as globalization and technology permits virtual workers to seek opportunities anywhere.

How will we lead a workforce and teams that can be almost anywhere? Before the infusion of technology in our lives, it was simple. People reported to work at a specific time of day and went home at a designated time. There was a supervisor or manager who made assignments and directed employee activity.

Today's employees work in flexible teams and need leaders who are coaches and mentors, leaders who provide tools to support collaboration, and leaders who can successfully create an atmosphere where ideas flow and creativity is heightened. How do we lead these bright people and teams? Successful leaders of today—and tomorrow—are leaders who have been able to evolve just as our workforce has evolved.

Cost pressures force leaders to focus on activities that can readily be automated, outsourced or off-shored to gain a cost advantage, but to create competitive advantage organizations need leadership that can drive value with ideas, intellectual property, process innovation, strategic insights, and personalization of services. In this innovative type of environment, winning organizations will find new ways to empower information workers with tools that amplify their human talents and connect them to information infrastructure. Leaders must allow the virtual workers to understand their role in the context of larger strategic objectives, find and collaborate with the right people, and make the best use of available information in their decision-making and work activities.

Teams are not the only factor impacting leadership of today and tomorrow. Technology dramatically impacts leadership. By 2010, it will be possible that the majority of the people in the industrial world and half in the developing world will be on-line. By 2050, it is possible that all the technological knowledge we work with today could represent only a very small percent of the knowledge that will be available at that time.

Today and tomorrow, there will be fewer managers to report to and fewer decisions that require their input. Workers will be empowered to make decisions, the question is—which decisions? And the question for us, as leaders, is and will be: "are we ready to face the leadership challenges of the virtual world of work?"

Chapter Summary
- For transformational change to be successful several conditions have to be created or nourished through exceptional leadership.
- With great leadership much can be accomplished.
- Leadership implies a relationship of power—the power to guide others.
- Work groups or teams without good leadership struggle and do not reach their potential.
- Most business failures can be traced back to a series of bad leadership decisions.
- There are only a handful of visionary technology leader for the whole world and if you listen and learn from them you will have a good idea of where you, your organizations and society are going.
- The question for this chapter is; how do organizations ensure the leadership and knowledge required to guide them in the transformational change to the new virtual world of work?
- James M. Burns introduced the idea of several different types of leaders: *transformational leadership, functional leadership, transactional leadership,* and *situational leadership.*
- Research indicates that a set of traits, a pattern of motives or the characteristics of followers can define a leader.

- Leaders are usually caught in a continuing game of balance between their concern for people and their concern for goal achievement.
- In today's highly competitive business environment, long term organizational success depends on the development of transformational leaders who can motivate and inspire their organizations to innovate and change in a continually evolving environment.
- Working in a single organization may not gain an individual the variety of experience required to lead in unpredictable times, through unchartered global waters.
- Words are cheap but over time a good role models actions and behavior will set the stage for trust and great leadership influence.
- A great leader makes every individual feel they are important to the outcome and that the leader understands and is interest in their role.
- There are many who are purveyors of gloom and negative energy that are very good at poking at things, picking things apart and creating negative ideas, but do not expect alternative visions, plans or suggestion of what to do from them.
- A transformational leader's job is to create and communicate a vivid vision so that a sufficient number will accept the vision as their own and be the force that enables a successful journey that brings the remaining employees along.
- Leaders use to enforce the bureaucracy; now they need to eliminate it.
- I like to relate organizational change as what an orthodontist does, just the right pressure and before long everything slides into place.
- Leaders are more generally concerned with direction, change and people, while managers are concerned more specifically with tasks, forecasts and performance.
- We can never lose sight of the fact that leaders need to focus on people every minute of every day.
- Great leadership and involvement by all = good business.
- Leadership is not for the fainthearted, it takes courage, integrity, dedication and business savvy.
- Whenever you see a successful business, someone once made a courageous decision.
- Labor is starting to flow freely around the world as globalization and technology permits virtual workers to seek opportunities anywhere.
- Today's employees work in teams and need leaders who are coaches and mentors, leaders who provide tools to support collaboration, and leaders who can successfully create an atmosphere where ideas flow and creativity is heightened.
- Successful leaders of today—and tomorrow—are leaders who have been able to evolve just as our workforce has evolved.

- Winning organizations will find new ways to empower information workers with tools that amplify their human talents and connect them to information infrastructure.

CHAPTER 28

COLLABORATION

The real business value from collaboration is team-generated innovation. Innovation in products, productivity, marketing, projects, and strategy will drive competitive advantage. For the virtual workers to make collaboration a success, they need software empowerment tools to deliver on the promise of innovation and team productivity. The time for virtual collaboration is now.

Hardware and software technology can enable and enhance virtual collaboration, but it is not sufficient to create it. It has much more to do with behavior in a social environment than a technology environment. To understand collaboration you need to examine the processes involved when people work together to accomplish an outcome that goes way beyond what could be accomplish by the same individuals working independently. Collaboration can apply to the work performed by individuals as part of a team or as a group working as one. We need the ability to store individual work, and the ability to automatically integrate the work into a single, community deliverable. Collaboration is more about putting the right people together than it is about the right technology. Technology is necessary but not sufficient.

The reason the word was not widely used earlier is that at one point the term held a very negative connotation. The use of the term *collaborator* meant, "Traitorous cooperation with the enemy." This negative meaning was popularized in the1940s by the French. In its original usage it made reference to the Vichy Regime, as well as the French civilians who sympathized with and fought for the Nazis against France. Since then, the words *collaboration* and *collaborateur* have a very pejorative meaning to the French; the shortened form *collabo* has an insulting meaning. Although I think col-

The Virtual World of Work, pages 251–259
Copyright © 2008 by Information Age Publishing
All rights of reproduction in any form reserved.

laboration is the path to our future and the correct term for us to use in this book, do not expect the French to easily accept the use of the word.

Research into the process of collaboration has intensified with its use in the computer software industry. It is commonly used to describe complex application development and maintenance approaches using globally distributed teams. It is used to describe a delivery model that often involves offshore service providers, outside contractors, suppliers, and internal employees all working together. The need for software that combines management and collaborative features has grown rapidly with the practice of now throwing software requirements "over-the-ocean" as opposed to the old practice of "over-the-wall."

There are many companies targeting the "working together theme" to create more useful and effective collaborative environments. Many technologies can support the sharing of work, but none address the complete integrated suite that is needed to meet the expectation of virtual collaboration. To choose the right technology for collaborative work, you currently must compliment your IT platforms with specialty products and support. The good news, because of the great need for performance, more and more people are investigating ways of achieving productivity improvements, and as such collaboration is coming under more intensive study as a viable work alternative.

The race is on to see who can deliver the best collaborative methods, techniques, tools and learning events. Remember, many are choosing different directions because there currently exists, no unifying general theory of collaboration to work with. Collaboration is a lot more than emails, messaging and video/voice communications; it is also more than information management, document management, business intelligence, search, and file sharing.

Before we can have a shared vision of what collaboration is, researchers will need to focus on answering some very basic questions:

- How does collaboration differ from other terms like—coordination, cooperation, sharing, teaming, working together, collective or community work, etc.?
- How do you define what collaboration is—do we need many definitive examples that make it clear what it is and is not?
- What qualifies as collaboration—is it a human process, is it really something different when it is done using technology virtually from anywhere on the planet?
- Is there a defined process describing alternate methods, techniques, and tools?

- What are the possible outcomes of collaboration—simple deliverables, complex deliverables, creative thinking, new knowledge, faster results, less cost, or better quality?
- How will our workers learn this skill—who is sponsoring, teaching, and perfecting these behaviors?

Let's look and see if we can discover a difference in what some of the words mean and how they are different. Collaborative work teams require a commitment to a shared objective and an even more important commitment to each other. There needs to be a sense of belonging and respect for the other participants. There must be a strong sense of trust that the team members provide the right mix of skills, knowledge and experience to be successful in achieving the shared objective or outcome.

Collaboration is a dynamic process engendering open communication and a great deal of flexibility coupled with mental agility. The team requires one member to be a good facilitator and fill this role. It is always useful for the members to already have experience and expertise in working in a collaborative environment. The team needs to be complementary yet diverse enough in their range of skills to provide for most contingencies. For a team to work effectively and efficiently, particularly in a virtual or partially virtual environment, there must be shared common platforms and tools, deployed and stable, which will support this style of work.

Collaborative work requires a high degree of interdependence yet allows the members to be trusted to tackle their tasks independently accommodating their individual talents. You do not require consensus on each decision if there exists total consensus or agreement on the shared outcomes, and a detailed understanding of the interdependences of the work process. I believe that new WMS (work management software) must handle these tasks for the members, and all coordination and integration of the work products.

The goal is to achieve collective results that the participants would be incapable of accomplishing working alone. An objective is to leverage each member's expertise to innovate and share in the pride that comes with successfully accomplishing extraordinary results. All process steps taken and all completed deliverables need to be captured into a knowledge repository for further measurements, analysis and re-use. The results, lessons learned and feedback must be shared with each member. It is not collaboration if one person is carrying the load for the team. Organizational collaborative efforts must be measurable in delivering higher quality, lower costs and improved enterprise value. It will change how people think; it is more than coordinating resources and tasks or encouraging cooperation.

How does collaboration compare to coordination. Coordination is the act or process of organizing the efforts of different parties of a project to deliver on a common outcome. The members do not need to carry on a working relationship beyond the accomplishment of the task. This is one of the jobs of the project manager involving schedules, plans and work breakdown structures. As indicated earlier this should be a task undertaken by the WMS. Coordination is usually associated with a lower level of trust between the members and the ones enforcing and assigning the work. It is not expected that the members will create new processes requiring initiative, creativity and risk in getting their work done. A valuable coordination task is to make sure everyone has everything they need to perform their work tasks.

Let's look at how cooperation is distinct from collaboration. Cooperation is something that can be done as an act of generosity, like what happens during a catastrophe and usually involves a diverse group of people. It provides a means to an end. Mutual trust and respect are not necessary, although helpful. In a work environment it can be associated with consultation and knowledge-sharing between participants. Cooperation will provide a mutual benefit from working together. The roles may be clearly defined or be based on more of a voluntary situation. The sharing or partitioning of work can provide a definite savings in time and costs. It is primarily a means to an end as opposed to how an organization does things. It would be difficult to imagine that a unique or innovative outcome would be achieved. When cooperating people are struggling to solve problems and make decisions, they will form relationships and become closer, this is a critical step in the journey to collaboration.

Open collaboration between partners requires much more than just non disclosure agreements to protect intellectual property rights. What we are talking about goes way beyond supply chain relationships or being a sub or prime on a project. The International Space Station is an example of what can be referred to as collaborative manufacturing. Here we see sharing of original knowledge, ideas and expertise so that the outcomes will dramatically advance human understanding. There is need for a level of precision in what each partner builds, so they can be delivered as completely intact components that will fit together and work the first time in a remote, harsh environment.

The Station provides a great example of a shared goal, commitment, trust and respect, specific mix of knowledge and capability, a dynamic process, flexibility, common processes and tools, high degree of interdependency, innovation, and pride of the achievement that could not have been accomplished separately. The creation of new knowledge and expertise is a critical outcome. There are becoming more examples of collaborative component manufacturing; this is why I am optimistic about collaboration being a necessary and successful practice in the virtual world of work.

There are many barriers to collaboration becoming the preferred way of getting complex work performed. Although organizations are increasingly using collaboration to operate at a competitive level, our education institutes under the university level are only just beginning to teach collaborative practices. We are more fixated on competition as a way of getting ahead and actively encourage individuals to do individual work in school. When I went through school sharing work with each other was so bad that you could fail if caught.

Although collaboration is natural in some societies, it is unnatural in western societies. Collaboration is difficult concept for new groups because it requires a level of trust that can take time to evolve or be earned. My experience is that the old "not invented here" syndrome is still a very strong mindset of many people. Other barriers include those individuals who hoard or will not share knowledge because this would diminish their perceived power. When these fears are coupled with, "stranger danger" or other insecurities, we recognize that this will take time to make collaboration a nature way of doing things in most organizations.

This is definitely not a technology problem it is a social issue that must be conquered, starting with the new generations. We need to encourage teaming and collaboration skills in our primary and secondary education. This is difficult when there is so much mistrust in our society. I am convinced that every sports hero is worshiped as an individual and the word "team" is spelt with many "I" today.

To implement collaboration it must be encouraged at the top and be supported down though the organization. Everyone should understand the desired outcome, the purpose, the plan and the impact on them. Let the people demonstrate the behavior, think and use group knowledge to solve problems, and deliver results. It works well as a grass roots movement working its way through an organization when encouraged by management. Word of mouth feedback is a key factor in its acceptance.

Although collaboration requires executive support from the top, people will get involved in the process in a bottom's up way, not a top's down way. As organizations start encouraging collaborative environments, there's a question of how do you get the right mix of what should be done top down versus what should be done bottom up.

The approach can be used to complete small projects or designs and build new products or services. It is also very useful in defining new organizations. The implementation of knowledge management and content management practices will integrate well with collaboration approaches. These approaches are about working together, feeding on the knowledge and expertise of each other, and to help workers find, use and share that knowledge across the organization.

In the IT market, the broader knowledge workplace trend is convergence of content management, portals and collaboration. The collaboration market is approaching $1 billion in new license revenue causing companies like IBM, Microsoft and Oracle to strengthening their collaborative offerings. Others like Interwoven and Collabnet are using Vignette techniques to hold onto their market position. Whatever you choose, you will require a common presentation layer, portal, browser, etc., operating in a run time infrastructure so you can share software, tools, storage, security, and services. Your challenge is how to create a vision, a strategy, and a plan that will encourage people to change their behavior. To successfully support collaboration, focus on the organization's culture, workers' attitudes and business processes, then buy the right technology.

If you are interested in some easy reads, Tamm, Austin, Straus, Schuman, all have authored books that provide well-organized guides to collaboration in a variety of situations. Many other books provide similar guides but these authors are a good choice to start with. There have been many recent Business Week articles that were interesting to read. They have predicted the decline of emails and the ascendancy of wikis for internal organizational communication. Wikis hold great potential for knowledge management and collaboration. A wiki is simply a website that can be edited by any authorized participant. It is ideal for collaborative document production. It will store all previous versions and the creation of new versions is as simple as assigning a new name. Notification is automatic whenever any version is changed, and it can track who made the change.

The industry research firms predict that wikis will become mainstream collaboration tools in this decade. This radically different model for communication and collaboration is another piece of technology that workers will need to learn and become skilled at. If you are going to implement wikis, have one person become familiar with them and have them mentor the other collaborative team members until the tool becomes familiar. Business Week and other sources have validated the tool but we are yet to see the full extent of the benefits to be realized by wikis or other tools like blogs in the virtual world of work. It does appear that once we get past our current dependence on emails, we will be taking another giant step toward "working together" in more productive virtual environments.

The workplace will increasingly be built to accommodate collaboration and connectivity. The physical space design will emphasis meeting rooms, chat rooms and workrooms for teams to gather in, the technology infrastructure will facilitate teams working together across time and space. Business will be accomplished through collaboration, success will become a team effort and the effectiveness of individuals will be increased by the networks they have at their disposal.

Friedman states,

It is now possible for more people than ever to collaborate and compete in real time with more people on more different kinds of work from more different corners of the planet and on a more equal footing than at any previous time in the history of the world.

He also provides us our urgency by iterating, "The world isn't going to be flat, it is flat." He wants all of us to understand these developments are desirable and unstoppable, and to know you're going to be trampled if you don't keep up with it.

Political and economic dynamics are forging a huge single global market. The market is made up of a global workforce, organizations, customers, partners, and suppliers. The market will require collaboration across time-zones, across organizations, across firewalls while meeting the challenge of maintaining security and confidentiality. Protection of the IP in an environment of increasing innovation and a nomadic global workforce of mobile and virtual resources, engaged through a variety of non-traditional employment arrangements, is a critical factor in nurturing collaboration.

A major challenge facing the "always on, always connected" world will be converting information into innovation. Collaborative environments will need to manage time while staying focused on high priority tasks, finding the right information and connecting with the right people in an organization via the best channels. For the individual information worker, staying on the same page as colleagues and managing the balance between work and family life must be a priority. These kinds of challenges require a new generation of collaborative work tools: ones that simplify rather than complicate, and automate many of the low-level tasks and decisions that currently clutter the lives and waste the time of information workers.

Collaboration is how we will accomplish future virtual work and technology is what we will use to leverage global knowledge, knowhow, and resources. Imagine the power that will be generated from the future virtual world of work when everyone can be connected and communicating in their own language and culture in a collaborative infrastructure.

Chapter Summary
- To understand collaboration you need to examine the processes involved when people work together over longer periods of time to accomplish an outcome that goes way beyond what could be accomplish by the same people working as individuals.
- Collaboration is more about putting the right people together than it is about the right technology.
- Research into the process of collaboration has intensified with its use and advancement in the computer software industry.

- Many technologies can support the sharing of work, but none address the complete integrated suite that is needed to meet the promise of collaboration.
- Collaboration work teams require a commitment to a shared objective and an even more important commitment to each other.
- For a team to work effectively and efficiently, particularly in a virtual or partially virtual environment, there must be shared common platforms and tools, deployed and stable, which will support this style of work.
- Collaborative work requires a high degree of interdependence yet allows the members to be trusted to tackle their tasks independently accommodating their individual talents.
- The goal is to achieve collective results that the participants would be incapable of accomplishing working alone and share in the pride that comes with successfully accomplishing extraordinary results.
- Collaboration will change how people think; it is more than coordinating resources and tasks or encouraging cooperation.
- The International Space Station is a great example of what can be referred to as collaborative manufacturing, where there exists a shared goal, commitment, trust and respect, specific mix of knowledge and capability, a dynamic process, flexibility, common processes and tools, high degree of interdependency, innovation, and pride of the achievement results that could not have been accomplished separately, and the creation of new knowledge and expertise for the future good of man.
- Although collaboration is natural in some societies, it is unnatural in western societies, we are more fixated on competition as a way of getting ahead and encouraging individuals to do their own work.
- Although collaboration requires executive support from the top, people will get involved in the process in a bottom up way, not a top down way.
- The collaboration market is approaching $1 billion in new license revenue causing companies like IBM, Microsoft and Oracle to strengthening their collaborative offerings.
- It is now possible for more people than ever to collaborate and compete in real time with more people on more different kinds of work from more different corners of the planet, and on a more equal footing than at any previous time in the history of the world.
- Protection of the IP in an environment of innovation and a nomadic global workforce of mobile and at-home employees, engaged through a variety of non-traditional employment arrangements, is a critical factor in nurturing collaboration.

- Staying on the same page as colleagues and managing the balance between work and family life must be a priority, and requires a new generation of collaborative work tools: ones that simplify rather than complicate, and automate many of the low-level tasks and decisions that currently clutter the lives and waste the time of information workers.
- Imagine the power that will be generated from the future virtual world of work when everyone can be connected and communicating in their own language and culture in a collaborative infrastructure.

Section Five

HOW TO ARCHITECT THE VIRTUAL WORLD OF WORK?

CHAPTER 29

SECTION INTRODUCTION

The first step in preparing for the future virtual world of work is to recognize things are changing so rapidly that you need to change now if you want to be part of this dynamic future. There has been no single, incredible event that is responsible for the change that is dramatically altering our society and how we work, nor can we see any single amazing event altering the near future. Over the last few decades there have been thousands of developments that are cumulatively changing our lives, our society, and particularly our jobs in extraordinary ways. The most significant to this study is that it is now feasible to be connected to work and work colleagues while remote from the traditional office. This has freed us to be mobility, allowing nearly anyplace to be a workplace.

The changes will continue at a more rapid pace going forward and will bring about new changes that are hard to imagine today. I hope the preceding chapters helped move you closer to this realization and ready for the quantum changes we are now part of. This realization is what obviously dictates the need for planned, immediate action in most organizations. This will directly cause individuals to change their lives. If I am correct, then why do studies show that few organizations recognize just how much the workplace has changed and unfortunately fewer still have done much about it? Organizations seem to be willing to be pulled along as and when they are ready, and do not have a clear well thought through strategy and plan to realize the benefits of the virtual world of work.

Mobility is already a fact of life, and working virtually is rapidly becoming the workplace of choice. The new work related processes, techniques and tools need to reflect this reality. Unless virtual collaboration does not work, globalization is stopped by security and political problems, the intro-

The Virtual World of Work, pages 263–270

duction of new technology is significantly slowed, attitudes harden and do not change, and demographics no longer matter; *you are going to change.* The odds that all of these powerful forces are neutralize at the same time is extremely slim. Let's continue with the assumption that the new virtual world of work is coming and we all need to prepare and architect ourselves and our organizations for this incredible future.

An initial observation was that this inevitable change is so all encompassing and different that traditional organizational change approaches would be inadequate to meet the need. After restudying many of the industry's change management methods, techniques and frameworks, I now believe that, with some obvious and not so obvious adaptations, they can in fact help us to succeed and achieve our goal of a better life for information workers and the organizations that want to make a timely change. It is difficult for individuals to ignore the changed world we will live in and impossible for organizations. The main decision facing all organizations is will their management be pulled along into the future or actively participate in architecting the future. One warning, with the current pace of change we are experiencing, to be pulled means you will arrive late to the party and will be held accountable for the consequences of your lack of foresight.

The change will be a continuous improvement process, progressively architected in many steps across many years. This involves a series of human changes and thus will be unique to each organization. The ultimate realization of the outcomes will *not* be achieved through a well-executed technology project. It will require a fundamental shift in how our workforces and organizations think. This change to a new virtual digital age will ultimately be greater than the changes experienced during the transformation to the Industrial Age because of the number of people now involved and the complexity of our business world.

The Industrial Revolution, over the last 200 years, was the major force in creating the urban society we live in and dictating where the majority of the industrialized workforces currently live. It changed how we thought about work and over time this has lead to the complexities of our present, physically connected world. The Digital Age is enabling an even more complex and virtually connected digital world that will change everything once again. The human race is already well into this new virtual age, enabling a basic change in how we think, communicate, play, learn, work, and live. This will bring about a seemingly infinite number of variables that will necessitate society to make countless adjustments as we proceed. These adjustments will, over time, create a totally new, and for most people, a much improved world.

In getting started there will be many decisions to make, and since these decisions will affect the entire workforce, including families, communication must take a top priority. Any significant journey requires understanding where you are, where you would like to be, preparing, and having a reliable means of getting there. Having a current map to follow will help. These words are obvious and extremely fundamental, but remember the devil is in the detail.

This will not be a simple or familiar journey for most. There are many critical issues which need to be well understood to make this journey a success. A few of the critical issues we need to consider are; how many people will participate in the journey, how far do we need to travel, and how fast do we need to go to complete the journey on time? All other decisions will be tied to the answers to these questions. Without this basic knowledge it would be impossible to plan, communicate, prepare and execute any complex organizational change.

Initially we should review any change planning previously undertaken and interview those involved to gain their perspective. We will need to survey the current workforce to assess what is happening on the existing landscape, what people think, their readiness for change, and what may already be planned. Prior to any interviews, surveys or assessments there must be communication to let everyone know what management is thinking, why and when this planning will take place, who will be involved, what will people be asked to do, how they can help, and how decisions will be made. In addition, an organizational context needs to be presented, including what is happening in similar organizations, industries, countries and society as a whole. It is also mandatory that an honest picture of a better future be depicted from the worker's perspective. Even if the picture is not complete, whatever is presented must be clear and believable.

This will help create buy-in, which is critical in gaining people's understanding, commitment, and support of the decisions and outcomes of a transformational change. Without buy-in you are almost certain to fail. You can't just dictate transformation. People will resist and even try to under mind a change program if such a strong-armed approach is attempted. After all, without buy-in you have not really convinced anyone that it is in their best interest to participate. I still believe people *will* change; they just resist *being* changed.

In today's world internal and external sentiment is everything! Abraham Lincoln said about public opinion, "With it, nothing can fail, without it, nothing can succeed." Public opinion in politics is analogous to buy-in at the organizational level. A useful technique to achieve buy-in is to use strategic stories and images of a positive future. This is like any sales or propaganda campaign; you must design, target and deliver an image or story that projects a positive future from the listener's perspective. Those listening to the message need to know what's in it for them, before they will believe, remember, and retell the stories.

The picture of the future must be clear and address the listener's agenda which means you need to understand what that is before the message is formulated. If you think this is something you can wing and adjust based on the audience's reaction, you are wrong, you will look weak and not confident in the message. With the endless number of organizational changes brought about by reorganizations, downsizing, acquisitions and mergers; very few people remember, could retell, or even appreciate the mystique that can be created by storytelling of past heroes and successes.

Many authors talk about leveraging experience as the best teacher and encourage the use of the age-old community practice of storytelling to pass on lessons and traditions. This learning method collects data from past experiences that demonstrate selected insight from the employee's perspective, and clearly puts it together in the form of a story to be used in discussion groups both internally or externally. In organizations where this has been used, it builds trust, provides an opportunity for collective reflection, and is an effective way to transfer knowledge. To help make this happen in your organization, provide incentives or rewards that will encourage employees to learn and help with the buy-in of chosen experiences.

If you take this simple approach to communications and gain buy-in, you will be halfway to achieving your goals. You will also be more successful in retaining this buy-in over the duration of a transformational change. If you empower the workforce to be involved in the process of improvement and contribute their massive capital to supporting the change, things will go more smoothly. To set the right outcomes for a complex organizational process improvement, business rules, incentives and measurements will need to change. Management will need to be more flexible, agile and make very tough decisions to realize the benefits of the new virtual world of work. Many will need to update their attitudes, habits and mental models before they will be able to willingly buy-in to a transformational change to the new virtual world of work.

When preparing an organization for a major change the value of social capital can go beyond creating competitive advantage and be beneficial to the change process itself. A useful framework for understanding the power and the role social capital can play in a business context was developed by Janine Nahapiet at Oxford University and Sumantra Ghoshal at the London Business School. They define social capital as, "The sum of the actual and potential resources embedded within, available through, and derived from the network of relationships possessed by an individual or social unit."

They describe social capital in these terms:

> There must be a series of connections that individuals have to others, individuals must perceive themselves to be part of a network, a sense of trust must

be developed across these connections and the members of the network must have a common interest or share a common goal.

Their research shows that organizations have begun to emphasize the sources and conditions of what has been described as organizational advantage through their social capital. They present several arguments that;

> Organizations are conducive to the development of high levels of social capital, social capital facilitates the creation of new intellectual capital, and those organizations with the most networks have a competitive advantage in creating and sharing intellectual capital.

A model is presented in a paperback book, *The Strategic Management of Intellectual Capital and Organizational Knowledge*, that draws from many authors and researchers to incorporate an overall argument in the form of a series of hypothesized relationships between different dimensions of social capital and the main mechanisms and processes necessary for the creation of intellectual capital. The editors of this work, Chun Wei Choo and Nick Bontis have selected from 30 articles, newly written for their book or from existing publications, which utilizes a knowledge-based approach to create a compellation of thinking that can be useful in structuring the journey to the virtual world of work.

I also discovered another piece of work that I found fascinating and thought provoking which speaks to the power that can be derived from a large, connect society. The book, *Emergence—The Connected Lives of Ants, Brains, Cities and Software*, is by Steven Johnson. He states that,

> An individual ant, like an individual neuron, cannot function or survive on its own, but if enough are connected into a greater scheme you get spontaneous intelligence. Ants, without leaders or explicit laws, organize themselves into highly complex colonies that adapt to the environment as a single entity. They have the necessary intellectual capital to alter the community's size and behavior to suit conditions exhibiting a weird collective intelligence, or what has come to be called emergence. Self-organizing clusters of shared interests and structured behavior has to do with feedback loops causing totally different behavior. When some threshold is passed, the nature of the system drastically changes.

It is my hope that at some point in the future our global connectivity or networks will contribute to the phenomenon of new emergent behavior for humanity. As our virtual world of work evolves it will develop to form a more complex, interconnected and dependent world that is better, but perhaps not readily apparent from today's constituent parts or virtual beginnings.

Included in this section are suggestions about how to organize virtual workforces to attain greater emergence. There is a great deal of literature about communities of practice (CoP) and how these integrate with virtual workers, virtual teams and virtual communities. I was able to find many authors that believe there is a direct connection between CoPs and organizational performance. Eric Lesser and John Storch of IBM, formed their conclusions based on a study of seven organizations where CoPs are acknowledged to be creating value. They believe,

> As organizations expand geographical scope, connectivity and complexity, it is increasingly apparent that sponsorship and support of communities of practice—groups whose members regularly engage in sharing and learning, based on common interests—can improve organizational performance.

They report,

> To build an understanding of how communities of practice create organizational value, we suggest thinking of a community as an engine for the development of social capital. We argue that the social capital resident in communities of practice leads to behavioral changes, which in turn positively influence business performance. We identify four specific performance outcomes associated with the communities of practice we studied and link these outcomes to the basic dimensions of social capital. These dimensions include connections among practitioners who may or may not be co-located; relationships that build a sense of trust and mutual obligation, and a common language and context that can be shared by community members.

Information workers today need to create and work in a different but better technological workplace. They are dealing with increased use of networks, people located in foreign countries, personal mobility, and working from a virtual home office. By being connected, resources are available for work functions no matter where they are located or what they are doing. This always on, always connected capability has led to a significant increase in the hours information workers work.

There is definitely work creep, and everyone is working harder right now because of email, wireless access and globalization. For those of you connected you can't even get a rest on the weekend. Worker advocates compare this trend to the automobile industry phenomenon of "*speedup*" in the 1920s. Personally I do not see the situation this way, sure there may be a similarity in the extension of the workday, but everything else is more flexible, fluid and totally different. The workforce is in much more control and has the opportunity to deal with this situation. Everyone needs to learn and leverage the greater flexibility so that in the future they can personally achieve a more satisfying work/life balance.

At the same time organizations are struggling to keep up with the need to deliver new workplaces to accommodate increased mobility, while attempting to save money in the process. Complexity, competition and financial pressures are at an all-time high. We have a compelling environment in which a virtual chain of events will cause a phenomenal change. The time is now, so let's review what we need to get ready to realize the benefits of a better virtual world of work.

In planning and guiding a transformational change we need to think of change as a continuous process that involves many different views or levels within an organization. We are not going to be successful by thinking of this change to a virtual world of work as a technology project or a single process improvement project. The path to a virtual work environment will lead to a fundamental change to how business is done. I have included a chapter on planning, using an approach that I have used successfully in my career. The approach involves how to plan and execute a transformation change from the strategic executive level, portfolio level, program level, project level and service management level. It includes useful techniques for aligning the efforts across all levels, and provides measurements for determining the degree to which all the activities contribute to the desired ultimate outcomes.

To help in this transformation a selection of lessons learned has been included. These have been derived from my own experience, from the experiences of others interviewed, and the published works from selected organizations. In Section Four there are cases studies, so in this section there is no attempt to provide the detailed context, just an extensive array of tips, hints, best practices, experiences, or what we used to call lessons learned. These are provided in a condensed format so as many as possible can be included. They are meant to remind readers of what has been covered, or to introduce new ideas that you need to think about and understand. If this knowledge helps you to succeed in your transformation to the new world of work, then I will sit back, relax, and feel proud of the information and knowledge delivered.

Section Introduction Summary
- The first step in preparing for the future world of work is to recognize that things are changing so rapidly that you need to change now.
- Mobility is already a fact of life, allowing nearly anyplace to be a workplace and working virtually is rapidly becoming the workplace of choice.
- We all need to prepare and architect ourselves and our organizations for the incredible virtual work future.

- The main decision facing all organizations is will their management be pulled along into the future or actively participate in architecting the future.
- The change to a new virtual digital age will ultimately be greater than the changes experienced during the transformation to the Industrial Age.
- The human race is already well into this new digital age, enabling a basic change in how we think, communicate, play, learn, work, and live.
- Prior to any interviews, surveys or assessments there must be communication to let everyone know what management is thinking, why and when this planning will be scheduled, who will be involved, what will people be asked to do, how they can help, and how decisions will be made.
- An honest picture of a better future will help create buy-in, which is the critical process in gaining people's understanding, commitment, and support of the decisions and outcomes of a transformational change.
- Public opinion in politics is analogous to buy-in at the organizational level and "With it, nothing can fail, without it, nothing can succeed."
- The picture of the future must be clear and address the listener's agenda which means you need to understand what that is before the message is formulated.
- Social capital is the sum of the actual and potential connections that individuals have to others and when the members of the network have a common interest or share a common goal, an organization can development a high level of social capital, social capital facilitates the creation of new intellectual capital, and those organizations with the most networks have a competitive advantage in creating and sharing intellectual capital.
- As organizations expand geographical scope, connectivity and complexity, it is increasingly apparent that sponsorship and support of communities of practice—groups whose members regularly engage in sharing and learning, based on common interests—can improve organizational performance.
- This always on, always connected has led to an increase in the hours information workers work.
- To help in this transformation I have put together a selection of lessons learned, derived from my own experience, from the experiences of others I have interviewed and the published words from selected organizations.

CHAPTER 30

GETTING STARTED

In this chapter we will cover communications, learning and development, surveys, assessments, and interviews, as the best places to start a transformational change program. You may have originated the best idea ever, thought through a complex problem, made a difficult decision, or created a roadmap to the future, but nothing can happen until these are communicated. Fortunately, today we have an unbelievably enhanced capability to effectively communicate in many new ways with incredible reach. Getting started with any transition, transformation, organization improvement or change starts with communication which works best when it is interactive, supported and encourages feedback. *Communication enables action!*

Internal communication exists in all organizations through many more unofficial channels than official communication channels. Communication deals with the exchange of information, creating understanding and behaviors within an organization. Communication promotes a wide-range of diverse effects, ultimately uniting the whole organization, or conversely paralyzing the organization. We want the internal communication to help improve the culture of an organization through active participation of all employees.

One-way, authoritative communication will not work with the future workforces. Organization wide communications usually involve such things as strategy, policy, actions, events, or results, and should be provided through the integrated use of multiple communication channels. The old adage works, tell people seven times, ideally all through different media, and they will remember. Tell them one time and they will forget. I am sure you have all heard people say, "I don't do anything until I have been told 3 times because they usually change their minds."

The Virtual World of Work, pages 271–283
Copyright © 2008 by Information Age Publishing

A good integrated internal communication strategy must use both media development (such as intranet web casts, conference broadcasts, newsletter, email, posters, etc.), and face-to-face meetings. Today we have the ability to have face-to-face meetings without being present in the flesh. This is very powerful because now leaders of larger dispersed organizations can have many more virtual personal contacts with the workforce either individually, in work teams, or in all hands geographic groupings than was feasible in the past.

There is literally no excuse for not meeting and communicating with anyone, or everyone, anywhere in the world. Thus, if your organization does not do this, it will be obvious that the leaders don't care, think the workforces doesn't care, don't see it as their job, or believe they are too busy. Every person from the top of the organization to the bottom can be in multiple places at the same time to listen, be heard or both in today's virtual world. We now have the incredible ability to visit employees, recruits, customers, suppliers, and investors in the same day anywhere in the world.

Internal communications departments, since the 1990's, often report directly to the organization's senior leadership or even the Board of Directors in some forward thinking organizations. Internal and external communications are being integrated, leading to the appointment of a Chief Communications Officer (CCO). In this way, all communications can be coordinated in one person, group or department, including marketing. At Fujitsu Consulting we also integrated the solution groups under the CCO. This coordination allows greater control over the corporate image, reinforcing its vision, values, and culture amongst employees. This helps ensure employees communicate a consistent message to potential clients, partners, investors, and new recruits.

The way in which messages are presented, remember Marshall McLuhan, "the media is the message," can have a major influence in how messages are perceived and accepted. The way messages are presented can have a negative or positive impact upon the reader or listener, regardless of the core content of the message. While this is sometimes referred to in the political environment as "spin" organizations need to avoid manipulative and ambiguous messages, as they destroy trust, resulting in the staff disbelieving all internal communications. If this happens, the people will seek information from other biased sources, the most inaccurate being the external press. The realization of good communication will contribute to a cohesive workforce, and foster loyalty and high-achievement. Great leaders will want to work with their workforce rather than simply have their workforce work for them. A great communicator will make you feel the message was focused for you.

Attributes of good internal communication that will help enable organization change will be:

- **Timely**—so that the employees hear it first from the leadership rather than the public media or the grapevine.
- **Relevant**—if the message is not relevant to the whole audience, individuals will checkout, and this can cause disruption or distraction for those interested.
- **Convenient**—it should be scheduled and delivered minimizing the time and effort required to participate. With today's tools this should be easier to accomplish. Time is a currency, and communications that cause disruption will cost the organization a lot more than the executive's time.
- **Clear**—the key messages must be obvious and easily understood. In the global world this may require the message to be modified to accommodate local culture, customs and/or language.
- **Concise**—people do not have time to read/listen to rambling communications. It should present the meat of the story quickly and efficiently, and then offer further details. Sometimes referred to as the inverted triangle style.
- **Informative**—the key messages should be presented to the audience to give them a new perspective, more information or clarify something.
- **Interesting**—communication needs to be interesting to be effective, particularly for large dispersed audiences. If possible, important communications should inform and motivate the participants through both the content and delivery.

The CCO and the internal communication departments are a focal point for interaction between official organization representatives and the receivers of the messages. This will help with adherence to standards that assure a level of consistency in the messages and how they are interpreted. They should also make sure that the person delivering the message is properly prepared, practiced and capable of delivering the message in an appropriate manner. I have witnessed numerous good managers fail to deliver because they felt they could get away with "winging it." Compliance to organizational values and consistency in how two-way communication and feedback will be accommodated will add familiarity and effectiveness to the process. The communication group should be responsible for developing and maintaining a number of channels, allowing effective and efficient communications to take place.

Many of these communication channels can also deliver training for those involved in the transformation to the new virtual world of work. Within the realm of organizational development, the related field of training and development deals with the design and delivery of learning events to improve performance within organizations and to support the workforce going through a major organizational change. In many organizations the term *Learning and Development* is now used instead of Training and Development in order to emphasize the importance of individuals taking the initiative for learning, as opposed to the organization taking responsibility for force feeding the content. The words emphasize more appropriately the fact that the experience of learning is the responsibility of the learner and not the instructor.

This separates the corporate world's efforts from the education industry in which most parents and others look to the teachers to hold this responsibility and not the students. There is also a significant difference between training and education. I attended a class where an instructor asked a simple question to emphasize the difference, "Would you prefer your child to take sex education or sex training at school?"

As I have pounded out in this book, the world is changing, thus training or learning must also adapt and change with the times to more effective methods, techniques, materials, and delivery mechanisms. The concept of a "typical learner" is quickly changing in the workforce. Today's learners have higher expectations that are strongly influenced by their experiences with technology and games, and the overload of information that is available to them. We will create 1.5 exabytes (1.5×10 to the power 18) of unique new information this year and technical information is doubling every two years, so learning will be more important than ever.

Today's learners more than any time in the past can, "vote with their feet." If your organization is not providing the latest technology or education on the newest tools, virtual teaming techniques, and work methods like knowledge collaboration, it will find itself behind the proverbial eight-ball. Virtual work realities will require more soft skill training, some of which should be available to both the workers and their families. These do not need to be extensive, but a concise interactive learning event and discussion will pay great dividends in limiting adjustment timeframes for change. Today's computing environments are essential to support today's organizational education objectives.

There are several important trends and new forces that are influencing education and learning. The new tools and digital content provide richer opportunities to interact with the content and the others participating in the learning. Vast stores of digital content can be retrieved through the Internet, but finding it is sometimes a challenge. One of the issues of this content you find on the Internet or intranet is how do you know the information is correct, current or the author's opinions can be trusted? At least if you are accessing information from internal repositories that are created and maintained by CoPs you should be OK.

Research does show that having an interactive learning environment, where it is possible to confirm understanding and provide and receive feedback in a timely manner, can improve learner satisfaction and learning outcomes. Most often in the new e-learning model the instructors are really learning facilitators and tutors, who are not there to spoon feed but help when there are questions. In the digital world it is easy to personalize, monitor and measure learning progress. The new architecture of the learning events makes it easier and more cost effective to create and maintain.

Learning can now be made accessible so that no matter the time or the place you can now work and learn when the time is best, and not just when it is scheduled. The same technologies that are used for work, play and entertainment are used for learning. Best of all, the transition between these activities can be natural and seamless. Learning from each other on virtual teams is the basis for on-the-job training. Learning-while-doing can be encouraged and well supported in a productive, collaborative work environment, especially when the teams are made up of members with varying levels of experience and expertise. I encourage each team to think through their approach and select a person to be assigned as the coach or lead for specific learning requirements. In this environment, learning opportunities may present themselves at any time.

Education and learning, coupled with access to experts and knowledge is one of the main benefits to the always on, mobile, secure, connected lifestyle we can now enjoy. The challenges of today's demand for workforce skill development has us adapting to a just-in-time, just-in-place and just-enough approach to learning. This approach should start the day recruits are considered for employment. Organizations are establishing functional skill standards and qualification testing for new hirers.

There are concerns that young recruits have not graduated from our education system with a firm grounding in the basics. Many do not have the functional skills necessary to write reports, prepare minutes, create presentations, and be able to deliver them. Organizations will need to provide this work-based learning to improve these skills, as well as job related specific task learning and skill development. Most young people do have great creativity and the ability to learn quickly, and can be motivated to do so (look at their incredible technology skills); they just have to be pushed to learn these skills.

I believe new hirers will need to be housed with others in a traditional office environment, allowing them to learn and prove themselves prior to working independently in a virtual work environment. They need to be indoctrinated with a culture of continuous self-improvement. Their flexibility, adaptability and superior familiarity with technology will allow them to flourish with the new organizational learning experience. The corporate world will definitely need to take the responsibility for educating and preparing our future virtual workforce.

There are so many terms that we see used to describe organizational learning experiences. They are called learning and skill development, quality improvement programs, e-learning, skills for life, functional learning, subject matter learning, task learning, briefing, education or training. There are also many organizations like the Learning and Skills Network that are trying to discover in detail what works and how, so that we can achieve improvements to existing activities or develop new programs for learning and skill development.

The Learning and Personal Development Center is also conducting research on learning and instruction with the aim of contributing to the advancement of education and training. Others like the Learning Research and Development Center has scholars from several disciplines contributing substantially to knowledge about human cognition, learning, and effective training. Research findings are applied, in collaboration with education practitioners, business and government enterprises, to reform and improve the instruction and training in schools and workplaces.

J.M. Chein and Walter Schneider of the University of Pittsburgh are mapping a cortical network of structures involved in simple learning, transitions that occur as skills are acquired, and how knowledge of results alters cortical processing and learning. At the National Science Foundation: Education and Human Resources, they are attempting to determine why highly effective forms of instruction, like human one-on-one tutoring work so well, and to develop computer-based constructive learning environments that foster equally impressive learning. Apple is also active in this field designing and delivering professional development programs that deal with digital literacy and technology infused learning.

Fujitsu put considerable investment into the development of a new approach to corporate learning development, called *Learning Events* (LEs), for their Macroscope methodologies. These bits of learning/skill development content can be personalized and assembled freely into learning paths and learning networks for specific task or job competency. The learning can then be tested (self or administered) for basic competency. This approach also streamlined the development and delivery practices enabling most LEs to be conducted on-line. Experience shows that many of the on-line LEs can be taken in a group or team session, virtually together or physically together, with an instructor, coach, mentor, or tutor available.

There is a very similar movement lead by several influential people and organizations in the industry that is gaining strength, called *Learning Objects* (LOs) that are similar to LEs. The experts are, Jim Spohrer of IBM who led the creation of the Education Object Exchange, Gerry Hanley of Cal State which houses the premier repository effort for higher education, Tom Carey of the University of Waterloo who is the leader of the Co-operative Learning Exchange and eduSource Canada projects. These individuals are some of the leaders in the development of LOs. Other practitioners and training managers from Microsoft, AT&T, Macromedia, Booz Allen Hamilton as well as others from University of Wisconsin, University of Wollongoog in Australia, the Defense Department's Advanced Distributed Learning Initiative and Learnativity Alliance are all passionate advocates of LOs.

The name is clever, actually derived from two terms: object-oriented—this is where programming has been simplified by using bits of code bundled together into reusable chunks that contain a discrete, simple set of logic or functionality, and the term learning objectives—which is a simple statement of desired learning that is specifically associated with performance outcomes so that the degree of learning can be measured and assured. These approaches are relevant to the notion of skills and not really knowledge or the concept of competency or the mastery of a job. Part of the credibility for LOs has been established because the development is initiated from professional practices. For more information go to: http://archive.nmc.org/projects/lo/repositories.shtml

Accenture's learning and development researchers are combining existing performance simulation applications with real-time gaming principles. They are creating next-generation training applications that are richer and more complex because they include the element of interaction with other live participants. Allowing people to log on and interact with others in a virtual learning world is becoming very popular. This is similar to the virtual game world which has well over half a million subscribers, and action games bring the participation numbers up to more than 40 million players.

By making the virtual double of the performance environment more faithful to the real one, workers can become more proficient at their jobs more quickly, in a safe environment. Cognitive research continually shows that learning retention is higher in a simulation environment if it involves an added dimension of rich interaction with others. Learning while doing, particularly in an environment where people are often doing tasks for the first time because of constant change, is the most effective way to learn and retain new skills. As Einstein said, "I never try to teach my students anything. I only try to create an environment in which they can learn." Imagine what he would say today considering our learning experiences enabled through technology.

The key in getting started for the virtual world of work is to decide on the types of communication and learning your organization will employ. Examine closely the content, when it is needed, whom it will be directed to, and how it will be delivered. If you do these things, you will be well on our way to ensuring everyone has the knowledge, skills and confidence to efficiently and effectively work in tomorrow's virtual world of work. The possibilities are infinite so you must choose what possibilities make sense for you and your organization.

Oh ya, how do we know where to start and with whom? It's all about the questions! All organizational changes start with an idea, but if you are going to go any further you need to understand the environment, the attitude of the people and identify as many of the issues and obstacles as possible. The best way to find out how everyone feels about a pending change is very simple, you ask them. This does not mean that determining the correct questions to ask will be simple. If you don't ask the right questions, in the right way, to the right people, you will not get the true answers you seek. This is why communications, learning and development and surveys, assessments, and interviews have been combined together under the topic, getting started. You just cannot successfully plan and start a journey without first understanding where you are currently, where you intend to go, how you will recognize the destination when you arrive, and the readiness of the participants.

You need to choose, through an interview process, an executive sponsor for the "getting started" program, also select who will be part of the program level transformational team, and the project level working teams; these selections then must be mapped to the roles each person will fill. There must be representation from the executives, lines of business, geographies, IT, HR, communications, learning and development, facilities, and of course the workforce itself. The goal is to accurately determine the readiness of the organization, and the individuals for such a life changing transformation to how and where they will work in the future. Questions need to be designed to not just get the hard facts about what is going on, but to dig deeper into the emotional aspects of how people think about the basics involved in the change. The better the assessments, the better the results will be!

The most difficult analysis will be with regard to predicting who will thrive in the virtual work style and who will not. This includes assessments of both the management and staff. We need to discover what they think about such critical issues as globalization, demographics, collaboration, connectivity, technology, technology skills, work/life balance, work flexibility, work socialization, security, work timeframes, commuting, their home workplace, and any other issue they believe to be relevant. These are the issues and the information that will define the change.

The transformation team will review the information gathered to start putting together a change management plan. The plan cannot obviously be completed without the requirements for the future environment being defined and architected. Once the current state and the future state are clearly understood, the nature of the differences can be factored into the planning. With appropriate analysis the gaps will indicate the work to be accomplished, the effort to be expended and the projected costs of the organizational change program.

To make any "go-no-go" decision or series of decisions will require a study of the benefits or outcomes of the change and the associated risks. There will be both hard and soft benefits. You should be able to attach a dollar value to all hard benefits and many of the soft or intangible predicted results. From personally looking at case studies, business cases and other findings over the last few years, I believe the positive results will clearly outweigh any negative risks and costs of the change. The aspect of staying competitive in the increasingly difficult resourcing and recruit global world, or the reality that this is simply a cost of doing business, may just tip the scales in favor of a bold transformational change.

Individual departments will need to be ready. One obvious department will be IT. The hardware platforms, software portfolios, information storage, network connectivity, and security will all need to operate proficiently on a global scale. The familiar and consistent infrastructure must allow only those with the correct authorization to connect with each other from anywhere at any time to work effectively and efficiently using a variety of different but, hopefully, compatible devices. This will be no small task for many organizations, particularly if they have not already made the transition to the world of wireless mobility.

The HR, benefits, resourcing and recruiting groups will need to have flexible policies and procedures to accommodate new classes of employees and contracted labor. The real-estate and facilities' groups will need to shed old workplaces and design new flexible work environments that can accommodate mobile individuals and teams in a virtual community environment. The facilities will be required to house group work, meeting space, drop in centers, schedulable hotelling workplaces, as well as traditional offices. Campus or building wireless capabilities must be available from the parking lot, outside benches, workplaces, meeting rooms, class rooms, cafeterias, hallways, and executive offices. Many of these changes will require not just new technology and procedures, but skill development and interactive orientation sessions as well.

The surveys need to pinpoint what is currently the extent of mobile and virtual work, who is doing it, from where, and using what technology. You want to discover any difficulties or issues people have encountered and how they were resolved or what work-arounds were needed. You need to get from them what they like and what they don't, and why. Collecting lessons learned from within your own organization is more valuable than those from other organizations.

An objective is to find success stories and opportunities for further successes. To get direct feedback on what is possible will make communications and planning much richer and more attainable. My experience is that when employees get involved, the goals become more aggressive as to what can be achieved.

It is inevitable that you will encounter blockers and those who have not yet made up their minds, and are on the fence. Both are important but will require different approaches. It is wise to encourage those that are negative to express their opinions. If they do not feel safe expressing themselves, they will simply operate underground or "under the radar" as they say, making them much more difficult to deal with. They also may have valid reasons for not supporting the change, perhaps a bad experience; it is usually worth understanding these and addressing them early before this information can spread and grow.

Those that are sitting on the fence can be more easily converted. Paying attention to why someone feels the way they do can help. But, having the fence sitters engaged with those that are positive, especially if they have had a good experience or know someone personally who has, will help alleviate some of their concerns. If you can identify some strong champions, make them visible and involve them in the communications and learning. A positive experience created through learning sessions can promote confidence and buy-in beyond what a management message can usually accomplish.

It is important to identify the innovators and the early adopter in the organization. Innovators tend to be enthusiastic about adopting new ways of doing things particularly when it involves using new hardware or software. They have a need to be at the leading edge of change and working in a changed way is seen as a challenge to be conquered. Their attention is on the implements of change more than the actual change itself. The innovator in this case will love to try something new and the virtual world holds tremendous intrigue for them.

The early adopters on the other hand are more likely to buy into a good vision of the future. The end state is what is appealing to them although they too are interested in adopting emerging approaches and technologies. They tend to focus on the positive aspects of the opportunity and less on the potential problems. They look for opportunities to learn and improve themselves. A key to success is dependent on the productivity attained by the innovators and the early adopters. The focus on productivity must shift to the output of deliverables which can be measured in performance improvement and not in how warm is their office chair or how often they were seen late at the office.

The final step in getting ready is to analyze the information that has been gathered and to draw conclusions. If patterns or trends can be identified, they will be of great use in the communication, learning and planning activities. One of the most critical conclusions will dictate the pace at which the deployment will be planned. This takes a delicate balance between the readiness of the organization, the need for the change, the benefits to be realized, and the risks that will be faced. It is fairly common to choose a different pace for different parts of the organization. Only those with limited choice should attempt an enterprise wide simultaneous roll-out. This generally creates a situation where too many people are focusing internally, which is never good for business. You can think of the pace of change options being divided into 3 speeds:

1. **Evolution**—let it happen naturally, at a pace that allows individual initiatives and supports the majority of the employees being comfortable.

2. **Planned**—lay out a road map, keep those involved well informed and progressively move forward realizing not everyone will be in favor—steady planned actions.

3. **Aggressive**—a strategic move to force the reposition of your organization by taking advantage of the virtual work possibilities—need to lead and be out front—understanding there will be issues to deal with, management has weighed the benefits against the risks and decided this change program is needed immediately.

The reason this section started with the notion, "it's all about the questions," is because the information gathered will dictate many of the conclusions that are required to design the best road map for your organization. Good question will produce good information. Identifying and choosing the most favorable opportunities will make the realization of the early benefits more likely. The best place to commence an organizational change program is with those that have the best attitude, are the most flexible, or have the most to gain. You will learn more during the early deployments from the individuals and groups than during all the planning. Be ready to understand and quickly react to feedback. This information will allow for fine tuning and help assure a smoother transformation to the future virtual world of work. Today it seems all targets are constantly moving, thus attempting to hit an end outcome without a strategy for monitoring and adjusting is a waste of time, effort and money. Remember the road to the future is always under construction.

Chapter Summary
- Communication deals with the exchange of information—creating understanding, opinions and behaviors, within an organization: communication enables action.
- Communication can ultimately unite an organization, or conversely paralyze an organization.

- Leaders of larger dispersed organizations can have many more virtual personal contacts with the workforce either individually, in work teams or in all hands geographic groupings than was feasible in the past.
- We now have the incredible ability to visit employees, recruits, customers, supplier and investors in the same day anywhere in the world.
- Internal and external communications are being integrated, leading to the appointment of a Chief Communications Officer (CCO) reporting directly to the organization's senior leadership.
- The way in which messages are presented will have a major influence in how they are perceived and accepted.
- Great leaders will want to work with their workforce rather than simply have their workforce work for them.
- Attributes of good communications are: Timely, Relevant, Convenient, Clear, Concise and Informative.
- The communication group should be responsible for developing and maintaining a number of *channels* allowing effective and efficient communications.
- Many of these communication channels can also deliver *Learning and Development* events.
- The experience of learning is the responsibility of the learner.
- Today's learners have higher expectations that are strongly influenced by their experiences with technology and games, and the overload of information that is available to them.
- Virtual work realities will require more soft skill training, some of which should be available to both the workers and their families.
- The new tools and digital content provide richer opportunities to interact with the content and the others participating in the learning.
- Most often in the new e-learning model the instructors are really learning facilitators and tutors, who are not there to spoon feed but help when there are questions.
- Learning while doing, can be encouraged and well supported in a productive, collaborative work environment.
- In the digital world it is easy to personalize, monitor and measure learning progress.
- The challenges of today's demand for workforce skill development has us adapting to a just-in-time, just-in-place and just-enough approach to learning.
- The corporate world will definitely need to take more responsibility for educating and preparing our future virtual workforce.
- The industry is delivering professional development programs that deal with digital literacy and technology infused learning.

- Several influential people and organizations are developing a new approach to education called Learning Objects (LOs).
- Researchers are combining existing performance simulation applications with real-time gaming principles to allow people to log on and interact with others in a virtual learning world.
- By making the virtual double of the performance environment more faithful to the real one, workers can become more proficient at their jobs, more quickly, in a safe environment.
- Learning while doing, particularly in an environment where people are often doing tasks for the first time because of constant change, is the most effective way to learn and retain new skills.
- You must combine communications, learning and development with surveys, assessments and interviews to properly get started—it's all about the questions.
- The most difficult analysis will be with regard to predicting who will thrive in the virtual work style and who will not.
- We need to discover what they think about such critical issues as globalization, collaboration, connectivity, technology, technology skills, work/life balance, work flexibility, work socialization, security, work timeframes, commuting, their home workplace, and any other issue they believe to be relevant.
- Once the current state and the future state are clearly understood the nature of the differences can be factored into the planning.
- To make any go-no-go decision or series of decisions will require a study of the benefits or outcomes of the change and the associated risks.
- Collecting lessons learned from within your own organization is more valuable than those from other organizations.
- My experience is that when employees get involved the goals become more aggressive as to what can be achieved.
- It is important to identify the innovators and the early adopter in the organization.
- One of the most critical conclusions will dictate the pace at which the deployment will be planned.
- The information gathered will dictate many of the conclusions that are required to design the best road map for your organization—*it's all about the questions.*
- You will learn more during the early deployments, from the individuals and groups than during all the planning—be ready to react.
- Remember the road to the future is always under construction.

CHAPTER 31

PLANNING FOR TRANSFORMATION

Understanding how to properly plan for transformational change is not well understood and there are few experts to call on in most organizations. Project management in contrast has many formal processes, techniques, tools and experts. The study of project management is extensive with international subject matter bodies such as PMI (Project Management Institute) and competency testing. Even with this huge body of knowledge, the watch dog agencies still report results from project delivery are very poor. So how do we conduct a successful transformational change which is significantly more complex than a single project? Let's look at an approach that will allow the creation of the appropriate artifacts to plan, manage, monitor and make effective adjustments. I will draw on my own experiences to describe an approach that I have used, and it works. The approach is explained in great detail in a colleague's book. John Thorp was the leader of DMR's (acquired by Fujitsu) Center for Strategic Leadership and the principal author of the book, *The Information Paradox*.

To undertake such a complex, challenging and potentially risky change requires involvement up and down the entire organizational chain. The organizational levels are broken down into five segments. The levels represent the necessary views that must exist across a change program. The top level is the *strategic* or *executive level*. At this lofty level a clear and well articulate vision must be delivered. It needs to encompass direction, structure, purpose, role, culture and a vivid description of the transformed organization in the future. These can be detailed in mission statements, strategic direction manuscripts and vision documents.

The Virtual World of Work, pages 285–292
Copyright © 2008 by Information Age Publishing
All rights of reproduction in any form reserved.

The *role* the organization will play in society is something that is often ignored but is increasingly critical for understanding why the organization exists. The role should be described in terms of the intended place the organization will fill for its customers, suppliers and the employees, as well as its position in the industry, community, region, nation, or global economy. This will provide a goal, objective or target for every other level to use as a guide for their plans.

Many organizations form a strategic council to be the entity that continually monitors the events that can cause the business, competition, customers or society to change, creating new opportunities or realities, thus requiring a change or adjustment to business plans. The executives need to have a deep understanding of current and future opportunities, and make decisions based on the customer view, the competitor view and their own ability to execute and to create a competitive advantage.

The *portfolio level* is where the organization will select their investment programs and chose the balance between need, risk and value. You can use portfolio techniques to decide what programs and projects will transform the organization and allow a balanced investment strategy to fulfill the vision and role of the organization. This level owns the issue of linking all lower activity to the value achievable by the organization. It is responsible for eliminating competing or overlapping initiatives.

There are always too many projects chancing too few resources. Some will be pet projects or "sacred cows," while others will be reactions to the squeaky wheel syndrome. Many will have good ROIs and well-supported business cases, but may not directly contribute or align with the strategic direction. It is wise to create a Value Management Office (VMO) to effectively deal with assuring the selected opportunities can be tied directly to targeted outcomes and organizational value.

It is difficult to align program benefits with value and direction. The portfolio and value assessment techniques described in Thorp's book can be greatly enhanced by creating models and multi dimensional graphs using software like that from ProSight. I have seen these models used effectively to provide objectivity when selecting investment choices and alignment. Although this portfolio approach used for transformational change is relatively new, its traditional use in the investment world is not. Balancing investment and alignment with financial worth and risk are the tasks at hand. Selecting the right investment areas will provide a framework and scope for the transformational change.

Program level management is better understood, but for those who have not used this level, its purpose is to enable meaningful coordination of multiple projects and initiatives within a program. It will allow the identification of all the elements of a complex change so that they can be managed. The portfolio view can contain many programs and each program can contain many projects. At the program level is where the responsibilities for the realization of outcomes and benefits reside. It is the structured grouping of projects that contribute to the chosen interim and ultimate business outcomes. It provides the alignment and contribution of the initiatives of an organizational change.

The Results Chain modeling techniques have been extensively used on many programs and projects. It provides techniques for making implicit thinking explicit. It can be very helpful in displaying a graphical view or big picture of all the initiatives or projects, and how they interrelate. I believe this view's most valuable contribution is that it diagrams a measure of the degree to which all initiatives, assumptions and interim outcomes contribute to the ultimate outcomes of a program. With this picture it is easier to select the best path that will provide the greatest contribution to a program. It will also allow you a better chance of determining the effect of change and adjustments during the change program.

This benefits method and techniques were developed with clients because it was painfully obvious that benefits do not just magically happen when a project is completed. There is a huge difference between enabling the opportunity for benefits and the realization of those benefits. Benefits must be managed and they rarely happen according to plan. Benefits management is a continuous benefit realization process that requires dynamic decision making. Research showed that organizations regularly invested in the order of 12 percent of a project budget for project management and zero to manage the benefit realization process.

Fujitsu's objective was to invest in researching the benefit realization process and to create a formal method, techniques and LEs that could be deployed internally and by their clients. Most clients now employ the use of a Program Management Office (PMO) to effectively conduct transformational change programs. The PMO targets business performance and results metrics that enable a better risk reward relationship.

The *project level* management is the most commonly practiced method. In a transformational change it is the delivery of the individual project steps that lead organizations from their current state to a future state. Since change is now epidemic there may never again be a stable state, thus change can never be a one-time event. Project Management (PM) is the practice of gathering requirements, designing a solution, testing what has been built or acquired and introducing the new functionality or capability into the workforce. It is where we create the change. I have seen PM planning used to manage facility construction, technology roll-out, re-engineering complex business processes, or the annual holiday party.

Typically projects are broken into multiple releases or smaller chunks of functionality that are regularly delivered in set block-points or timeframes. This has created the need for a Project Office (PO) to be responsible for such functions as metrics, documentation, requirement traceability, resources, coaches, methods, techniques, tools, quality testing, functionality testing, re-use, visibility rooms, libraries, etc. Generally projects are judged against a budget and schedule but there are many more valuable measures involving delivering the expected functionality, earned value techniques concerning deliverables, defects, resourcing effectiveness, just to name a few. It is important to track effort and schedule but they tend not to indicate the true success of a project. PM is necessary but not sufficient to manage the scope of transformational change.

You may not be familiar with the term, service management. The *service level* is critical to the functioning of any sizable organization. This is the operational level that provisions, supports and maintains the software, hardware, networks and security that support your daily work efforts. Think of it as the utility that delivers the infrastructure. There are more measures for this critical area than any other. Although the heroes in this area primarily function in the background, their efforts make the difference to how effective and efficient the organization operates.

Service level management is critical because the workforce is dependent on the infrastructure and jobs simply cannot be done without it. This is increasingly true the further we move toward a completely wired, digital, virtual world of work. As we consider the pace of change and how our work world has become more dispersed, complex and flexible, we should appreciate the job it takes to keep it functioning, but we don't. When services are operating flawlessly, we act like it is our right to have them and when there is a problem we get instantly frustrated and irritable.

When all these levels are integrated and they become a common way to manage change, you can then focus your efforts on full-cycle governance. Your change programs will be governed by value, alignment, outcomes, contribution, benefits, delivery and service levels, not activities, opinions, power plays, and other common practices. The blended investment view, alignment view, value view, contribution view, operational proficiency view and earned value view will allow all involved to keep the pulse of the change. To be able to measure the degree to which each of these views are providing a picture of progress is a necessary and powerful tool for managing transformational change. These practices will enable organizations to move more quickly and successfully to the new virtual world of work.

Metrics and measurements have been popular business tools for many decades. The ultimate goal of transformational metrics is to demonstrate that the investments and the changes are translated into economic gains for the organization. *Concept to cash!* In the world of the virtual worker they must also show personal improvement for the individual. Taking new measurements is not about producing more information; it is about deriving the right information. The right metrics will allow better decisions providing they are timely enough to be useful.

Earlier metrics tended to be focused primarily on financial measures, such as profit, profitability, earnings per share, and return on investment. This meant they were backward-looking measures, but they served the purpose. Senior executives have used financial metrics to communicate performance to shareholders, bankers, media and the government (IRS). Over time business metrics have become more complex and organizations are now forced to look both back and forward. This forward looking view is predictive and deals with driving future performance. There is a focus on future projections and guidance of future results.

It seems today projections are more powerful indicators and preferred over current results. The focus on the future has brought about many improvement programs involving re-engineering, continuous improvement initiatives, process improvement projects, and a focus on creating future value. These changes force organizations to reexamine their core business objectives and the processes needed to control and measure them. Many businesses are trying to unite the business under a common set of metrics to demonstrate they are driving future value. Their resolve, they hope, will showcase their focus and communicate success. This requires organizations to be capable of understanding how each business activity is linked together and how each is aligned with the organizational goals.

Metrics involving change management, present us with two troubling dilemmas. First, the experts still feel there is a real lack of correlation between change spending and performance improvement. I personally find this difficult to accept this motion because in my experience very few people would be happy going back to the old way of doing things.

The second dilemma is that all the statistics show the majority of all projects are less than successful. Forrester has tracked IT project statistics for several decades with little change to the poor performance of delivering on project expectations. Benefit measurements from IT enabled change have evolved during my working life from operational metrics, to tactical, to strategic and now to determining what role the organization is playing in the global economy. Our emphasis has changed from tracking technology challenges, to business challenges and now to global and society challenges. No wonder there is a renewed emphasis on transparency and the SOX (Sarbanes–Oxley) initiatives.

It is popular to use these metrics to create a new internal language to gain buy-in to their importance and resolve. Managers need to be careful to translate or explain the language when communicating to external sources. Often new terms can be used to create the illusion of new activity and mystique for the organization. This certainly has been the case in the technology sector and the consulting field. It is important to at least keep up with the latest terminology to show you understand and are in the know.

People use to say, I don't know or it depends, but now you hear it is "situationally dependent." My experience is that only the most senior and confident people speak in a straightforward dialog. Have you ever listened to Mr. Buffet speak? Those with the most knowledge ask the simplest questions. Now, if we could only get to simple answers we would be well on our way to understanding what is happening.

Some of the most common approaches to metrics started in manufacturing, but today people in many businesses are using Six Sigma or other approaches to measure critical processes against industry standard. They are used to decrease variability, defects and wasted effort or compliance across business processes. If you are trying to change something major in your organization, you should start with the metrics you will use and how you will calibrate a base line to measure against. Be careful though, measurement can affect behavior in profound ways.

To take advantage of this, we need to measure the outcomes of the business before and after an organizational change. The metrics need to encompass measurements associated with results, the processes and the trends over time. There are methods, techniques and tools to help with the process of connecting outcomes and the measurements you will need to support change. The *Results Chain* technique, explained in John Thorp's book, is a familiar approach that will demonstrate the connections between initiatives and the resulting outcomes.

Chapter Summary
- A useful way to plan for a transformational change is to examine the views that are necessary from the different levels within an organization.
- The strategic or executive level must provide a clear and well articulate vision that should encompass direction, structure, purpose, role, culture statements, and a vivid description of the organization in the future.
- The role should be described in terms of the intended place the organization will fill for its customers, suppliers and the employees, as well as its position in the industry, community, region, nation, or global economy.
- Form a strategic council to continually monitors the events that can cause the business, competition, customers, or society to change.
- It is at the portfolio level that you decide what programs and projects will transform the organization, and allow a balanced investment strategy to fulfill the vision and role of the organization.

- This level owns the issue of linking all lower activity to the value achievable by the organization and eliminate competing or overlapping initiatives.
- It is wise to create a Value Management Office (VMO) to effectively deal with assuring the selected opportunities can be tied or aligned directly to targeted organizational value.
- Balancing investment and alignment with financial worth and risk are the tasks at hand.
- At the program level is where multiple projects and initiatives are coordinated and where the responsibilities for the realization of outcomes and benefits reside.
- You need an approach that makes implicit thinking explicit, and a graphical view of all the initiatives or projects and how they interrelate.
- A Program Management Office (PMO) must measure of the degree to which all initiatives, assumptions and interim outcomes contribute to the ultimate outcomes of a program—allowing a better chance of determining the effect of changes and adjustments during the change program.
- The project level management is the delivery of the functionality that is architected to lead organizations from their current state to a future state.
- The project level is where we create the change and since change is continuous never again will there be a sustained current state.
- A Project Office (PO) is responsible for such functions as metrics, documentation, requirement traceability, resources, coaches, methods, techniques, tools, quality testing, functionality testing, re-use, visibility rooms, libraries, etc.
- The service level is the operational level that provisions, supports and maintains the software, hardware, networks and security that support your work efforts every day—the utility or infrastructure.
- When all these levels are integrated and they become a common way to manage change, you can then focus your efforts to full-cycle governance.
- These practices will enable organizations to move more quickly and successfully to the new virtual world of work.
- The ultimate goal of transformational metrics is to demonstrate that the investments and the changes are translated into economic gains for the organization and in the world of the virtual worker, to show personal improvement for the individual.
- The right metrics will allow better decisions.
- Over time business metrics have become more complex and organizations are now forced to look both back and forward.

- Metrics and measures require organizations to be capable of understanding how each business activity is linked together and how each is aligned with the organizational goals.
- There is a real lack of correlation between change spending and business performance.
- The statistics show that the majority of projects are less than successful.
- Benefits measurements from IT enabled change have evolved during my working life from operational metrics, to tactical, to strategic and now to determining what role the organization is playing in the global economy.
- It is popular to use these metrics to create a new internal language to gain buy-in to their importance and resolve.
- Those with the most knowledge and confidence ask the simplest questions.
- If you are trying to change something major in your organization you should start with the metrics you will use and how you will calibrate a base line to measure against—be careful, measurement can affect behavior in profound ways.
- Metrics need to encompass measurements associated with results, the processes and the trends over time.
- There are methods, techniques and tools to help with the process of connecting initiatives to outcomes and the measurements you will need to support change.

CHAPTER 32

THE EMOTIONS OF CHANGE

Change, change, change—this seems to be the mantra that we hear from everyone. We are continuing to trade the status quo, stability and predictability, for better opportunities, flexibility and productivity. We call this progress! It is what humans do, have always done, and as far as we can see will continue to do, but at a greatly accelerated pace. The current pace and complexity do not afford the luxury of allowing change to happen in an evolutionary way. In fact, the better term now is revolutionary, and this puts a great burden on those responsible for *change management.*

People naturally think and focus on the delivery and risks of a change program, but there is something even more difficult to manage, the emotion of change. Emotion is a fact of life; in fact with change and risk comes some powerful emotions. The reality is that approximately half of the organizations managed risk and the associated emotions poorly. Those organizations that attempt to avoid risk are missing the point; this will limit the entrepreneurial spirit which will impact enterprise value. You cannot eliminate the risks and emotions of change, but you can monitor and manage them. Reacting quickly with corrective actions, if you know what you are doing, will make the difference in successful change programs.

Drs. Jaffe and Scott are experts in the field of change management. They describe change as a natural progression through a series of four phases: Denial, Resistance, Exploration, and Commitment. To successfully deal with change, employees must pass through all four phases. Their Change Curve Model is based on the following principles of change:

- Change is an ongoing process rather than an event.

The Virtual World of Work, pages 293–299

- There is a progressive sequence of change behaviors that need to be experienced and mastered to be effective in handling change.
- Seemingly negative behaviors such as denial, apprehension, anger, and resistance, are normal and adaptive elements in the change process.
- There are specific strategies available to increase change mastery.
- The progression through the phases of change represents an opportunity for growth and responsible risk taking.

In Wikipedia, organizational change management is,

> Change management that includes processes and tools for managing the people side of the change at an organizational level. These tools include a structured approach that can be used to effectively transition groups or organizations through change. When combined with an understanding of individual change management, these tools provide a framework for managing the people side of change.

Change management can be reactive, in which case management is responding to pressures from inside or outside the organization. This usually means they are reacting late and perhaps reluctantly to just keep up. In the world of virtual work, this may mean the personal virtual initiates undertaken by the employees are what have brought the situation to a head. The alternative is proactive, in which management is initiating the change in order to achieve a desired goal. This normally means they are not content with a strategy of simply following others, but desire to be a leader in what they do. Change management is most often organized on a program-by-program basis, but these programs are most successful when conducted in an organization that has a culture of continuous learning and changing, so that change is viewed as innovation, opportunity and growth, as opposed to negative emotions like upheaval, disruptive or just bad business. Emotion can be a powerful enemy or ally of transformational change.

Successfully implementing organizational change must involve all departments to contribute their expertise, but the major focus involves overcoming resistance to change which is fundamentally a human issue. To understand and predict how people will react is difficult. Why individuals react will be influenced by their psychological make-up, the actions controlled by management, and the specific nature of the change itself. A good change management program will assess the impact on the workforce, including management, and be ready with appropriate support mechanisms as they go through the change process. This must be continued to the point of change acceptance. An individual's attitude toward change tends to evolve as they become more familiar with it.

There are specific levels of change attainment in the IT field that are used, such as Carnegie Mellon University's Software Engineering Institute (SEI) Software Capability Maturity Models (CMM), and the Information Technology Infrastructure Library (ITIL) that are used in measuring and reporting on change progress.

There are many authors who have a wealth of experience describing change in similar ways that we can adopt for our own use in organizational change. One obvious choice is G. A. Moore, (1991) *"Crossing the Chasm,"* where he focuses on the challenge of technology acceptance and the segmentation of those involved in a bell curve. Another famous change curve model has been developed by Elizabeth Kubler-Ross to deal with grief and tragedy. Her model has been reworked and adopted as a means of getting workforces through major change processes. The subsequent model describes the stages that a person must proceed through when adapted for organizational change. The premise is that all people have to experience the same emotional feelings before they can move on. Nine states of emotion are organized into three stages:

Stage 1: Shock, Denial, Numbness.

Stage 2: Fear, Anger, Depression.

Stage 3: Understanding, Acceptance, Moving on.

Peter Drucker, the most prolific writer on management principles, has often been quoted as speaking about the change process. He believes whether change is perceived as positive or negative, will always encounter a certain degree of challenge, resistance, and scrutiny. Thus, an organizational change process needs to be as painless and smooth as possible. To paraphrase one of his thoughts, change is not about what you put into it— it is what you get out of it that is important.

Business challenges and day-to-day responsibilities do not cease to exist just because there is a major change. No matter how ineffective the current way of conducting business may be, it is familiar, and the workforce understands how to make it work. I once had the President of a large client put it in terms we could all understand, "Please help us improve our processes but whatever you do, don't break the current process." Oh yeah, he used the "F" word for emphasis in the original discussion.

The prospect of a new way of doing things represents a level of uncertainty which can be very real and somewhat threatening. This means understanding both the underpinnings and objectives of the change activities. Everyone must realize that the workforce is being placed into a position of partial *incompetence* during the change and there needs to be plans to reduce the sensitivity and concern on the part of everyone. One of the most senior consultants I worked with used the "freezing" approach, which was an early model of change developed by Kurt Lewin to describe change. Our consultant would say,

> We need to unfreeze the current process, quickly change it and refreeze it before it runs all over the floor. So let's do this in manageable chunks. A modular approach to change should stretch us but it also must be achievable.

Jeanie Daniel Duck's, *The Change Monster: The Human Forces that Fuel or Foil Corporate Transformation and Change.* Her book deals with the understanding of how people cope with both the reality of change and the manner in which it is brought about. Though targeted at the change management drivers of the business world it is infused with a sense of the effects of change in all areas of life. This is a summary of her work:

1. **Shock/Surprise**—this is the initial reaction to change and depending on the change readiness, this reaction may range anywhere from barely noticeable to highly traumatic outpouring of emotion. It is a normal reaction to the possibility of a change to the established status quo. The change managers should be somewhat empathetic, but they should not attempt to minimize the real effect of the change.

2. **Denial**—the next reaction tends to be one of disbelief or denial. This is the classic "maybe if I don't think about it—it will go away" response. This can cause the worker to simply drop out of the process, withholding their support and participation to such an extent that the proposed change becomes very difficult to implement. Involvement in exploring options to make the upcoming change work within the business environment can help.

3. **Hostility/Anger**—once confronted with the reality, many may express their displeasure either through subtle negative reactions, or through more open and direct challenges. Watch for those that get mad for they will need help to get through the change.

4. **Negotiation**—as implementation nears, some may look for concessions. This may be the last ditch effort to stop the momentum so you must not comprise the change program unless clearly what is proposed is beneficial.

5. **Depression**—with the realization that the change is actually going to happen, a feeling of depression may set in. This is a kind of mourning for the familiar way of doing things, and a slight fear of the unknown. Communications and learning events will assist the workforce feel that they will be able to cope with the new situation.

6. **Trial**—this is the day the workforce starts working in the new environment, (perhaps virtual). This is the time for encouragement and maximum mentoring, coaching and support to give the workforce a

hand in reaching success. This is like the launch of a new product line or business.

7. **Acceptance**—once things begin to settle down the change management teams need to monitor performance and do lessons learned to prepare for the next change.

There are other similar approaches incorporated in organizations that involve process improvement. These tend to focus more on the efficiency of skills and productivity attained through a change in the actual process. The same change management understanding can be used for processes improvement programs, change management, or organizational change programs. The change we are dealing with in this book is one of greater proficiency of the information worker through flexibility in where they work, when they work and how they utilize technology, collaboration, knowledge, and other work techniques. Where process improvement in the classical sense are the changes to a business process like collaborative manufacturing or on-line involvement of customers, suppliers, employees, partners, or the public through new portals.

Process improvement initiatives will require many of the same activities and deliverable to be supported from top management down through the organization. Experienced change leaders that can pick the right objectives and focus on the right processes are equally beneficial in any major change to an organization. Change improvement requires change leaders that are familiar with process improvement methods, tools and techniques (such as Six Sigma) to effectively facilitate change teams. For a reasonable shot at success, everyone will need to be involved and committed to the whole process of change.

There are two contrasting basic strategies for organizing change, the push and the pull. Most traditional managers feel comfortable with the push strategy to create focused, innovative, organizational change. A push method is a top-down approach to change and is often characterized as a more centralized or rigid change program. This approach is used and defended by these ideas which we have all heard expressed:

- It is top management job so they need to have control.
- Top-management know best what needs be done.
- The push approach will be more efficient.
- This will make it easier to mobilize resources and control any impact on performance.

What it does not do is engender participation by the workforce or have them take responsibility for the results. In our more distributed, flexible corporate world it does not take advantage of the global networked environment and the local skills that are available. It actually can slow the process by creating bottlenecks because others down the organizational ladder do not feel empowered to take decisions on their own.

Today, there are an increasing number of change programs that can be characterized as utilizing the pull strategy. This more versatile approach tends to be more far-reaching and designed to be more modular. Through global decentralization a greater diversity of participants are connected with responsibility for the program. As pull programs become more common, executives will need to redefine their role and measure whether these new disbursed approaches are better at initiating innovative organizational change and creating competitive advantage. My personal experience is that organizations which employ good principles and practices, and are high performing organizations, will use the same expertise to succeed at change and the reverse is also true.

Another fact that should be acknowledged is the discoveries generated by the complexity sciences. There is emerging evidence that complex groupings of people can exhibit different behavior than the individuals that make up the group. This is seen at sporting events, on the floor of the stock exchange, at auctions, and at rallies or demonstrations. A group mentality can take over and change the actions of the majority. In periods of heightened tension, group emotions need to be carefully monitored because they have the potential to be very positive or extremely negative to a major change program.

In a situation of heightened alertness messages can pass through a group with incredible speed. Human beings create reality through language, images and experiences—this is what we referred to earlier in the book as mental models. They are a product of their individual life experiences and are constantly reinforced by unconscious filters determining the information we process. It is these mental models, habits and attitudes that very often determine how successful process improvement can be in an organization. These individual attributes need to be assessed and plans modified by the reality of the findings. Moving to a new virtual world of work will require the kind of analysis and tactical planning to manage the events and the emotions of a change program.

Chapter Summary
- We are continuing to trade stability, consistency and predictability for better opportunities, flexibility and productivity—we call this progress.
- Change management—the process of developing a planned approach to change in an organization.
- There are Change Curve Models that identify a series of phases people will go through—Denial, Resistance, Exploration, and Commitment.

- The discipline of change management deals primarily with the human aspect of change which can be reactive or proactive.
- Overcoming resistance to change is fundamentally a human issue, making it difficult to understand and predict how people will react.
- A good change management program will assess the impact on the workforce, including the management, and be ready with appropriate support mechanisms.
- Change is not about what you put into it—it is what you get out of it that is important.
- The prospect of a new way of doing things represents a level of uncertainty which can be very real and somewhat threatening.
- Everyone must realize that the workforce is being placed into a position of partial *incompetence* during the change, and there needs to be plans to reduce the sensitivity and concern on the part of everyone.
- It is critical to understand how people cope with both the reality of change and the manner in which it is brought about.
- There are two contrasting basic strategies for organizing change, the push and the pull.
- My personal experience is that organizations which employ good principles and practices, and are high performing organizations, will use the same expertise to succeed at change and the reverse is also true.
- Complexity science is discovering emerging evidence that complex groupings of people can exhibit different behavior than the individuals that make up the group.
- In periods of heightened tension, group emotions need to be carefully monitored because they have the potential to be very positive or extremely negative to a major change program.

CHAPTER 33

HOW TO ORGANIZE

As the virtual world unfolds with new technologies and connectivity capabilities, we have a new found ability to adjust how we work. Pretty much anyplace can be a workplace, and we can discontinue the tradition of physically gathering together to work effectively. Because we can connect people together with little effort, it means we can virtually team with each other no matter the location. This teaming presents us with new opportunities to dynamically create small pools of expertise and knowledge with ease. This will allow us to benefit through the use of collaboration and to better utilize an array of capabilities from disbursed resources as easily as those that are co-located.

If we can quickly and conveniently apply the best resources to a problem, we will have enabled the best environment for getting the job done right, the first time. To be really effective and efficient we need to leverage these resources for short bursts of effort. This will be a challenge because organizations are not structured to create multiple virtual teams and have them work together on multiple assignments over short periods of time. Teams will eventually be expected to form and disband in a matter of minutes in the new virtual world of work.

This will be challenging, but imagine the productivity and what we will be able to accomplish. As virtual work becomes the standard, people will be free to rethink where they would like to reside. This will free us to reverse the urbanization trend that greatly influences where we live today. Change creates opportunities and risks, and with enough change the possibilities become infinite. I hope everyone agrees that everything is changing and that we all need to help those that are stuck in their status quo.

The Virtual World of Work, pages 301–309
Copyright © 2008 by Information Age Publishing
All rights of reproduction in any form reserved.

A tremendous advantage will be realized through new techniques leveraging knowledge whether it is digitized, printed, or in someone's head. These sources of knowledge exist in all organizations but it is the exchange between each source that is needed to create new knowledge. We now have the infrastructures to do this, what we lack is the culture that encourages frequent dialogue, communication and virtual teaming. The best way to distribute new knowledge is by letting the employees experiment with new innovation from across the organization, so they too will feel they own it. It is through working with others, or as we can call them, "networkers," that will encourage the creation of knowledge networks that can lead to knowledge communities.

IBM researches, Lesser and Storch, created some interesting observations during their studies:

- Team relationships are established when the organization assigns people to be team members, while community relationships are formed around practice.
- Similarly, authority relationships within the team are organizationally determined. Authority relationships in a community of practice emerge through interaction around expertise.
- Teams have goals, which are often established by people not on the team. Communities on the other hand are only responsible to their members.
- Teams rely on work and reporting processes that are organizationally defined, while communities develop their own processes.

Communities of Practice (CoP) are able to influence organizational performance through the intellectual capital generated, distributed and used by the members. Belonging to a CoP can enable relationships that build a sense of trust and mutual obligation between members. They not only create know-how and the adoption from outside of new ideas, they promote a context for a common language that encourages the disbursement of the know-how throughout the organization.

The CoP must not become an elite intellectual club; each member must commit to being the catalyst to improve the productivity of the entire workforce. They can do this by being actively involved in work groups, projects and sponsoring Special Interest Groups (SIGs). Their worth should be measured by the overall performance of their area of expertise, not on the number of articles or industry presentations they deliver in a year. Each member must demonstrate their contribution and positive impact, on improving the learning curve, fostering innovation, and eliminating the "not invented here attitude." These must be done to support the transformation to the new virtual world of work.

It is importance that the CoP fosters an environment of learning, research, experimentation, and innovation. Quinn, Anderson, and Finkelstein, authors of, *Managing Professional Intellect: Making the Most of the Best*, describes this as a working culture of self-motivated creativity within an organization. The strength of this kind of culture can be expanded by recruiting, providing extensive learning and development, encouraging a higher level of risk in trying new approaches and by establishing professional levels of certification. Membership in a CoP, if earned through measured expertise, can be a strong motivator, particularly if the members are looked up to for their skills and what they have been able to accomplish. This is an area that is conducive to storytelling about great deeds. CoPs should be an important part to how you organize critical expertise in virtual organizations.

In other areas of organizational development, Jeff Raikes, Group Vice President of Microsoft's Information Worker Group, recently talked about the addition of Groove. "Together, Microsoft and Groove will make any-time, anywhere collaboration a more natural extension of how information workers coordinate their projects and document-centric work." Today over half of all information workers do their jobs out of the traditional "office," at least part of the time. Most of those who are relatively stationary in a traditional office have to interact with virtual workers in order to get their jobs done. In today's work world we need new capabilities because getting our jobs done is not easy. The workforce needs these new tools to help the workers negotiate a maze of network connections, firewalls, file systems, tools, applications, databases, voicemails, and emails.

We spend most of our time trying to find information, reach people, and very little time is left to actually do productive work. This is a major contributor to work creep. When I worked in a traditional office, I had to wait for the distractions to go away before I could be truly productive. As I have stated before, I believe the traditional office environment is a most unproductive place to work on a regular basis.

Many organizations are expending a great deal of time, effort, and money trying to make the work environment more flexible. Most companies are trying strategies that include portals, extranets, blogs, and chat features, but at best they have been only partially successful. The inability to always have a broadband connection and access to the requisite servers has made life for the early virtual teams complicated and frustrating. This causes a reduction of organizational productivity, effectiveness and individual efficiency. Many individual workers are caught in a situation which has them trying to recover by stealing time from their personal life, including sleep time. What is needed in our new virtual workplace is a way to totally eliminate the old model of the physical office, and create a new virtual environment where everybody and everything are easily available from anywhere at any time.

Ideally the virtual workplace will support bringing together team members from both inside and outside the organization, with little effort, IT assistance, or wasted time spent navigating firewalls, servers, security, and network access. This will allow virtual workers to get things done quickly, in a collaborative environment, where they always know the location of each virtual member and whether they are available.

All relevant information will be available in one place for everyone to access, eliminating the problem of multiple sources and limited transparency. Each member can see what they are doing and what the others are working on. All calendaring, version control, hand-offs and deliverable integration will be handled by the new software. Everyone will always have secure, high speed connectivity.

It's crazy to think virtual teams can be created and function effectively without, new rules, training and an understanding of the unique conditions this adds to doing business. Virtual workers are not given education on how to work efficiently in virtual teams, because no one knows what to teach them. So for the moment there is a "learn as you go" attitude because people intuitively believe it to be the right thing to do, but there is little experience to draw on in most organizations.

Virtual teams will be able to easily involve multiple members in different cities and countries that normally work in different languages. Imagine for a moment that you are in charge of such a team operating on both sides of the dateline, with different cultures and conflicting government regulations. Routine tasks like scheduling conferences and collaborative work sessions take on new challenges when one person is just starting their day, another is having dinner, and still another group is fast asleep. This is looking at the glass half empty, from the half-full perspective some teams can have members working diligently around the clock.

We need to think differently and work in totally new ways. I think the really weak point is the hand-offs in this kind of situations. It will require workers being much more disciplined than in physically attended work sessions. For example, how will you handle the situation when the information you need is on someone else's desk who is sleeping, because they thought you either did not need it or already had it. People will be people, so we are going to need new tools that help take care of our little oversights when working virtually. To run such work sessions will require new levels of tact, cultural sensitivity and creativity.

Today we try to combine old and new techniques for teleconferences. How many times have you seen a group huddled around a speaker phone trying to meet with others in a similar position? I did not agree with what I am recommending a few years ago but now I would encourage everyone to participate from their own workplace. It will take time for people to adjust but in the long-run things will work better, everyone will be more comfortable and have a better chance to participate.

Make sure your organization has the tools to allow this; many do not because of cost or capacity. Make sure your systems allows for messaging, side talk between participants, and that everyone has access to the information, files or documents they are discussing or referring to. It personally took me time to listen more astutely and be sensitive to the quieter participants. Similar to traditional meetings, allow time for greetings, chit chat, or just familiarizing the group with each other. It can be very beneficial to have topics or questions that will help to get each member engaged prior to the formal session. Having people learn personal things about each other makes the virtual relationship more intimate, causing greater patients, understanding, and cooperation within the group. Use these techniques to make sure the quiet or the disinterested members are brought into the session. They may just have the most contribution to make on a particular topic.

Informal conversations will help those with language deficiencies, practice speaking and listening, and if done well will build trust within the group. Remember that those not participating in their native language will need to work harder and will become more tired, quicker. Try to have a balance of both written and verbal content. People will quickly be able to identify each other by the sound of their voice and what expertise they bring to the team.

Every individual filters input through their own experience and culture. This can be problematic because the same words to one may be direct, but to another may be blunt or even rude. Some may need to brainstorm together but in other cultures this may be seen as a weakness. Some people are very subtle in their requests or suggestions, while others seem to be "*in your face.*" Email is not a good answer for virtual teams; long extended trails are not good enough. We need new collaboration software but until that time, blogs, wikis and other shared databases are helping.

I have heard experts and personally experienced three different types of team conflicts:

1. **Relationship**—This type of conflict is very damaging to the team; it includes personality differences, hostility, and annoyance between individuals. Personality conflicts.

2. **Task**—This type of conflict is an awareness of differences in viewpoints pertaining to the team's task. A conflict of ideas is what should be encouraged, and a heated discussion of opposing ideas usually leads to the best idea emerging.

3. **Process**—This type of conflict includes disagreements regarding how to do the task or how to delegate resources. These conflicts can waste an enormous amount of time.

Conflict can be frightening, but it can also be very useful. You have to ensure that conflicts of ideas do not become relationship clashes. New virtual teams may have a harder time distinguishing between the types of conflict. The solution to ensuring that a battle of ideas does not grow into a battle of egos is to engender as much trust as possible between the individuals before the idea conflicts start to fly. The issue of trust is everyone's responsibility and something a leader or facilitator must be very cognitive about. Humans seem to build trust easier in face-to-face encounters, so spend part of the budget and bring the members together if possible.

The dynamics of working in a team are more complex than working alone, and virtual team dynamics are more complicated still. Members of virtual teams need to be especially vigilant and pay attention to how the team functions. Problems resulting from miscommunications that may be easily corrected through face-to-face interaction can take on a life of their own in the virtual environment. The greatest advantage to virtual teams is that they do not limit you to physical proximity in choosing team participants. This is tremendously significant for organizations and will surely allow virtual teams to outperform teams that must co-locate and be selected from the local pool.

Jeffrey Pfeffer in his 1998 book, *The Human Equation: Building Profits by Putting People First,* found there is mounting evidence that giving people more responsibility for making decisions in their jobs generates greater productivity, morale, and commitment. Yet, in spite of the substantial economic returns to decentralization and delegation, many American managers resist such practices in favor of traditional command-and-control approaches to managing people. Pfeffer believes this problem stems in part from a contemporary obsession with traditional leadership.models. "There is a cultural, socially learned belief in leadership."

Many studies have examined how decentralization and trust affect the people who are subject to these management approaches, but he has recently examined the effect of control, or its absence, on their bosses. Pfeffer explains,

If you've been actively involved in producing something, it's going to look better to you. Conversely, something in which you have been less involved looks worse. It's a common cognitive bias motivated by the desire for self-enhancement.

Ironically, he says, "This faith in supervision is often misplaced, because creative and intellectual activity can be undermined by close supervision." Because of the tendency to inflate the worth of work produced with one's direct involvement, it may be necessary to force delegation. One way to help make this happen is to put managers in a situation where they have to delegate. Pfeffer suggests, "Give them a large number of direct reports and thereby force decentralization."

Effective organizations put people in groups that manage themselves while leaders develop and nourish the corporate culture, while promoting an atmosphere that values learning, innovation, and accomplishment. Instead of telling people what to do and breathing down their necks to make sure they do it, good managers train and support their people, and give them the resources to make their own decisions.

Recent research by Deborah Gruenfeld, associate professor of organizational behavior at Stanford Graduate School of Business, suggests that teams encompassing at least two separate points of view on a particular question make better decisions, because the pressure of the minority forces the majority to think more complexly and consider diverse evidence. Moreover Gruenfeld also found that close majorities tend to be more open minded in their reasoning than majorities holding a larger balance of power. This, of course, suggests that token diversity of opinion is probably less effective than true diversity. "I was interested in showing that the dynamics of relationships among people who work together in groups are a stronger determinant of their behavior than personality."

As we move closer and closer to the virtual world of work we will change where we live and eventually the make-up of our communities. Those organizations that move to a model or culture emulating a true virtual community will be in the power seat.

If you read, *Linked: The New Science of Networks*, a book by Albert-Laszlo Barabasi of Notre Dame, the networked and connected society will gradually create a complete interconnected web of life. Linked presents the next step in complexity theory and Barabasi argues that just about everything is disseminated through a complex series of networks made up of interconnected hubs. He explains the basic history of network theory, and then shows how his own work has turned it into a closer model of reality, a model that most of us will recognize. These networks are replicated in every facet of human life; there is a path between any two neurons in our brain, between any two companies in the global economy, between any two chemicals in our body, and between any two individuals. This premise, called the six degrees phenomenon, was developed in 1967 by sociology professor Stanley Milgram. While at Harvard, he conducted the small-world experiment (the source of the six degrees of separation concept). We are quickly moving to a life where we work, play, learn, establish relationships, and live in a combined virtual/physical world. Did you know that one in eight of those married in 2006 met on the Internet?

Chapter Summary
- Pretty much anyplace can be a workplace, thus we can discontinue the tradition of physically gathering together to work effectively.
- Teaming presents us with new opportunities to dynamically create small pools of expertise and knowledge with ease.
- This will be a challenge because organizations are not structured to create multiple virtual teams and have them work together on multiple assignments over short periods of time.
- As virtual work becomes the standard, people will be free to rethink where they would like to reside—reversing the urbanization trend.
- A tremendous advantage will be realized through new techniques leveraging knowledge whether it is digitized (explicit) or in someone's head (tacit).
- The best way to distribute new knowledge is by letting the employees experiment with new innovation from across the organization so they too will feel they own it.
- Communities of Practice (CoP) are able to influence organizational performance through the intellectual capital generated, distributed and used by the members. Belonging to a CoP can enable relationships that build a sense of trust and mutual obligation between members.
- The CoP must not become an elite intellectual club; each member must commit to being the catalyst to improving the productivity of the entire workforce.
- Today over half of all information workers do their jobs out of the traditional office.
- I believe the traditional office environment is the most unproductive place to work on a regular basis.
- Ideally the virtual workplace will support bringing together team members from both inside and outside the organization, with little effort, IT assistance, or wasted time spent navigating firewalls, servers, security, and network access.
- In the new virtual world of work all relevant information will be available in one place for everyone to access.
- Virtual teams will be able to easily involve multiple members in different cities and countries that normally work in different languages, causing most to think differently and work in totally new ways.
- Allow time for greetings, chit chat, or just familiarizing the group with each other, this will build trust within a virtual group.

- Those not participating in their native language will need to work harder and will become more tired, quicker, so have a balance of both written and verbal content.
- Every individual filters input through their own experience and culture.

CHAPTER 34

LESSONS LEARNED

The key lessons learned have been gathered through personal experience, and the wealth of expertise now offered by authors and early adopters as they settle into the mobile and virtual work environments. The knowledge accumulated is depicting a picture of a better future for employees and organizations. The data is positive and becoming compelling, making it viable that in the future the majority of the information workers will work from home offices, and when necessary nearly anywhere will function as a productive, occasional workplace.

Eventually flexibility in the workplace will be thought of as the working norm. This will change where virtual workers elect to live, and in turn will change our urban society to a more disbursed balance between crowded neighborhoods and expanded suburbs. Just imagine if the need to live close to the office did not exist, if everyday commutes were a thing of the past. Where would you choose to live?

Few organizations seem to actually understand just how much the workplace has changed and fewer still have done anything about it. Studies show that with the increased mobility afforded by technology, much less time is being spent in offices and cubicles. Take a look where you work, probably something like 25 percent to 50 percent of the desks are unoccupied at any given time. Inside and outside meetings, conferences, training, sick days, vacations, working from home, and other travel commitments have made these empty workplaces an expensive reality.

Do your own study, the data you derive may surprise some and it will surely help those in doubt to understand that the present workforce is already more mobile than most realized. Organizations need to change how real estate and facilities are thought of and how we refer to them. If we

The Virtual World of Work, pages 311–325
Copyright © 2008 by Information Age Publishing
All rights of reproduction in any form reserved.

think of them as workplace resources and not workplace entitlement, then people will gradually broaden their mental models about the need for expensive, physical space. None of this is possible if the right web-based portable tools, technology infrastructure, communication and security are not in place.

Once the mental models start to change or are forced to change, then new ideas can emerge about what the work environment could become and how we envision work. Early adaptors to the virtual world of work are redesigning their campuses and buildings to be more accommodating to the new workforce. Some are creating a more flexible community environment than the traditional structured work enclosures. These include cubicles, offices and meeting rooms that can be dedicated to both those that need to reserve them and those that are available on a first-come basis. There are more casual free-forming areas both inside and outside that can accommodate those that are between meetings and away from their normal workspace.

The idea is to create a more flexible atmosphere for those that are mobile and intersperse these flexible zones with those that remain fixed to a physical space. A few companies are dispersing smaller and more flexible facilities across a broader geography so they will be available closer to where employees live. Many are simply using places like Starbucks to meet. The objective is to take advantage of what technology gives us to be more efficient and agile; flexibility, and our choices will enable greater productivity that creates improved business performance. In addition to productivity these flexible environments are designed to encourage greater creativity which can be channeled into innovation.

An important statistic to identify is the vacancy rates for office space. With the number of reorganization exercises, the vacancy rate may be higher than expected. Many large organizations are finding these rates to be in the order of 10 percent to 30 percent. The numbers that currently exist for each organization will be different, but experience shows that in the new virtual world of work these ratios can be reduced substantially. With collaboration dictating the forming and reforming of work teams, the new flexible workspace designs will provide a real advantage to organizations who find themselves in constantly changing business environments.

Managing a remote workforce or team will provide new challenges, and how well you adapt to these changes will determine your success in the future virtual world of work. Changes in goals, course corrections, resourcing, conflicts, and conflicting priorities can be more difficult to handle in a virtual environment. Let's look at what some of the leaders are doing.

Sun Microsystems through their "Work From Home (WFH) Program," have collected their lessons learned and organized the results around the common challenges that are specifically relevant to the remote manager.

Set clear goals, objectives and direction.

1. Always hold the kick-off team meeting face-to-face!
2. Share the team's vision and gain the commitment of all team members during the kick-off meeting.
3. Set a specific deadline to develop the team's final goals. Take time to develop the goals thoroughly, and not just finalize them at the end of a staff meeting. Document any goal decisions in your meeting notes. Align your team goals with the corporate direction.
4. Develop a methodology for gathering and analyzing data so team members understand how the goals were achieved and agree as to whether the desired outcome was achieved.
5. Meet quarterly to review goal progress and remaining actions. Situations change quickly; therefore, it is important to review and update goals regularly.

Establishing operating agreements on communication and collaboration.

1. Establish a "Members Only" password web site with a page for everyone's contact information and distribute pocket-sized paper copies.
2. Hold monthly conference calls with the entire team.
3. Conduct quarterly meetings face-to-face with the team if possible.
4. Arrange for direct reports to travel to each other's areas if possible.
5. Use webcast or video conferencing for team meetings.
6. Keep an hour free immediately following conference calls with your team, should any of your employees want to follow up on something.
7. Make a special effort to enable people from other cultures to communicate. Remember: A Western opinion tends to be expressed more strongly. Ask people from other cultures what they think. Allow everyone to be heard.
8. Suggest to direct reports, who have difficulty communicating in English during a conference call, that they send their comments in an email after the call.
9. Agree as a team to define a written plan for communication and collaboration, and performance tracking and assessment of progress toward goals.
10. Rotate the drivers and facilitators for the conference calls or face-to-face meetings. Record notes and send them to the team.
11. Agree on response times to messages. Examples: Return all phone calls and emails within 24 hours, and mark or tag urgent emails and voice mails.

Building and maintaining remote relationships.

1. Devote quarterly face-to-face team meetings just for team-building activities. Send informational content through email or email attachments. Don't use up the time in the meetings.

2. Learn how to celebrate "*virtually*." Use video conferencing for team building; choose a "*theme*" such as having everyone dress in Hawaiian shirts. Try a virtual "happy hour"—a phone or video conference where no work is allowed—just conversation.

3. Get to know employees or potential team members before you form a team. It helps to understand what the interpersonal and team dynamics might be when you put together a team.

4. Have your team members take the Myers-Briggs test (or similar personality test) and brainstorm ideas on how to communicate better with each other.

5. Invite special guests (such as second-level managers) to attend face-to-face team meetings.

6. Have the whole team welcome new members. If appropriate, provide a local mentor.

7. Schedule a get-together in one location (if fiscally possible) for the whole team at least once a year to take advantage of team-building classes that the group can attend. Or set up a training session just for your team.

8. Launch your regular team conference calls with some light hearted banter. This depends on the manager's style, but it usually works well.

9. Be sensitive of the various time zones when holding a meeting. Don't always hold a meeting when the same person has to attend late at night. Rotate the calls during different times.

10. Ask for advice from your direct reports who are in different geographic areas to learn about their cultures and customs.

11. Use team conference calls to discuss problems and ask the entire team for suggestions. This helps to build team spirit and allows team members to get to know each other.

12. Set up councils (for example, an engineering council or managers' council) to talk about issues and make decisions. Allow members to work out the issues they need to decide upon as a group. Instruct the councils to share their decisions about issues with you.

13. Establish practice forums (for example, an engineering forum). You'll find that these groups will become empowered and share ideas. This not only helps to build relationships between your profes-

sional and technical staffs, but it also helps with developing junior staff members.

14. Share results from your management performance feedback tool, and ask for advice and input from your direct reports.

15. Be very direct, either verbally or electronically, when managing conflict. If two groups of people are on either side of an issue, make sure they speak with each other on the phone. Participants can't rely on physical clues because they can't see them. Therefore, they have to ask a lot of questions to make sure they understand the full scope of the problem.

Assessing work remotely, measuring progress against goals.

1. Ask the team to create a performance scorecard that can be used to measure goal performance.

2. Constantly ask the team if your requests are too aggressive and then allow for an open dialogue about how to accomplish tasks and projects in a timely fashion. Always keep an open dialogue.

3. Use a project-planning tool. It will help with managing a project within a dispersed team. Everyone will have visibility around project milestones, required actions, deliverables, and dependencies.

Rewarding, motivating, coaching, and career development.

1. Rotate direct reports into other jobs within the team so that they are constantly learning new skills and developing themselves.

2. Become familiar with HR global processes and always look for ways to help your direct reports.

3. Share good news and recognition from upper management with the entire team and other stakeholders. Celebrate successes. Send gift certificates to remote employees to show your appreciation.

Here are 5 tips to allow for better communications for those working from home. Even if you have the right tools and the ability to have face-to-face meetings when necessary, communicating with co-workers and team members from home is still different from working in the office. Since communication is the key to virtual success here are a few suggestions to improve how you communicate with others from a home workplace:

- **Make appointments.** You set aside time to meet with someone in person, so why not make appointments for important telephone calls? By booking a specific time, you can be assured that your co-worker will be prepared and more focused on the conversation. They may also have done some prep work beforehand to make the call more productive.

- **Stay focused in phone conferences**. It's easy to stray when meetings get long, but keep multitasking to a minimum during phone conferences. The other party can almost certainly hear that keyboard clicking while you respond to someone else's email. Use the mute feature when not talking.
- **Attend weekly staff meetings**. If you work at home full-time, try to attend as many meetings as possible. The key is to keep in touch with others, virtually or in person, so they are aware of your presents.
- **Stay online as much as possible**. If you're not there, it's likely that people may not think you're working, even if you're working more than 40 hours a week. Responding quickly to email will help remind people you're still there and can be depended on.
- **Be assertive**. Don't always wait for people to contact you. Ask for information if you don't feel like you've received it. Most feel they can be more assertive electronically so take advantage of this fact.

Microsoft published an article on May 22, 2007, "Workers Eager for Flexibility, Optimistic About Technology's Role," that can be retrieved from their Website. The article states:

> As commutes grow and cubicles shrink, workers in the United States are eagerly exploring the potential of flexible work arrangements. Likewise, more and more employers are considering policies that allow employees to work whenever and wherever they can be most productive. A new survey commissioned by Microsoft Corp.'s Windows Vista® mobility team to study attitudes toward this trend found that 77 percent of American office workers interviewed would like the opportunity to shift their work hours or to work remotely. While 37 percent said they consider technology to be their biggest barrier, workers also are optimistic about new advances—with 87 percent reporting that new technology usually made their job easier.

> For employers considering mobile, flexible work policies, the survey suggested that employee satisfaction could be the biggest benefit; with two out of three respondents (66 percent) reporting the arrangement would give them a more positive attitude toward their work. And workers who have tried flextime were overwhelmingly positive about the benefits, with 74 percent reporting that having more flexibility gave them a more positive outlook toward their job.

> A majority of workers (55 percent) interested in flexible working arrangements and working remotely were focused on the expected savings of time and money currently spent on their commute to work, far outpacing other benefits such as the ability to set their own work hours (12 percent), spending more time with their family (9 percent) and being more productive (7 percent).

While 69 percent of those interested in workplace flexibility expected it would be easy to set up their laptop to work remotely, survey respondents conveyed lingering concerns about those arrangements. Two out of three respondents were still concerned with the security of sending confidential e-mails or documents from outside the office. One in five said they feared they would feel "out of the loop" if they worked in a flexible environment. Similar concerns are often cited by employers who have not yet embraced flextime and remote work arrangements.

Even once the technology is in place, employers are often not as excited about flextime arrangements as employees, but they should be," said Patricia Roehling, a professor of psychology at Hope College and the former director of research at the Cornell Employment and Family Careers Institute.

Studies have found that between 75 and 85 percent of workers were more productive when working in a flexible environment, and that employers can trim absenteeism by 60 percent which, in one study, saved an employer up to $2,000 per employee per year. Finally, workers who are allowed to work remotely report greater job satisfaction and commitment, and are less likely to voluntarily leave their job or look for another job," Roehling said.

In addition, the Windows Vista survey found that almost half of those surveyed (45 percent) would be willing to put in a few extra hours per week if they could work on a flextime schedule.

Roehling offered these tips for those exploring flextime or remote work arrangements:

For employees:

- Have clearly defined times during which work life does not intrude into family life.
- Arrange your remote office so you are not vulnerable to outside distractions during your identified work hours.
- Set up regular times to connect with managers and co-workers, either in the home or the office, or via phone or Windows® Live Messenger.
- Check in regularly with your supervisor and keep your employer up-to-date about the work you have produced.
- Have reliable, high-speed connections to the Internet, preferably using virtual private networking (VPN) to connect to company servers more securely.
- Consider using a Windows Mobile®-powered Smartphone, which allows you to easily access all your critical business information while you are away from your home or office PC.

For employers:

- Clearly define roles and functions, and set guidelines for regular communication between flex workers and supervisors.
- Have clear expectations around starting and ending work times.

- Require new employees to work from the office initially so managers and coworkers can get to know and trust each other, and so the employee can learn about the company culture.
- Clearly identify the expected work outcomes and evaluation criteria.

IBM has also published lessons learned about working from home, which they and many others still refer to as telecommuting. Their experience indicates that there is an adjustment period when first starting to work from home on a regular basis. Their studies show to expect adjustment durations of normally between 30–90 days, and that even the most organized and conscientious worker will need some time to learn and become comfortable. IBM's research shows the benefits, challenges and tips to working from home:

Benefits

1. Increased flexibility.
2. Improved work/life balance.
3. Reduced commuting time.
4. Reduced stress.
5. Increased personal control.
6. Increased individual productivity.

Challenges & Tips

Isolation—Telecommuters working at home may miss the camaraderie and support of coworkers.

1. Communicate regularly with coworkers and managers using e-mail, voice-mail, Profs notes, telephone.
2. Attend all team meetings and conference calls.
3. Join a Telecommuter Professional Association.
4. Consider part-time telecommuting.
5. Form a telecommuting support group.
6. Have good social networks outside work.

Difficulty Managing Time—Without formal structure that the workplace provides, it may be difficult for telecommuters to work efficiently.

7. Maintain a regular schedule.
8. Set up a workspace with all equipment/materials within reach.
9. Periodically make a list of objectives.
10. Make a prioritized "to-do" list with discrete duties.
11. Keep your work organized.
12. Contact office daily and agreed upon number of times.
13. Take planned breaks.

Burnout/Overwork—Since telecommuting gives 24 hour access to work, workaholics may work to excess.

14. Establish routine to structure your work time.
15. Set firm starting and stopping times.
16. Inform coworkers of your working hours.
17. Take regular breaks.
18. Set reasonable expectations of your day's work.

Household Distractions—Blurred boundaries between work and family may interfere with telecommuter productivity.

19. Have dedicated work space at home, preferably with a door that locks.
20. The work space door should give the family the message that the telecommuter is working and is not to be disturbed.
21. Teach family members when it is OK and not OK to interrupt.
22. Make sure a plan is in place for children to be cared for while you are working.

Career Advancement Concerns—Telecommuters may worry that their reduced visibility will limit their potential for advancement.

23. Schedule regular meetings with your manager to assess needs, get feedback, and discuss problems.
24. Keep your manager informed about status of work/projects.
25. Let manager know about work successes.

In doing the research for this book I came across a paper online at Microsoft's Small Business Center that I would like to share. It is by Jeff Wuorio and it asks and discusses a fundamental question about the upcoming virtual world of work:

"Are you self-assured enough to be a telecommuter?" "I knew I was suited when I realized I never once missed the office gossip and sports chatter." Here are a few selected points from his paper that are particularly relevant.

Wuorio continues, "You must decide if you (or your employees) are genuinely suited to the dynamics of working away from the office on a regular basis. Not only is that a critical question to help ensure that a telecommuter is both happy and productive, it is central to deciding whether a telecommuting arrangement makes sense for your company as well. It's no surprise that the best telecommuters thrive on autonomy and prefer not having a supervisor looking over their shoulder. Often, the best workers in the office make the best telecommuters. They're dependable, independent and self-motivated.

I did uncover an issue that a would-be telecommuter would do well to address: a potential lack of visibility within the company can harm an employee's chances of promotion; it may be best to stick to the office if getting ahead for you outweighs the pluses of telecommuting, at least until it becomes commonplace in the organization.

Still another element to consider is availability. Many office-bound employees feel more than comfortable about turning off their cell phones in the evenings. Since telecommuters are physically removed from the office, some telecommuters say that they must be prepared to remain accessible. You can't walk down the hall to talk to a boss or co-worker, and they can't do the same with you. So communication for and with telecommuters often has to occur at odd hours of the day. You pretty much have to make yourself available whenever you are needed.

Telecommuters who flourish also are adept communicators. But that skill goes beyond simple chit-chat to include a knack for being able to interpret things without face-to-face contact. If necessary ask meeting participants to describe facial expressions and other aspects of body language, they may tell you volumes about a person.

Telecommuters must address whether their employers are leery about a key member of the team working off-site. First, it's essential to grasp the "myth of accessibility," the notion that just because someone works in the building, they're always available is definitely not true.

Many telecommuters are happy to be at the ready 24/7—but it's also critical to bear in mind that telecommuting is probably the worst possible work dodge-around. While an in-house worker can often hide within the hive, a telecommuter who doesn't pull their weight leaves evidence everywhere, from unreturned phone calls to e-mails that die on the vine. That means a telecommuter is likely a top performer who stands ready to prove the arrangement both comfortable and productive.

Organizations are focused on mega projects and programs with huge investments in consolidating data centers, outsourcing to India, implementing SAP, migrating legacy applications, or supply chain improvements. What this book is about is a reminder that focusing on personal support systems may in fact provide a greater return. Sometimes the best value can be achieved with the programs that concentrate on human centric improvements, like the move to the virtual work world. The issue is that the employee improvement programs may not seems as urgent to the senior executives as the mega investments. The emphasis should be on making the information workers more creative and productive, and not on some obscure data warehousing project, especially if you take into count the bad experience organizations have had with delivering on mega projects. It is not that large projects are not important; it is they should not overshadow the need for organizations to transform to the new virtual world of work. There is always a need to distinguish what is important and what is critical.

Virtual business tools break down the barriers created by geography, language and time. This is a huge change, but once these barriers are eliminated the seamless virtual environments will deliver on the awesome productivity potential by getting more value from the mobile and virtual information workers. After all what is a great idea, an enthusiastic employee, or lots of extra effort worth? I believe a lot!

Ken's Tips—How to Prepare for the Virtual World of Work

Things you need to do

1. Set up your home-based workplace as a permanent work solution.
2. Imagine you are opening a mini branch office.
3. Select a work location that has a door and can be shut-off from the rest of the home.
4. Convince everyone your new workplace is the "office," not home.
5. Make your home office look and feel like a business office.
6. Always utilize the best equipment possible and have everything you need conveniently located, ergonomics are important.
7. Establish a good working relationship with the tech support people.
8. Schedule regular contacts with co-workers to replace hallway chats, coffee breaks and lunches.
9. Plan breaks or "holi-hours" into your work schedule.
10. Get the best and fastest communication network possible, never use dial-up or home phone lines.
11. Eliminate, minimize or manage home distractions.
12. Start working from home on a part-time basis if possible, ease into the new routine.
13. Celebrate the elimination of the commuting time, costs and frustrations.
14. Enjoy the time saving from eliminating the "getting ready for work" routine.
15. Talk to your family and friends about the change to your work, and explain what to expect and what they can do to help.
16. Understand why the change is taking place in your organization.
17. Find out who else is transitioning to a home worker status and establish a support group.

18. Review and understand any organization policies, procedures and guidelines that apply to the new work routine.

19. Find out what others are doing and what they negotiated.

20. Seek out and join a virtual worker SIG or outside support group.

21. Have an agreement with your employer on all capital, expense, support, and maintenance items.

22. Reduce work creep through focusing on a personal work/life balance strategy.

23. Take advantage of the increased flexibility.

24. Enjoy the satisfaction earned from greater productivity.

25. Stay in touch, keep yourself in the minds of others.

Things you need to know

26. Your attitude is critical—start with a positive, open mind.

27. Do not expect things to be the same as in the traditional office.

28. Understand that your family, friends and colleagues will also need time to adjust.

29. In a virtual workplace you may work alone but you need never be alone.

30. At first you will feel awkward, isolated and you're working relationships may feel impersonal.

31. Understand the change to a virtual worker will require an adjustment period of at least one to three months on average.

32. You will need better than average communication and organizational skills.

33. You will need to be more assertive with contacting and scheduling coworkers.

34. Technology is there to enhance your capabilities, not hinder them.

35. Remember self-imposed pressure for the virtual worker is often greater than office pressures, leading to increased frustration and stress, watch for these signs.

36. You will be connected and available for work across more of the day, stay connected and available.

37. It is harder to hide a lack of work effort in the virtual world.

38. Virtual capabilities make working more convenient—manage the temptation—you will definitely work longer hours.

39. Competition between virtual workers is real and will happen.

40. Group dynamics will impact individual behavior.

41. You will need to work harder at bonding and building camaraderie.

42. Virtual team dynamics are more complicated than traditional teams.

43. Ensure conflict over ideas do not expand into ego-based conflicts.

44. Conflicts over process can be more common in the virtual world wasting time and energy.

45. Encourage and participate in all organization team building activities.

46. Be proactive about reporting and identifying your value, this will help in building working relationships and trust.

47. Be flexible—always start team-oriented collaborative work with common processes and then tailor them to the specific situation.

48. Plan post team meeting free time for individual discussions and follow-ups.

49. Pay attention to how teams function and what roles people tend to play.

50. Miscommunication is more common in virtual teams and may take on a life of their own if not addressed immediately and managed carefully.

51. The change to a virtual worker will position you on the main path to the future.

52. As a virtual worker you must be available and responsive when people try to contact you.

53. Establish a balance of written and voice communication.

54. Your work contributions will be more scrutinized and visible.

55. Use shared or common databases if possible, instead of email attachments for collaborative team work.

Things you need to learn

56. Learn to make the rapid transition between work, personal time and back—there is no commute time to windup or down.

57. You must learn to read people without the benefit of body language.

58. Self motivation—you are responsibility for your time and productivity.

59. You must develop a strong desire to perform and improve your abilities—set goals and objectives.

60. Multitasking is a "must learn" skill.

61. Self-discipline—ability to set goals, establish to-do lists, focus your efforts, schedule time, and make commitments.

62. Organized—have access to what assets and people you need.

63. Willingness to plan your day and all calls/meetings, use automated reminders and lists.

64. Be current on how to reach people, set up networks and stay in touch.

65. Become an expert in using all your technology tools—technical competency equals less frustration and greater productivity.
66. Listen more astutely and be sensitive to quieter participants and foreign team members.
67. Allow time for greetings, chit-chat on conference calls to build familiarity and gain trust.
68. Familiarizing yourself with your colleagues—make the effort to get to know them.
69. Exercise greater patientce particularly with international members.
70. You must be able to build trust without face-to-face contact.
71. Learn to work longer hours spread across a longer day.
72. Learn to estimate time and effort for project deliverables.
73. Learn to set realistic expectations and value the power of persistence.
74. Learn to celebrate as a dispersed team.

Things the organizational should do

75. Recognize that the virtual workplace can provide competitive advantage.
76. Review the current status of what's in place to support the virtual worker—focus on IT, HR, Finance, Facilities, Learning and Development, Recruiting, Resourcing, Legal, Communications and the Executive Suite.
77. Create an oversight transformational change committee.
78. Create a strategy and vision for the future virtual world of work.
79. Prepare communications plans.
80. Conduct readiness assessments for each of the targeted workforces.
81. Put together an enterprise view ResultsChain or equivalent picture.
82. Put together an initial program level plan based on the ResultsChain.
83. Have each department produce project plans for deployment and training based on the program plan.
84. Complete a portfolio review of the plans, selecting the appropriate investments, alignment and deployment decisions.
85. Produce all appropriate guidelines, polices, procedures, and agreements necessary to support a dispersed virtual workforce.
86. Have a kick-off meeting to launch the transformational change program.
87. Commence the governance of the program including the measurements and metrics necessary to guide the monitoring and adjustment processes.

88. Put together support groups for the transitioning staff and their families.
89. Create the necessary technology help desk to support the virtual workforce.
90. Team building is best done face-to-face—don't forget to budget travel.
91. Create standardized skills profiles, processes and deliverables.
92. The greatest advantage to virtual teams is that they do not limit organizations to physical proximity in choosing team participants.
93. Celebrate successes.

KEY MESSAGES

The President of the United States of America is our most visible virtual worker. President Bush has the infrastructure that provides him the flexibility to work equally well whether in the Oval Office, traveling on Air Force One, vacationing at Camp David, or at his home in Crawford, Texas. These capabilities are now being extended to many virtual workers; they can be connected and available for work regardless of location or time. Technology has enabled ordinary people to live and work in an amazing mobile infrastructure. Mobility has made it possible for business to flourish in a dispersed model, allowing workers everywhere to work on virtual global teams. This is what is called the *virtual world of work!*

I was very fortunate to have enjoyed my career during a period of rich change, but not as fortunate as those just starting their careers. I am very optimistic about the future and convinced the next generation will experience a period of even greater unprecedented technological advances, social changes and wealth creation. This will naturally add more stress to their lives, and sure there are plenty of bad things you can worry about, but there are even more wonderful things just waiting to be discovered that will continue to enhance and improve human abilities. With all the information technology, automation, and outsourcing, we do not need the net-gens to keep us on the current path, work harder, or be more dedicated to work; what we need from them is to be more creative, adaptive and free to innovate. Things are changing so rapidly the future will be a surprise, so be flexible, observe, understand, and adapt. Adaptation is fundamental to survival and success!

I was an eager early adopter from the beginning of the Information Worker Stage, through the Mobile Worker Stage, and into the early part of the Virtual Worker Stage. I will watch with envy as the Virtual Stage matures and the Knowledge Worker Stage unfolds. My career is now behind me and I gladly hand-off the baton to the next generation of workers to journey

The Virtual World of Work, pages 327–335
Copyright © 2008 by Information Age Publishing
All rights of reproduction in any form reserved.

into the exciting possibilities of the future world of work. Pay attention to each new social and technical development for change will come at you fast. Take a position, make a statement, but most of all purposefully contribute to your future so it can be shared with billions of other people.

Just consider for a moment the unimaginable changes enabled by technology since the start of the Information Worker Stage (only 40 or so years ago), and then think about how much society, and our family life has changed in that same period. My parents and some of our friends existed in a time of more traditional roles and responsibilities. They were comfortable and had very little problem understanding the transition between when to work and when not to work. In fact, the transition time between when one is working or not, in the virtual work world can be instantaneous. For those working at home there is no drive time to think, reflect and unwind before moving into their alternate role. This is yet another adjustment you will need to adapt to. In my generation many women took on the additional responsibility of working outside the home but they still fulfilled most of the traditional responsibilities of a wife and mother within the home.

Today our children are blending and optimizing their relationships and family roles in new ways. Not by preserving our parents thinking, but by being flexible and adapting their lives to the opportunities and circumstances they face. Their family roles are flexible, not completely understood or defined, but much more blended. They view their partnerships as one between equals with both responsible for the family roles and earning the pay checks. The flexibility allows the roles to continue to change based on circumstances and what works best at any point in time. This is a profound change and it is already influencing all aspects of their lives and our society. The need for good communication is much greater than when roles were defined by tradition.

This same generation is the one now struggling with the work/life balance challenge brought about by work creep and the always connected world of technology. The same technology contributing to the work creep problem is also providing us with a solution (working with greater flexibly from home). Looking back to our parents again, it appears they were guided more by less flexible traditions, while today people are dealing with lives that are more fluid, flexible and continuing to change. Each new generation has to become better at adapting more quickly to changing environments and the stress of uncertainty that comes from constantly changing circumstances. The coming generations will live in an environment that is not predictable so more people will live on the edge.

If you couple these personal changes with the global ones enabling the creation of an economic community that now includes 2/3rds of the world's population, the possibilities are truly infinite. Early in my career no one imagined what China and India did economically could impact our markets and daily working lives in this country. Who imagined Russia would be our partner on such an immense undertaking as building the International Space Station. These countries are developing incredible new wealth and knowledge through exploding middle classes. They are taking their place in the global economic community most recently dominated by the U.S., Europe and Japan. This presents us with enormous opportunities but will require most of us to change and unfortunately some to lose. As the global economy grows it will impact us in the U.S. far more than we will influence it. We all need to realize this and adapt appropriately.

We now have the opportunity to network together millions of people, or any two, regardless of geography, time, technology, language, politic boundaries, or culture. The "networkers" will work together, exchange ideas and create new knowledge for the betterment of the human race. Our challenge is to make sure we do not step backwards in an effort to try to preserve or recover the past status quo. We must go forward learning, innovating, teaching, and sharing so we can optimize our potential. There will be those that want to stop this trend to a global, flexible, connected world because it impacts their control, power, jobs, or finances. I believe that to continue to develop the wealth that funds our future opportunities, we must keep expanding our thinking, our markets, and adapt to the realities of the new virtual world of work and everything it means.

The synopsis of my research is that I am very confident in the future, and the opportunity to make this world a better place. Technology, attitudes, globalization, and demographics are the key forces that are changing and influencing the future. To prosper each person and each organization needs to understand this new landscape and adapt. You have the opportunity to be a beneficiary or a victim of the future virtual world of work. What will you choose?

The book is organized around five very basic questions. In the book these questions are structured as sections each with relevant and supporting chapters. The introduction sets the context followed by observations, conclusions, key messages and a glimpse into the future. Lets review the questions:

1. What is the virtual world of work?

It is a technology centric flexible work environment that can be efficiently and effectively utilized by information workers whether they are at the traditional office, traveling, or located at their primary workplace in the home. It allows high speed, secure connectivity to all work related information, resources and colleagues, whether they are located within the organizational facilities or outside. Work can be accomplished individually, but increasingly most work is done using collaborative methods, techniques and technologies. The emphasis will be on forming small agile teams with a common understanding of a shared objective. Although management will provide the strategy, direction, context and funding, the teams will be largely self managed and responsible for the timely delivery of quality deliverables that are aligned with the planned organizational outcomes.

A clear definition is provided for the main words used so that we can have clarity in what is meant by their use. Some original thinking is presented to create the evolutionary stages of worker development to provide a context to where individuals and organizations are in their transformation to the virtual world of work. These stages are built from the workers perspective based on the increasing technological enabled capabilities enjoyed by them in each unique stage. This section includes a brief review of where we have come from, where we are, and most importantly where we will be going in the future.

2. What factors have enabled the virtual world of work?

The forces that have propelled us to the reality of an emerging virtual workforce are compelling and continuing to grow in strength by rapidly accumulating new supporters. The main reason most are moving to this more flexible virtual world is because they can.

We have a number of important and powerful factors (technology, attitudes, globalization and demographics) that are coalescing at the same time and are fundamental to the formation of the virtual world of work.

One of the most essential factors changing is the attitude of the workforce. It is not only the new generation that has new ideas, attitudes, habits and mental models, all age groups are changing. The problem is that they are not all changing at the same rate or to the same degree. People change when the situation dictates a need that is sufficient to enable change that otherwise would not take place. This is what is taking place and the pace of these changes is what is really taxing the workforce in particular and society in general. To accommodate the incredible pace of technology development organizations are employing new approaches to rapid deployment like, technology insertion.

The economic pressures are definitely encouraging both organizations and individuals to change. The relentless need for quarterly performance improvements are causing organizations to search for ways to penetrate new markets, introduce new products and services, reduce costs, and improve productivity. At the same time, individuals are continuing to want more of the "good life." These pressures are forcing increased work hours and nearly full-time connectivity. This work creep is requiring new approaches to achieve work/life balance.

3. Will the virtual world of work continue?

The total acceptance of technological change into both our work life and our personal life make regression improbable. Our eagerness to adapt and accept these changes is a good indicator that we can handle more. We are demanding more technological capabilities and devouring these into our lives overnight. I did not believe it possible for a society to change so quickly until we had the pleasure to visit China three times across the 1980s and 1990s. On our first visit we saw very few foreigners, cars, retail shops, hotels or restaurants. Most people wore MAO outfits and the people did not speak English, requiring us to travel as part of a group tour. The last time we arrived at the Beijing Airport there were hundreds of taxis, cars plugging the streets, merchants were selling everything, a seemingly endless number of high rise buildings were going up, hotels and restaurants were plentiful, and most people wore western style clothes. The young people spoke English allowing us to make our own arrangements and we traveled on our own.

If the Chinese can change that quickly, then we can surely change to the new virtual world of work; in fact, if we don't and they do, they will surpass us at our own game. It is imperative that we study our virtual experience and examine what others are doing to better understand the possibilities. The value and returns from doing business in a global virtual environment will be tremendous. We cannot succeed without embracing globalization and adjusting to what it will mean. The nations that do not fully participate in the global economy and resource pools will do so at their own peril.

Demographics are dictating a rapid change in the workforce. We will integrate international resources of all ages and cultures into a fluid workforce to meet the coming demand. Once connected this workforce will leverage global knowledge and function in collaborative teams to complete assignments. Organizations and employees will redefine the definition of an employee and have greater flexibility to arrange new work locations, work hours and work methods. There is no going back to some past familiar state, we all must observe, understand, adjust, and move forward into the virtual world of work.

4. How does the virtual world work?

To see how the virtual world of work will work we need to examine the tremendous advances in all aspects of technology and their combined effect. The technology environment encompasses connectivity, software, hardware and security. The ability to connect primarily through the Internet has enabled people to talk, exchange information and work together leveraging humanity's huge global store of knowledge and expertise. It is increasingly difficult to discern where the technology capabilities exist. Is the security in the hardware, the connections or the software? Is the information stored and accessed by the hardware, software or communications? Is the power in the network? The point is they all work together to enable the virtual capabilities we depend on.

For the global virtual world of work to function we need national security, technology security and the security of our information. If we cannot transmit our information and knowledge between approved virtual workers securely, the new networked environment will not work. We have plenty of tech idiots, criminals, rogue nations, and international terrorist trying to compromise the systems for completely different reasons. We need different methods to stop the attacks, prosecute the bad guys and enforce the security. I believe our biggest threat is not from a dirty bomb it is from cyber attacks.

The new flexible virtual way of working requires new management and leadership for us to reach our potential. Each individual and organization will need to rethink how the new virtual approach to business will work and what contribution they will make to it. It will require all of us to adjust and adapt to new collaborative ways to do our jobs. Those that adjust to teaming across locations, time, boundaries and technologies will seize the opportunity and lead our global society into the future. Many will work from home in the near future; they will work alone without ever being alone. The key to the future will be the networks we leverage.

5. How to architect the virtual world of work?

Most people feel the pressure to change and are thus experiencing the emotions engendered by these coming changes, but few are actually being proactive to change themselves or their organizations. My reviews show many are either resisting, abstaining or simply waiting for someone else to do something. In a recent discussion I learned that a very advanced virtual organization allows most employees to work remotely but the administrative staff must only work from an office. How can this be? What are people thinking? There is still time but you must get started now. You need to review what is already happening, why it has happened or what is preventing the transformation to the new virtual world of work in your environment. Discuss and communicate the transformational messages through your workforce and across all areas of the organization. To adapt is to survive.

Once you have a good understanding of the current state then you can start the planning activities to optimize the transformation to a new virtual world of work. This transformation is different from that required to produce a new product, service or line of business. The focus is to improved human centric productivity of the entire workforce through new experiments in flexibility. This will require new metrics and measurements to gauge progress and success, but the measures must be sensitive to the emotions of those changing or lagging behind. There are a number of organizations and individuals already operating in the virtual world of work. Take the time to understand how they have organized and what lessons they have learned so you do not need to make all of the change discoveries for yourself.

The Future

Let's take another look at the emerging virtual world of work and imagine what it will be like. Most everyone participating in the prosperous global economy will have new and more powerful technology that will enable all digital activities to be mobile. The virtual worker workplace platforms are currently dominated by Microsoft, IBM and Oracle. Whether it will be these technology leaders, others, the businesses, or the individual virtual workers that lead us to the future; what is clear is that the adoption to the new virtual world of work will be quicker than most expect. I believe that the majority (more than 100 million) of all U.S. workers will spend time working from home each month in the future.

The high-performance virtual workplace is focused on people centric performance, whether they are employees, customers, partners, or suppliers. The virtual workplace strategies will take the next generation beyond productivity to encompass innovation and organizational transformation.

Extremely high speed networks will dynamically connect everyone whether for business, learning, communications, entertainment, sports, politics, or for whatever the participants desire. New more powerful and sophisticated security will exist to protect all hardware, software, communications, business information, and personal data from unwanted threats. Interfaces with technology will be interactive and allow people to communicate in a much more humanistic way with computers, devices, books, etc. These artificial intelligence interfaces will involve holographic images so we can operate using all of our senses. Imagine for a moment that your computer will have a unique name, face, shape, sound, touch, and even smell. It will know who you are and understand you from the perspective of how you prefer to work, what you do, who you normally interface with, and have the knowledge to anticipate the context in which you live your life.

When working we will have work management software that performs all of the functions of a team of personal assistants. For a collaborative team the software will organize what the entire team is doing to make sure all work integrates, contributes to the stated outcomes and objectives, and all interfaces and hand-offs are efficient and effective. The software will be responsible for organizing the work, connecting to all digital resources, and keeping track of who is available and working on what. It keeps all contact information and the libraries for deliverables not yet complete, their status, as well as all completed deliverables available for re-use. Those with the right technology and security clearance can attend meetings in several different modes (voice, data, video conference, hologram, or combinations) with the most sophisticated being a personal hologram.

Management will have adapted to managing by deliverables and productivity, not time and attendance. Management will be modeling the virtual behaviors themselves and be more available to the employees through digital techniques. The employees will have adjusted to their home being a normal workplace and not where you go to escape work. The always connected world will adjust to a logical balance between work and life demands. Gradually people will change their homes to accommodate work and will locate their homes where they would prefer to live, as opposed to where they needed to live based on commute times. This will allow dispersed families to be much closer. Those employees struggling with the necessary drive and discipline to work virtually will be weeded out of the virtual workforce.

A major portion of the world will be connected and working together to freely collaborate and share resource expertise. Sophisticated language handling software will make it normal to work in diverse teams that live in different parts of the world, speak different languages, and honor different cultures. Technology will be making things easier, by handling routine tasks, allowing workers time to be more creative. More and more of the retirement eligible workforce will remain working, but under new employment arrangements.

The "not invented here" attitude will be replaced by a global commitment to capturing knowledge and sharing that knowledge. This will happen when it is easier to find and re-use stored work products (deliverables) rather than just doing it yourself from scratch (this unfortunately is not the case today). The incredible advantages achieved through connecting global resources will become a reality not just a promise. Knowledge is our link to the past and our path to the future.

Individuals will make personal decisions on how far they are willing to go to enhance themselves. There will be incredible new ways to enhance our capabilities. We will witness advances in performance enhancing drugs, external (wearable) and internal (bio-tech) technologies, and DNA engineering. We will reach the point, whether legal or illegal, that we will have two types of workers, enhanced and natural. This is simply an extension of our current situation, what is in question is how fast and how far these changes will be acceptable.

On this personal journey, and through my research, I have referenced a tremendous number of different sources to enrich the credibility and to demonstrate the opportunities enabled by the new virtual world of work. I hope you have learned something of value that will help you in your journey to a better work world. My advice is to learn and accept the new technologies, be free to explore new ideas and discover new attitudes, habits and mental models, understand the impacts created by global workforce demographics, and open your mind to the infinite possibilities enabled by globalization. Good success in your transformation to the new virtual world of work. See you there!

REFERENCES

American Telecommuting Association. (2006, August 22). *The American telecommuting association invites you to eliminate your commute!* Retrieved October 14, 2006, from http://www.yourata.com/index.html

Argyris, C. (Digital 2007). *Teaching smart people how to learn* (HBR Onpoint enhanced edition). From http://www.amazon.com/Teaching-Smart-People-OnPoint-Enhanced/dp/B00005REHM/ref=pd_bbs_sr_1/102-0006885-8863372?ie=UTF8&s=books&qid=1182352784&sr=1-1

Barabasi, A-L. (2003). *Linked: How everything is connected to everything else and what it means.* New York: Plume.

Benjamin, D., & Simon, S. (2002). *The age of sacred terror: Radical Islam's war against America.* New York: Random House.

Beveridge, C. (2003, January 14). *The new workplace.* Abstract retrieved December 10, 2005, from http://www.sun.com/2003-0114/feature/

Burns, J. M. (1997). *Leadership.* New York: Harper & Row.

Change management. (2005). *Organizational change management.* Retrieved April 22, 2005, from http://en.wikipedia.org/wiki/Change_management#Organizational_Change_Management

Chein, J. M., & Schneider, W. (2005). Neuroimaging studies of practice-related change: fMRI and meta-analytic evidence of a domain-general control network for learning. *Cognitive Brain Research, 25*(3), 607–623.

Choo, C. W., & Bontis, N. (2002). *The strategic management of intellectual capital and organizational knowledge.* New York, NY: Oxford University Press.

Committee on Information Trustworthiness, National Research Council. (1999). *Trust in cyberspace.* Retrieved September 19, 2005, from http://books.nap.edu/catalog.php?record_id=6161

Conlin, M. (2006, December 11). Smashing the clock. *Business Week,* 60–68.

Duck, J. D. (2001). *The change monster: The human forces that fuel or foil corporate transformation and change.* New York: Three Rivers Press.

Drucker, P. F. (1999). *Management challenges for the 21st century.* New York: Harper-Collins.

The Virtual World of Work, pages 337–341
Copyright © 2008 by Information Age Publishing
All rights of reproduction in any form reserved.

Dychtwald, K., & Flower, J. (1990). *The age wave: How the most important trend of our time can change your future.* New York: Bantam Books.

Epistemology. (2006, November). *Theory of knowledge.* Abstract retrieved January 5, 2007, from http://en.wikipedia.org/wiki/Epistemology

Families and Work Institute. (2004). *Overwork in America: When the way we work becomes too much.* Abstract retrieved February 12, 2006, from http://www.familiesandwork.org/index.asp?PageAction=VIEWPROD&ProdID36

Farley, T. (1995). *Telephone history series.* Abstract retrieved May 17, 2005, from http://www.privateline.com/mt_telephonehistory/

Fischetti, M. (2006). Working knowledge: Going vertical. *Scientific American Magazine,* August 2006 2 Page(s). Retrieved November 20, 2006, from http://www.sciamdigital.com/index.cfm?fa=Products.ViewIssuePreview&ARTICLEID_CHAR=49EDF4AD-2B35-221B-6CE6BDE388FCAD45&sc= I100322

Friedman, T. L. (2006). *The world is flat: A brief history of the twenty-first century.* New York: Farrar, Straus and Giroux.

Fujitsu Consulting. (2007). *Macroscope learning events.* Retrieved July 14, 2007, from http:www.fujitsu.com/us/services/consulting/method/macroscope/index_p3.html

Galinsky, E. (2002). *A new generation at work.* Abstract retrieved February 12, 2006, from http://www.abcdependentcare.com/docs/ABC-generation-gender-workplace.pdf

Garreau, J. (2005). *Radical evolution: The promise and peril of enhancing our minds, our bodies—and what it means to be human.* New York: Doubleday.

Garvin, D. A. (1993). *Building a learning organization.* Boston: Harvard Business School Press.

Gates, B. (2005, May 19). *Digital workstyle: The new world of work.* Paper presented at the 2005 Microsoft CEO Summit. Abstract retrieved May 30, 2005, from http://www.microsoft.com/events/executives/billgates.mspx

German, J. (2004, November). New level of 'working together'—7E7 program benefits from collaboration methods. *Boeing News, 3*(7). Abstract retrieved May 14, 2005, from http://www.boeing.com/news/frontiers/archive/2004/november/i_ca1.htm

Gruenfeld, D. (2004, April). *Better decisions through teamwork.* Abstract retrieved November 7, 2006, from http://www.gsb.stanford.edu/news/research/ob_teamdecisionmaking.shtml

Hardware. (2004). *Computer hardware.* Abstract retrieved April 22, 2005, from http://en.wikipedia.org/wiki/Hardware Wikipedia.

House, R. J., & Podsakoff, P. M. (2004). *Leadership.* Abstract retrieved March 21, 2006, from http://en.wikipedia.org/wiki/Leadership.

Hughes, T. P. (2000). *Technological momentum.* Retrieved September 22, 2005, from http://en.wikipedia.org/wiki/Technological_momentum

Huntington, S. P. (1996). *Clash of civilizations and the remaking of world order.* New York: Touchstone.

IBM. (2006). *Stress management for telecommuters.* Retrieved September 7 2006, http://www.pc.ibm.com/ww/healthycomputing/stress.html

Intel Corporation. (2003, November). *Effects of wireless mobile technology on employee productivity: Wireless mobility changes the way employees work.* Abstract retrieved

March 19, 2005, from http://cache-www.intel.com/cd/00/00/08/45/84501_
wireless_productivity.pdf

The International Monitory Fund (IMF). (2006, October 31, last update). *Glossary of selected financial terms: terms and definitions—globalization.* Retrieved May 18, 2006, from http://www.imf.org/external/np/exr/glossary/showTerm.asp#91

Internet. (2004). *History of the internet.* Abstract retrieved April 22, 2005, from http://en.wikipedia.org/wiki/History_of_the_internet

Jaffe, A. H., & Scott, V. (1968). *Studies in the short story.* Austin, TX: Holt Rinehart and Winston.

Johnson, S. (2001). *Emergence: The connected lives of ants, brains, cities and software.* New York: Touchstone.

Kelly, E. L., & Moen, P. (2006). *Schedule control rethinking the clockwork of work: Why schedule control may pay off at work and at home.* Abstract retrieved May 2, 2007from University of Minnesota, Department of Sociology Web site: http://www.part-timemba.carlsonschool.umn.edu/assets/88387.pdf

Koellner, L. (2002, June 19). *Leaders—are we ready for the future?* Retrieved September 22, 2005, from http://www.boeing.com/news/speeches/2002/koellner_020619.html

Kubler-Ross, E. (1996). *The five stages of grief.* Retrieved June 10, 2007from http://en.wikipedia.org/wiki/K%C3%BCbler-Ross_model

Kurzweil, R. (1999). *The age of spiritual machines: When computers exceed human intelligence.* New York: Penguin.

Leonard, D., & Straus, S. (Digital 2007). *Putting your company's whole brain to work* (HBR Onpoint enhanced edition). Boston: Harvard Business School Press. http://www.amazon.com/Putting-Companys-Whole-OnPoint-Enhanced/dp/B00005REH9/ref=sr_1_1/102-0006885-8863372?ie=UTF8&s=books&qid=1182352908&sr=1-1

Lesser, E. (2005, May). *The mobile working experience: A European perspective.* Somers, NY: IBM Global Services.

Lesser, E. & Storch, J. (2001, November 4). *Communities of practice and organizational performance.* Abstract retrieved March 14, 2005, from http://researchweb.watson.ibm.com/journal/sj/404/lesser.html

Lingle, K. (2005, January 21). Work/life balance. Interview retrieved March 10, 2005, from http://www.usatoday.com/community/chat/2002-03-25-lingle.htm

Microsoft. (2007, May 22). *Workers eager for flexibility, optimistic about technology's role.* Retrieved June 10, 2007 from http://www.microsoft.com/presspass/press/2007/may07/05-22FlextimeSurveyPR.mspx?rss_fdn=Press%20Releases

Milgram, S. (2004). *Small world phenomenon: Six degrees of separation.* Abstract retrieve October 7, 2005, from http://en.wikipedia.org/wiki/Stanley_milgram

Mobile phones. (2004). *History of mobile phones.* Abstract retrieved April 22, 2005, from http://en.wikipedia.org/wiki/History_of_mobile_phones

Moore, G.A. (2002). *Crossing the chasm.* New York: HarperCollins.

Mowshowitz, A. (2002). *Virtual organization: Towards a theory of societal transformation stimulated by information technology.* Westport, CT: Quorum.

Nahapiet, J., with Ghoshal, S. (1998). *Social capital, intellectual capital and the organizational advantage* (Oxford Institute of Strategic and International Manage-

ment—Interview). Abstract retrieved October 2, 2005, from www.templeton
.ox.ac.uk/news/pdf/ViewsHilary2000.pdf

Nissan Motor Company. (2005, June 2). *Case study: Nissan boosts global communication
and collaboration, cutting time-to-market.* Abstract retrieved May 30, 2005, from
http://www.microsoft.com/casestudies/casestudy.aspx?casestudyid=53861

Nonaka, I. (1995). *The knowledge-creating company: How Japanese companies create the
dynamics innovation.* New York: Oxford University Press.

Nunns, A. (2006, May 23). *Advancing the platform. Chevron presentation at the Microsoft
2006 CEO Summit.* Abstract retrieved June 23, 2006, from http://www
.microsoft.com/presspass/exec/billg/speeches/2006/05-23WinHEC.mspx

Oerter, R. (2006). *The theory of almost everything: The standard model, the unsung tri-
umph of modern physics.* New York: Pearson Education.

Peck, M. S. (1998). *The different drum: Community making and peace* (2nd ed.) New
York: Touchstone.

Pfeffer, J. (1998). *The human equation: Building profits by putting people first.* Boston:
Harvard Business School Press.

Porter, G., & Kakabadse, N. K. (2006). HRM perspectives on addiction to technology and work. *Journal of Management Development, 25.*

Quinn, J B., Anderson, P., & Finkelstein, S. (Digital 2007). *Managing professional intellect: Making the most of the best.* Boston: Harvard Business School Press: http://www
.amazon.com/Managing-Professional-Intellect-Making-Most/dp/B00005RZ5T/
ref=sr_1_1/102-0006885-8863372?ie=UTF8&s=books&qid=1182612953&sr=1-1

Raikes, J. (2005, March 10). *Microsoft—Groove networks to combine forces to create anytime, anywhere collaboration.* Abstract retrieved June 10, 2005, from http://
www.microsoft.com/presspass/features/2005/mar05/03-10GrooveQA.mspx

Ray, B. D. (2006). *The National Home Education Research Institute's Web site.* Abstract
retrieved December 10, 2006, from http://www.nheri.org/

Rayman, M., Varghese, P., Lehman, D., & Livesay, L. (1999). *Results from the Deep
Space 1 technology validation mission* [Electronic version]. Abstract retrieved
November 15, 2005 from http://nmp-techval-reports.jpl.nasa.gov/DS1/
DS1_Results.pdf

Rheingold, H. (1993). *Virtual Community: Homesteading on the electronic frontier.* Boston: Addison Wesley.

Richta, R. (1995). *Technological evolution.* Retrieved October 7, 2005, from http://
en.wikipedia.org/wiki/Technological_evolution

Ringo, T., & Rosenfeld, E. (2005). *The changing face of simulations.* Abstract retrieved
January   23,   2006,   from   http://www.accenture.com/Global/Services/
By_Subject/Business_Process_Outsourcing/Accenture_Learning/R_and_I/
FaceofSimulations.htm

Schaefer, J., Berger, L., Mejia, S., & Suda, T. (2005, June 2). *Case study: Nissan boosts
global communication and collaboration, cutting time-to-market.* Abstract retrieved
June 5, 2006, from http://www.microsoft.com/casestudy/casestudy.aspx?case-
studyid=53861

Schuman, H., & Scott, J. (1989). *Study of U.S. generational cohorts.* Abstract retrieved
July 14, 2005, from http://en.wikipedia.org/wiki/Demographics

Software. (2004). *Computer software.* Abstract retrieved April 22, 2005, from http://
en.wikipedia.org/wiki/Software

Sun Microsystems. (2005). *How will you manage? Best practices for the remote manager.* Abstract retrieved December 19, 2005, from http://developers.sun.com/toolkits/articles/manage.html

Tapscott, D. (1998). *Growing up digital: The rise of the net generation.* New York: McGraw-Hill.

Telematic. (2002). *Vehicle telematics.* Abstract retrieved September 22, 2005, from http://en.wikipedia.org/wiki/Telematic

Thorp, J. (2003). *The information paradox: Realizing the business benefits of information technology.* Toronto: McGraw-Hill Ryerson.

Vinge, V. (1992). *A fire upon the deep (Gollancz).* New York: Tom Doherty, Associates.

Washington States Ferries. (2005). *Washington State ferries provide wireless over water.* Abstract retrieved October 7, 2006, from http://enterprise.usa.siemens.com/products/solutions/hipathwireless/mainColumnParagraphs/05/document/Washington.pdf

Webster, N. (1912). *Webster imperial dictionary of the English language.* New York: Saalfield Publishing.

Welch, J. (2005). *Winning.* New York: HarperCollins

Whaley, L. J. (2006). *Prisoners of technology.* Bloomington, IN: RoofTop.

Wilber, K. (1982). *The holographic paradigm and other paradoxes.* Boston: Shambhala Publishing.

The World Bank. (2000, April). *Assessing globalization.* Abstract retrieved May 18, 2006, from http://www1.worldbank.org/economicpolicy/globalization/documents/AssessingGlobalizationP1.pdf

Wuorio, J. (2006). *Are you self-assured enough to be a telecommuter?* Retrieved June 5, 2006, from http://www.microsoft.com/smallbusiness/resources/management/pay_benefits/are_you_selfassured_enough_to_be_telecommuter.mspx

Printed in the United States
99338LV00002B/181-186/A